DESIRING WOMEN WRITING:
ENGLISH RENAISSANCE EXAMPLES

Desiring

JONATHAN GOLDBERG

Writing Women,

ENGLISH RENAISSANCE EXAMPLES

STANFORD UNIVERSITY PRESS
STANFORD, CALIFORNIA
1997

Stanford University Press
Stanford, California

Printed in the United States of America

CIP data appear at the end of the book

ACKNOWLEDGMENTS

Portions of this book have appeared in essay form: "The Countess of Pembroke's Literal Translation" in *Subject and Object in Renaissance Culture*, ed. Margreta de Grazia, Maureen Quilligan, and Peter Stallybrass (Cambridge, 1996); a version of "Mary Shelton's Hand" as "Writing as a Woman / The Female Pen" in *Language Machines*, ed. Jeff Masten, Peter Stallybrass, and Nancy Vickers (Routledge, 1997).

It would have been impossible for me to have written this book without the collaborative efforts of my students at The Johns Hopkins University and, more recently, at Duke, where Angela Burns and Lara Bovilsky have been especially inspiring interlocutors. The pleasure of reading Cary's *Mariam* remains forever marked for me by discussions with Anthony Scott and Elizabeth Hewitt occasioned by their essays on the play; so, too, David Glimp's work on Margaret Roper must be reflected in my understanding of her *Pater Noster*. Working with Jennifer Summit on her dissertation on the emergence of gendered categories of authorship has also been an important experience that lies behind the writing of this book.

Daniel Gil and Lenore Messick made a seminar on seventeenth-century women writers a memorable experience. R. Asad Raza was, undoubtedly, the most brilliant undergraduate to challenge and help me refine my thoughts on a number of these texts; his colleagues, especially Leah Stern, Wei-Li F. X. Tjong, and Tien Vu, also deserve mention here, as do other students from years past, especially Sarah Morton and Kimberley Thompson.

I am grateful for opportunities to present parts of this book: to Margreta de Grazia, Maureen Quilligan, and Peter Stallybrass for an invitation to the Renaissance Object / Early Modern Subject conference at the University of Pennsylvania and to Peter, again, for an opportunity to present part of this book at the English Institute; to Margo Hendricks and her colleagues at the University of California, Santa Cruz; to Karen Newman, for an appearance at MLA; to Gary Taylor and his colleagues at the University of Alabama (Tuscaloosa), especially Elizabeth Meese, Richard Rand, and Harold Weber, who provided spirited and lively conversation; and to Sharon Marcus at the University of California, Berkeley, and her splendid colleagues.

Mary Poovey and Jonathan Kramnick each engaged me in important discussions that have guided me in framing this project; my gratitude to them extends well beyond those conversations. Jonathan also provided an exacting and valuable reading of a portion of this book, as did Margaret Ferguson and Laurie Shannon, which I am happy to acknowledge here. I extend my thanks to Margo Hendricks and David Riggs, the readers for the press, for their enthusiastic endorsement of this work. It has surprised me to find myself writing about religion in this book, and I owe to the work of Richard Rambuss much inspiration and confirmation; I also happily note here the importance to me of our friendship. Judith Butler was in the audience at the English Institute and raised some questions there that, I hope, she finds answered here (I'm sure that the question she raised at Berkeley remains unanswered); her work has informed my own, and her friendship is something I cherish. I must, as always, acknowledge how much my work is made possible by Eve Sedgwick's, and how I value her friendship. Michael Moon has been the unfailing reader of these pages and always the most supportive and loving partner; his gifts will never be recompensed by a sentence on a page of acknowledgments. Finally, Helen Tartar, my extraordinary editor at Stanford, read the entire book with care, and touchingly thanked me for writing it, and not just as my publisher, as she put it. I return the thanks here, by dedicating this book to her, and not just as my editor, in gratitude for her support over the years, and for her remarkable intelligence.

CONTENTS

One THE LEGEND OF GOOD WOMEN

INTRODUCTION

After little more than a decade of enormously consequential work—including anthologies of texts, editions, major critical assessments, critical anthologies, bibliographies—the desire that women writers should be seen as contributors to English Renaissance literature should be uncontentious. If this work began, as Elaine Hobby says about the impulses governing her groundbreaking *Virtue of Necessity*, "simply" with a desire "to know what was there" (such archival work is by no means complete)—and to share her discoveries with other women—what to make of this emerging body of material remains in question.[1] For Hobby, this question is raised by the very historical context of her own work. Begun initially through her involvement in the Women's Liberation movement, her understanding of the texts she explored was shaped by living under an increasingly conservative British government in the 1980s (the U.S. parallel goes without saying) and by a splintering within the women's movement that inevitably complicated the sense of gender solidarity that provided Hobby's initial impulse. Hobby points, in criticizing her own work, to its failure to engage questions of race and its lack of pressure on assumptions about women's desires that inevitably configure them within the norms of heterosexuality; these issues are, of course, recognizably those that split the women's movement as it came to be seen as articulating programs that were aimed at white, middle-class, heterosexual women.[2] "Women" in the movement was not an umbrella term but housed restrictions. Moreover, as Hobby also points out, in the 1980s feminists came to articulate definitions of women's "nature" that were often complicit with the very systems of oppression under attack—women as naturally docile and loving, for instance, characterizations not all that far from the conservative politics that wished to undo the women's movement and return women to home and family. As Hobby puts it succinctly: "Since dominant ideas about 'women's nature' also define us as nurturing, sexually passive beings, I am not convinced that anti-sex, anti-violence feminist positions are really that radical at all" (p. 205). In the United States, the clearest site of these complicities has been in the unholy alliance of MacKinnonite feminism—which, in these conservative times, is fast becoming identical to feminism—and repressive, intrusive legislation around pornography.[3]

Although these developments within feminism could be thought of as quite distant from an archival program, Hobby is quite forthright in stating what should be obvious: that we come to materials of the past from our positions in the present. Hobby's gesture toward race and sexuality as necessarily on the agenda of any progressive attempt to read these early materials points in a number of directions: it recognizes that "women" is not a self-identical category, and hence that gender analysis is inevitably complicated by other questions, other ways in which gendered subjects are positioned. It points, too, to the fact that these locations are not only gendered, that inevitably gender is a relational category that exceeds the binary men/women.[4] For, of course, racial, class, or sexual positions are markers that are not confined to gender, although they are, obviously enough, inflected by gender.

When (mainly male) legislators sign pieces of MacKinnonite legislation, we witness one site in which feminist agendas are not solely a single gender issue. "When I began this study," Hobby writes, "I was working on 'forgotten women.' By the time it was finished, I was concerned with the problem of what happens to subordinate groups living under reactionary regimes; and what happens to radicals when they lose their vision, their sense of purpose" (p. 205). While fine tuning is needed not to collapse all subordinate groups (women, workers, Blacks, queers) into parallel positions of oppression, it is also important to note that Hobby's shift in focus represents an expansion of her project: finding lost women for other women is no longer enough.

To raise these issues allows one to note that much of the work of recovery of early women writers has not progressed in the directions that Hobby indicates.[5] Rather, the prevailing trend has been tantamount to the recovery of morally pure, suffering subjects whose goodness is legible in the terms that Hobby reveals.[6] (Hence, the earliest kind of studies of women—the tradition of Women Worthies, as Natalie Zemon Davis labeled this approach, or what I am calling here the legend of good women—remains strongest among literary historians.)[7] What to be done with these writers—beyond proclaiming their virtue—has translated into an endeavor whose conservatism is easily marked, indeed perhaps is implicit in any attempt aimed at recovery, which is definitionally an act of conservation: the desire to make canonical space for these writers, to "counterbalance the canon," as one recent anthology offers as its goal.[8] One question, Hobby notes, that she was often asked about her authors was "Were they any good?" Rejecting the question out of hand for its complicity with "dominant literary and educational cultures" and for the ways in which so-called "good writing" supports the values of "white, heterosexual, middle-class men" (p. 25), Hobby's refusal of the canonical issue raises difficult questions: Must the inclusion of these texts in the canon necessarily support dominant values and the oppressive regimes they foster? Will a refusal of the canonical question inevitably constitute these texts in a canonical relationship of marginality and minority? If so, what interests are served by such a subordination?

The first of these questions is implicated in a recent and ambitious volume, Barbara Kiefer Lewalski's *Writing Women in Jacobean England.* One has to be struck by the fact that every chapter nominates its literary subject as a "first"—Rachel Speght is "the first Englishwoman to identify herself, unmistakably and by name, as a polemicist and critic of contemporary gender ideology" (p. 153); Elizabeth Cary is not only "the first Englishwoman to write a tragedy," but also "the first Englishwoman to write a full-scale history" (p. 179); Aemilia Lanyer is "the first Englishwoman to publish a substantial volume of original poems" (p. 213); Mary Wroth writes "the first prose romance and the first sonnet sequence" (p. 243); these "firsts" add up to a group of women commandeering traditional forms and genres. Many of these "firsts" are fudged in their qualifications—what does "substantial" or "original" mean? What is the value of a name? Why privilege print over manuscripts? Why ignore continental precedents? One is struck, too, by Lewalski's continuing evaluative gestures, and, as Margaret Ferguson notes acutely in a review of the book, by the ways in which these always qualified affirmations of value continually measure these texts against "male" standards of literary performance and with an eye to high canonical values; so, too, Lewalski's book imagines its readership to be men who need to be convinced that these texts by women are worth their attention. Lewalski's rhetoric, Ferguson concludes, concedes much; indeed, "some feminists will feel it's the whole shop."[9] How is one to argue the value of these texts? How are these texts to be read *in* the English Renaissance?

These questions are approached in the two chapters that follow, the first occasioned by the inclusion of selections from Lanyer's *Salve Deus Rex Judaeorum* (1611) in recent editions of the *Norton Anthology of English Literature*—a sign, surely, of canonization. There are, of course, good reasons to distrust canonization—those that Hobby lists seem to me compelling—especially when canonization succumbs to these valuations. In his recent, stringent contribution to the canon debate, John Guillory has sought to argue that exclusions from the canon are not to be understood in terms of the social categories that Hobby names, and that the inclusion of the excluded will not automatically restructure social and political relations. While Guillory's arguments are far too complex to be engaged here in a systematic fashion, I would turn to his caveats about the inclusion of "lost" women writers in the canon as one path toward an answer to the question of what is to be made of these newly discovered writers. For Guillory, to include these early women writers would be an ahistorical act, a response to present concerns (about gender equality) cast in modern terms.[10] However, to argue that the inclusion of women writers in the canon merely responds to a demand for the addition of works representative of "*new* social identities and new writers" (p. 15), as Guillory does, is to take the fact that from the nineteenth century on women have been visibly productive authors as a supposed historical warrant for the marginalization of earlier writing by women (for Guillory they can only be the subject of what he refers to as a research program). Although Guillory argues, correctly, that women-as-women is a problematic category and that Renaissance women writers represent only a fraction of the population (most women were illiterate), this was also, if less massively so, the case for men (and for canonical male authors). Certainly Renaissance women writers cannot be taken to represent all women, but there is no problem in considering the writings of women in this period as part of the scene of literary production—or of what will come to be seen as literary production (Renaissance authors did not write for modern-day classrooms, nor are many of their texts now canonized marked by high literary aspirations). To relegate women writers to the status of the noncanonical is to reproduce the very activity of canon formation as it has been commandeered by the school and particularly by the university curriculum in the twentieth century. While Guillory's aim to situate canon formation as part of a history of schooling and literacy is certainly admirable, it also leads him to ignore all the other sites that produce canonicity—editions of works, anthologies, encyclopedias, biographies—and the complex negotiations between these publications and their readers and the texts assigned in schools.

About Aemilia Lanyer it is therefore salutary to recall the evidence that Margaret Ezell has assembled, documenting the widespread dissemination of early modern women authors through the eighteenth and nineteenth centuries.[11] In that context one must note that George Ballard's 1752 *Memoirs of Several Ladies of Great Britain*, a set of lives of sixty-three learned and literary women from the sixteenth through the early eighteenth century (a book in the Women Worthies tradition), includes Lanyer's name in the preface along with fifteen other seventeenth-century figures (including Mary Wroth), whom, he writes, "I well know to have been persons of distinguished parts and learning, but have been able to collect very little else relating to them."[12] Thus, more than a century after the publication of *Salve Deus Rex Judaeorum*, Lanyer's name—and presumably her poem—were known to Ballard. Given the protocols of Ballard's project, which, as Ezell argues, presents a definition of the woman of letters allied to "the domestic, the melancholic, and the impulse for self-sacrifice over the public, the witty, or the defiant (not to mention the erotic)" (p. 88)—and in which women authors too racy for this definition, or authors who wrote for profit go unnamed—Aphra Behn is one notable example here, and the chapter below considers ways in which even recent radical re-estimations of Behn fall sway to some Ballardlike protocols—it is difficult to know whether the failure to do more than name Lanyer arises from the possibility that Ballard knew the kinds of facts about her biography that pose an obstacle to declaring her virtue. Whether or not that was the case (and the chapter that follows takes up some of the ways in which recent critics handle the biographical evidence), to the point here is the recognition that

Lanyer's name still had some currency in the middle of the eighteenth century. Ballard's book, in fact, includes several of the figures studied in the pages that follow—Margaret Roper and the Countess of Pembroke, for instance—as well as a number that would now be studied in any full-scale treatment of Renaissance women writers—among them, Elizabeth I, Margaret Cavendish, Mary Astell, Katherine Philips—as well as numerous others yet to be given critical attention. What this forcibly suggests is that the recovery of women authors from the early modern period in many instances means nothing more than the belated recognition in the academy of texts that once were more widely known and the inclusion of writers that once were canonical. (By "canonical" I mean nothing more than that the names of these writers were recognizable items on a list of early modern authors.) As Ezell argues, the history of the publication of early women writers involved a continuing process of separating male from female writers, a narrowing of the scope of what counted as feminine and thus the increasing marginalization and decreasing publication of earlier women writers as the nineteenth century progressed. The exclusion of women authors from the standard curriculum, as much as the refusal to acknowledge anything but heteronormativity as the foundational plot of literature, are contributions of the academy and the canon as it came to be formed from the moment when vernacular literature was included in the university syllabus (the Greeks and Romans had already been bowdlerized). Because her work really is part of the history of English literature, if for no other reason, Aemilia Lanyer's canonization, and the inclusion of other early women writers, is justified. No arguments about literary value need be made; no assumptions that the university inevitably reproduces dominant values have to be endorsed.[13]

In the chapters that follow, one aim is to consider how the arguments for the value of Lanyer and of Aphra Behn have been shaped by the Worthies tradition, how they are constituted as good writers by being shown to be good women. In exploring these questions for Lanyer, I take my cue from an important essay by Ann Baynes Coiro, a study that nonetheless could fall prey to Guillory's caveat insofar as Coiro's salutary attention to class difference as inevitably fracturing any definition of "women" seeks to claim Lanyer as a spokesperson for her class; a modern notion of class solidarity intrudes in the argument and produces its own suspect hagiographic effect. I follow as well an agenda in reading Lanyer (and Behn, as well as the other authors considered in later chapters) that points to the second meaning in the title of this book—an exploration of the desires represented in these texts. Here I seek to further the project that Hobby names when she points to her ongoing work on Katherine Philips "as part of a new project around seventeenth-century sexuality, and especially homosexuality"; in this context, she writes: "I doubt if my statements about romantic love will look the same once this thinking has gone further" (p. 205).[14] Not only romantic love but also the presumption that the only desire possible to discern in these texts is one shaped by the obligations of marriage must come into question: questions of other structures of desire inevitably point to forms of social relationship other than those dictated by the hierarchical relations of men and women that marriage means to assure.[15] Once again, one has to note how infrequently considerations of sexuality are pursued in recent criticism.[16] Thus, in the chapter on Lanyer, while I find much to further my argument in the work of Wendy Wall, it has to be said that her important observations about gender transitivity, cross-gender positions and identifications never lead her outside a matrix of heteronormativity.[17] This blockage around gender, and the inevitable reproduction of normative definitions of femininity that it entails, certainly relates to the strain of feminist thinking that Hobby identifies; but there are, of course, other vibrant feminist contributions that lead to considerations of questions of sexuality, and it is these that guide my path (it will be regrettable if this approach appears to some as a repudiation of feminism). Guillory would no doubt censure such considerations of sex and gender for their reliance on modern categories of identity. My argument in this book, as in *Sodometries*, is not meant to declare anything about anyone's "sexual orientation"; indeed, I am as wary as anyone when identity categories become sites of what Wendy Brown incisively labels "wounded attachments," that is, when identities are embraced as sites of victimage demanding redress. To formulate identity in this way inevitably reifies power as entirely in the hands of others; it reduces identity to the field of experience in which claiming an identity amounts to little more than announcing victimhood and in which collectivity (or community) is achieved by limiting membership to those who will testify to their status in the terms that the group demands.[18]

To point the relevance of these concerns to the topic of inquiry here, we might recall Lewalski's "firsts," which is one way in which she produces an identity category—female "autonomy." This is a suspect category, as Margaret Ferguson argues at length, and not least when applied to the gentry and aristocratic women studied, whose "freedom" is often a matter of their social status rather than a sign of rebellion. But if gender is taken as *eo ipse* oppressive, then there is no other way to understand how a woman could ever be empowered enough to write and publish. Any other answer would need to reckon with their power positions. Individualizing answers beg such questions. These "firsts" arise as Worthy Women, exceptional women triumphing over the constraints of gender. As Ferguson puts it wryly, it's the Horatio Alger story one more time, "this time for women" (p. 361); more bleakly, one could say that such celebrations of proto-bourgeois individualism mystify the conditions of oppression of modern society, ignoring how "autonomy" for some entails oppression for most others; one might also recall that the Alger story has erotic valences quite at odds with its normative capitalistic venture.[19]

The constitution of a legend of good women as the prevailing narrative of early women writers is comprehensible not only in terms of the kinds of conservatism that Hobby underscores but as a reaction to prevailing descriptions of women in the period as sites of unbridled desire. Because female desire was described in the most stigmatized ways, and as the excuse for institutionalized forms of control—including control over publication—scholarship has often sought to argue against such imputations, to assure the propriety of women and the decorum of their public appearances in print. These protocols have served, however, as constraints; by rescuing women from oblivion and stigma, normative women, bound in a community of interests as women, have become a standard topos. If one looks, for instance, to the introduction that Sandra Gilbert and Susan Gubar provide for the volumes in their Women of Letters series published by Indiana University Press, one finds exactly the same kind of celebration of firsts found in Lewalski. Gilbert and Gubar found their "female literary tradition" on "the first feminist utopia," Christine de Pisan's *Book of the City of Ladies*, and it has immediately to be noted that they thereby ignore the placement of Christine performed by Natalie Zemon Davis, who lists her as a latecomer in a tradition going back to Plutarch and his book on eminent women. Each woman writer is treated as a particular "individual," yet all are "citizens" of Christine's city. "Such a City has always existed," Gilbert and Gubar affirm: this is a transhistorical community of women united in their suffering and abjection.[20] Gender is conserved as a site of pain. Gilbert and Gubar's women are, moreover, a highly selective lot: only those texts that can be read this way fit this canon. Guillory's misapprehension about the history of women writers is amply confirmed as well by their labors on *The Norton Anthology of Women Writers*, excoriated by Ezell precisely for furthering Victorian aims: the anthology includes few early women writers, and it preserves texts in which women write about properly female topics.[21]

Something more needs to be done, then, as any number of feminist historians, literary critics, and theorists would urge: considerations of this writing within social relations that widen an understanding of the work that gender does; a realization that texts by women are not simply ones in which the only thing to be considered is their representation of women; more than the occasional noting that something other than heterosexuality is involved in these texts. Although one could be heartened, for instance, to find Louise Schleiner opening her recent study of women's communities and their practices of reading and writing, *Tudor and Stuart Women Writers*, by entertaining the possibility that these relationships were "sometimes lesbian"—and I agree with her that "a social-power differential in a warm personal relationship, whether homosexual or heterosexual, typically carries a potential for erotic loading" (p. 251*n*7)—it is disappointing to find that speculation immediately foreclosed: "Direct clues on that point will have to be left to other studies" (p. 3). "Clues," of course, may not exactly be what is needed; biographical proof that some of these writers were lesbians misses the point. As Valerie Traub has incisively argued, it is not the case that lesbian desire and its representation are transparently available to any critic, or that "lesbians" can simply be produced by the critic out of the archives.[22]

One of the things that makes Hobby's work so important is that, unlike many other studies, its focus is not on individual authors, and it does not aim at biographical readings, in which women's texts are indices to their lives or the lives of women *tout court*, inevitably cast in privative terms. Genre and historical developments on a broad social scale place the writing that Hobby examines. Granted, it is far easier to do this in a book about mid-seventeenth-century writing than with earlier texts; in *The Currency of Eros*, Ann Rosalind Jones solves this problem by pairing her writers in terms of strategies of writing, class position, and across national boundaries. Jones's book is also among the few that engage texts in terms of the desires they enunciate. Her work is motivated by the recognition that cultural production arises out of sites of negotiation and contestation, that prescriptions against women's desires or women's writings are not simply repressive mechanisms whose force must be acknowledged, but sites inevitably engaged and rescripted by the writing produced by women in the period, women who, thanks to their literacy, cannot be considered simply as marginalized or oppressed members of their culture. I take my cue from Jones in the pages that follow—I, too, "want to resist interpretive frameworks that doom women of the past—or the present—to a relentlessly disempowered relation to political and cultural practices" (p. 9).

Although the book that follows does not match Hobby or Jones in its ambition or scope, I hope to make possible explorations no longer bound to the prevailing protocols of reading. In the two chapters in this section, I engage the possibility of reading Lanyer and Behn beyond the constraints I have noted above. "Translating Women" looks at writing by Margaret More Roper and Mary Sidney, Countess of Pembroke, beyond the usual view that tends to dismiss translation—precisely because it was a permitted sphere—as therefore necessarily trivial as a writing activity. The last section of this book engages the question of the thematization of the woman writer in Elizabeth Cary's work, as well as seeking to problematize it through a manuscript that may—or may not—be an example of writing by a woman. These chapters are guided by the double desire that titles this book—the desire that there should be women writers in the Renaissance and that the desires articulated in their texts be acknowledged. These are not perfectly congruent desires: the former takes its impulse from the feminist critique of the canon that has, working in pincers fashion, as Eve Kosofsky Sedgwick puts it, insisted both on the addition of works by women to the canon and on rereading canonical texts in ways that apply pressure so that they can no longer disguise themselves as repositories of truth but must be read as "*a* particular canon, a canon of mastery, in this case of men's mastery over, and mastery against, women."[23] To read these texts on the lookout for their structures of desire, is, to follow Sedgwick, to acknowledge "that no one *can* know *in advance* where the limits of gay-centered inquiry are to be drawn" (p. 53). That is: such questions can be asked of any text. Although this book confines itself to a few examples rather than attempt a survey of writing by English women in the sixteenth and seventeenth centuries, I hope, through readings as attentive as I am able to perform, to widen the possibilities for an understanding of the place of these texts in the social and cultural formation called the English Renaissance.[24]

CANONIZING AEMILIA LANYER

In the opening paragraph of an essay offering an important rejoinder to the emphasis on "idealized sisterhood" in "current studies devoted to early modern women writers" (an intervention that guides the pages that follow), Ann Baynes Coiro notes a remarkable fact about one of these writers: in the most recent (sixth) edition of *The Norton Anthology of English Literature* (1993), Aemilia Lanyer appears "as a major author," ready for, if not granted, canonization by her inclusion.[1] Coiro does not mention the fact that the headnote introducing Lanyer is, save for a single phrase, identical to the one that prefaced the piece of her writing that had appeared in the previous edition of the *Norton Anthology* (1986). There she had been included as a sixteenth-century prose writer, and one of the three prose pieces in her *Salve Deus Rex Judaeorum* (1611) had served to represent her. Lanyer's elevation in the sixth edition involves dropping her preface "To the Virtuous Reader" and replacing it with a stretch of some 100 lines from the main poem plus the entirety of the final poem in the volume, "The Description of Cooke-ham." To be a "major author," Lanyer must be represented, it seems clear, as a poet (this, of course, does not misrepresent her volume, whose prose pieces are a minute portion of a text whose verse runs to 3,000 lines). Whether as major poet or as minor prose figure, the same headnote, it seems, can serve to introduce her.

In both editions of the *Norton Anthology*, the claim for Lanyer's inclusion is made in terms of the thesis that Coiro calls into question: she is described as a writer of work with "a decidedly feminist thrust" realized in her depictions of "a community of contemporary good women" and in a historical project that rereads the Bible to offer paradigms of "good women" to counter "weak and evil men" and that turns in the poem on Cookham to offer "an Edenic paradise of women, now lost."[2] Thus, an undifferentiated sisterhood among contemporaries and stretching across centuries is the mark of Lanyer's feminism and the sign of her value as a woman writer. In the fifth edition, Lanyer's prose selection presents her as a feminist contributor to the *querelle des femmes*, whereas in the sixth, it is her poetic defense of Eve that fills this slot.[3] One may have some doubts whether a claim to major authorship can be made when literary value is tantamount to a paraphrasable content as available in prose as verse. More to the point, however, is to wonder what to make of a "feminist thrust," in which, to quote Coiro, "sisterhood" ignores "highly varied configurations of women." By grouping women (writers) together "simply as women," Coiro argues, "a disservice to women writers and a distortion of their real power" results (p. 358). Even as the *Norton Anthology* offers Lanyer up to canonization, the terms for such an elevation can be seen, following Coiro, as wanting.[4]

Lanyer's contribution to the *querelle des femmes* is described as "spirited and forceful" in the Norton headnotes, and it is not difficult to see that a taxonomy of good forceful women versus weak bad men is taken to represent her feminism, where "spirited" is only a hairsbreadth away from "spiritual." "Women" qua women is thus modified by the insistent adjective "good." Yet, the attribution of force and "thrust" to women may make legible a certain displacement of a conventional attribute of masculinity in this definition of the *femme fort*. In this context, it is worth noting that when the headnote adduces other texts from the *querelle* to situate Lanyer's, all of them are male-authored.[5] The listing of texts by Chaucer and Shakespeare puts Lanyer in canonical company. The Wife of Bath or the shrew Kate, it would seem, are strong women *tout court*, no matter the gender of the authors or the politics of their writing.

This move—in which "male" values are excoriated and appropriated for the woman writer—has its counterpart, in fact, in Lanyer's own defense of Eve, the text taken to represent her strong and gender separatist feminism. It is precisely the failure of Adam as strong man that extenuates weak Eve's fall:

> But surely Adam cannot be excused;
> Her [Eve's] fault though great, yet he was most to blame;
> What weakness offered, strength might have refused,
> Being lord of all, the greater was his shame.
>
> (*Norton Anthology*, "Eve's Apology," ll. 33–36)

Lanyer's suspicious deployment of conventional male/strength, female/weakness equations suggests that the seemingly tautological "women . . . as women" formulations that seek to guarantee Lanyer's feminist value are not quite Lanyer's terms. It is certainly the case, as Janel Mueller has argued, that Lanyer calls male strength into question: how strong was Adam if he fell to the seduction of Eve, she asks? How culpable was Eve, made from Adam's rib, and thus "the ground of all" (l. 66)? How could her offer of knowledge to ignorant man or her display of love be blamed when compared to the part men played in the crucifixion? It was one thing when in her "weaknesse" (l. 72) Eve was lured by the serpent, another when men demonically sacrificed God.[6] Much as Lanyer questions male/strength, female/weakness equations, she also preserves them even as she works her reversal: "Then let us have our liberty again, / And challenge to yourselves no sovereignty. / You came not in the world without our pain" (ll. 81–83). The reversal of priority here—in which women produce men—also overturns the fully ideological biblical narrative, in which the first man produces the first woman. These reversals of priority and of sovereignty seize upon woman's childbearing capacity and its attendant pain. The latter, however, is a consequence of the fall. So, too, there is no way of fathoming what prior state of liberty is imagined since it results from a redistribution and redeployment of the gendered terms of value (strength/weakness) based in the foundational biblical narrative. If weakness emerges to be valued over strength, it is along the lines of identification between the suffering, humiliated Christ and female powerlessness: it is this identification that makes for "good" women.

If the transvaluation of Eve involves a redeployment of sovereignty and priority, the question of the possibility of a separate sphere of female value, uncontaminated by masculinity, must inevitably arise. This problem can be recognized as the familiar dilemma attending any radical break with prior systems of conceptualization and social organization that cannot entirely frame itself without using the very terms it seeks to evade. (In this instance, Lanyer's reversal, however radically it rereads the Bible to wrest from it its patriarchal bias, nonetheless also preserves many of the crucial terms that link women to suffering and passivity.) This dilemma need not lead to the argument that such new possibilities inevitably reproduce old systems; rather, it may mean that the resources for the future are already available within them. My point here is not to suggest that Lanyer's text is incompatible with a feminist revaluation, but to begin to notice some complications in her presentation of gender that have not been recognized by the arguments around ideal sisterhood; as I have also indicated, there is some reason to wonder whether those arguments are as woman-centered as they appear to be.

Coiro provides further terms for this inquiry and moves us from the ethical register ("good women") to the social: "women" in this period cannot be thought of as a category in itself; "it is virtually impossible to separate out gender as a category unrelated to class position" (p. 358), Coiro writes, thus insisting that Lanyer's address to patrons represents not one good woman speaking to others but a negotiation across highly differentiated positions of power. Community, if achieved, must be a socially mediated activity; as Coiro sees it, class resentment cannot be overcome. Hence, to return to Lanyer's defense of Eve, it could be argued that her elevation to sovereignty and the production of her goodness resonates with Lanyer's celebration of her aristocratic patrons. Eve's sovereignty and liberty make her a "great Lady"; such, indeed, is Lanyer's explicit claim in the first of the prefatory poems to *Salve Deus*, dedicated to Queen Anne, where the Eve of her revisionary text is offered especially to Anne as a "great Lady" (l. 79) whom the Queen may "delight to looke upon" (l. 82), as if Lady Eve were one of her court attendants reflecting back her majesty even as she serves as a kind of exemplary mirror for the Queen.[7]

Just as one must recognize the nexus of class and gender in defining "good" women, so, too, elements of power that are conventionally treated simply as an attribute of gender need to be rethought. Eve's "male" sovereignty could be instructively compared to the praise of Queen Anne, who descends through "the blood of Kings" (l. 18) and is herself "Most gratious Mother of succeeding Kings" (l. 2). Even in her most radical formulation of genealogy, in the dedicatory poem to Anne Clifford, in which Lanyer offers the argument that virtue rather than class defines true nobility, female perfection has a male lineage. Lanyer replaces blood there with the honor of male ancestors, and when she declares Anne Clifford "Gods Steward" (l. 57), she locates her in "that place to him assign'd" (l. 54): the good woman occupies the place of a man "fit for honour, or command" (l. 49). Lanyer's argument at this point is part of her complicated representation of Clifford's right to the inheritance she had been barred from thanks to her father's will. Denying on the one hand the basis for Clifford's claim in blood, she reasserts it in a genealogy of masculinized virtue. What Coiro refers to as a "levelling" argument here is perhaps better understood as the way in which such a formulation represents Lanyer's attempt to find a ground of address across the divide of social position. What this intimates about the community of virtuous women can be noted as well in the antagonism between women in the dedicatory poem to the Countess of Pembroke, in which the struggle between the goddesses Nature and Art is resolved to "perfit unity" (l. 90), a suspension of "subjection" (l. 92) resulting in "equall sov'raigntie" (l. 93). Equalization here, like the mirroring relationship between Eve and Queen Anne, is part of Lanyer's project to put herself on a footing with her patrons as a good woman. What this involves, however, is a wresting of "male" sovereignty for female equality; the imaginary projection of virtue that "levels" class difference does not guarantee female community. Rather, it is offered against the implacable divide of social status.

"Goodness" and the supposed community of good women is an ideological project that serves Lanyer and her patrons differentially. Insofar as it points to Lanyer's position as a writer, it needs to be decoupled from the standard plot that Coiro adduces, the "shared difficulty" of women writers of "speaking in a male-dominated discourse" (p. 358), a plot that lends itself to hagiographic gestures celebrating those able to overcome this difficulty, or those like Mary Wroth, excoriated when they did so. As Coiro briefly notes, however, print is a contested sphere in the period; indeed, the insistent effort to gender print as an exclusively male venue is precisely that, an effort that registers the co-implications of gender construction with the definition of a public space supposedly denied to women and, more generally, an attempt to secure writing as a masculine activity against feminizing implications. Coiro puts the point succinctly, that "we must now in these latter days acknowledge, women, as well as men, were authors" (p. 360) and therefore explore the systems of possibility rather than frame each instance of a woman writing as the unique triumph over constraint. In *The Imprint of*

Gender, Wendy Wall has brilliantly documented the ways in which a gendered plot emerges with print culture, one that would seek to preclude women as authors or to make their appearance suspect. But, as she also demonstrates, difficulties are not impossibilities: women authors do write and publish, and this sometimes involves the negotiation of the terms of exclusion. These negotiations may also call into question the absolutism of gender division. Women who *can* write and do publish may not simply be assimilable to the supposedly self-identical category of gender; as Coiro pointedly asks, "To what extent would a woman be *breaking* company with other women by publishing?" (p. 360)

Oddly enough, when the *Norton Anthology* headnote identifies Lanyer as "the daughter and wife of gentlemen musicians attached to the courts of Elizabeth I and James I," it might seem to point to this "break."[8] Coiro's main argument about Lanyer is to insist on her (lower-)class position and on the difficulties of her transportation to the milieu (that in which canonical male verse is produced in the period) in which the headnote effortlessly locates her by way of her father and husband. Although it is certainly true that both Lanyer's father and husband were court musicians, whether they were exactly "gentle" and what that might mean needs to be asked (one might note that Lanyer herself seizes upon something like the strategy of the headnote on the title page of *Salve Deus*, which names her as "wife to Captaine *Alfonso Lanyer*," although even then it only further describes him as "Servant to the Kings Majestie," not as a gentleman). Moreover, court musicians were males, and their offices were passed down from fathers to sons; locating Lanyer in this male genealogy does not point to a set of affordances to her as a writer. The headnote's legitimation of Lanyer by way of a husband and father with court connections, one must suspect, serves to cover over the omission of some biographical facts: that it is not certain that Lanyer's parents were legally married; that Lanyer's marriage to Alfonso Lanyer was arranged by her lover, Lord Hunsdon, when he discovered that she was pregnant with his child. The headnote seems to evade what Lorna Hutson refers to as Lanyer's "notorious past" and to deny what Hutson takes to be undeniable: "No-one denies that she was promiscuous."[9] Indeed, the headnote risks patriarchal complicity in order to guarantee Lanyer's status as good woman.

The reasons for this are not far to seek. Lanyer's notoriety has been common knowledge ever since A. L. Rowse invidiously linked the supposed fact that "she was illegitimate to begin with" to her "promiscuity" and to her "rampant feminism."[10] It is to Rowse, after all, that scholars are indebted for most of the information retrieved thus far about Lanyer. In the context of arguments everywhere belied by false syllogisms, Rowse claimed that Lanyer was Shakespeare's dark lady and that her volume of poems constituted her angry response to Shakespeare's representations of her—and especially of her promiscuity—in the 1609 volume of his sonnets. The "logic" of this is transparently false; that Lanyer was Lord Hunsdon's mistress and Hunsdon was Lord Chamberlain when Shakespeare's company was under his patronage, hardly proves that Lanyer had sex with Shakespeare.[11] Rowse "found" Lanyer in his research into Simon Forman's manuscripts, discovered that she had visited him several times in the late 1590s, and that in the course of consultations had revealed her former liaison with Hunsdon and her forced marriage. (Forman's notes also reveal, *pace* Coiro, that Lanyer was hopeful that she might regain her social status lost when she married Lanyer, rather than that "she self-consciously identified herself with the laboring classes," [p. 363] as Coiro claims.)[12] In the recent edition of Lanyer's poems in the new Oxford series Women Writers in English, 1350–1850, a few slips in transcription have been noted, but its editor, Susanne Woods, basically follows Rowse, attempting, however, to read the diary entries to produce a "good" woman from them. One has to be sympathetic to this endeavor insofar as Rowse's imagination continually borders on the salacious and pornographic. It is nonetheless worthwhile pausing over Woods's arguments because they are symptomatic of the endeavor to produce Lanyer as a good woman, the seeming prerequisite for her canonization as a writer.

In seeking to exonerate Lanyer from Forman's charge, Woods makes the question of Lanyer's sexual behavior entirely a moral issue. She thus passes hastily over Lanyer's liaison with Hunsdon rather than developing the case that even Rowse makes intermittently, that Lanyer was the prey of powerful men; nor does she consider that sex work may also have been one of Lanyer's few options for advancement at court. (Coiro's argument that Lanyer experienced service to powerful women as demeaning is, of course, not entertained, since Woods subscribes to the thesis about female community.) Woods points out that the entry that Rowse takes as proof that Lanyer and Forman had sex does not explicitly make that claim. Forman was not usually reticent about recording his conquests and indicating when sexual intercourse occurred; it seems clear that Lanyer refused to have intercourse with him, and that when she persisted in her refusal he became angry and abusive. As Woods puts it: "Forman's frustration is evident as he reports that Lanyer was friendly to him, apparently enjoyed his company, let him kiss her, but would not 'halek' [Forman's code for intercourse] and 'he never obteyned his purpose.' His reaction suggests that he is not interested in friendship on her terms. His calling her a 'hore' who 'delt evill with him' must be taken in the context of his disappointment" (p. xxiii). Fair enough. Yet what were the terms of "friendship" that Lanyer offered, according to Forman?

Woods rather euphemizes the situation that Forman describes, in which he "staid all night. and she was familiar & friendlie to him in all thinges. But only she wold not halek. Yet he tolde all parts of her body wilingly. & kyssed her often" (Woods, pp. xxii–xxiii). If the diary is to be trusted, Lanyer gave Forman access to her body in every way short of intercourse; her "friendship" had only that limit. Although Rowse thinks that eventually Lanyer did have sex with Forman, Woods instead advises her reader that "one might better imagine that she came for a consultation" (p. xxiii). Lanyer undoubtedly did have Forman cast her horoscope, but this is clearly not an either/or situation. How one chooses to understand what they did in bed, however, must be more complicated than the question of how far they went. Sex short of intercourse is still sex; sexual behavior needs to be understood in its social circumstances, not simply as a moral question; even if Lanyer had intercourse with Forman, that would not prove that she was a bad, promiscuous woman.[13]

How far Woods goes to present Lanyer as a "good" woman is suggested by a rather bizarre gloss she offers to explain Forman's comment about Lanyer, that "it seams for Lucrese sake [Lanyer] wilbe a good fellowe for necessity doth compell." Here is Woods's note: "*Lucrese*: lucre, money. Possibly also a cryptic reference to Lucrece, whose rape by a member of the ruling family caused the downfall of early imperial Rome" (p. xxi*n*20). Forman nowhere mentions paying Lanyer; if she refused to have intercourse, perhaps it was because she expected to be paid. If this means that she was literally someone who sold her body, even Forman offers a way of understanding this outside of moral judgment: "necessity doth compell." Woods turns lucre into Lucrece, metamorphosing the woman who (it is claimed) would sell her body into a rape victim whose suicide guarantees her status as a foundational figure of chastity. What is unencrypted in this supposed allusion is the assurance, thus, of Lanyer's exemplary moral status. Yet, as Stephanie Jed has taught us to appreciate, the complicity of rape with the exaltation of the chaste (and suicidal) Lucrece is a moment to be reread under feminist suspicion; what way is this to constitute the good, chaste woman?

Not the least disturbing fact about this strange emergence of Lucrece into Woods's text is its possible prompting by a moment in Lanyer's poem where Lucrece appears in the context of a list of women whose beauty led to their downfall and the destruction of civilizations:

> Twas Beautie bred in *Troy* the ten years strife,
> And carried *Hellen* from her lawfull Lord;

Twas Beautie made chast *Lucrece* loose her life,
For which prowd *Tarquins* fact was so abhorr'd:
Beautie the cause *Antonius* wrong'd his wife,
Which could not be decided but by sword:
  Great *Cleopatraes* Beautie and defects
  Did worke *Octaviaes* wrongs, and his neglects.
(*Salve Deus*, ll. 209–16)

Lorna Hutson handles this difficult moment in the poem by arguing that through it Lanyer shows that not even the exemplary chaste woman is safe from male depradation. Hutson claims that Lanyer needs to develop a tactic in writing in which female beauty is not just a counter in male rivalry. Such a reading grants to Lanyer something like Jed's feminist insight, although this form of revealing the fate of Lucrece in the male imaginary is tantamount to consigning her to the locus of "bad" women—temptresses and homewreckers like Helen or Cleopatra; the strategies employed in the defense of Eve are not mobilized here toward a revaluation of these women. Hutson argues that Lanyer deploys Lucrece in this fashion in order to "avoid the articulation of . . . virtue as the incriminating display of the female body" (p. 30), but the path of "avoidance" also involves criminalizing Lucrece. This strategy of removing good women from being counters in male negotiation (Hutson's critical project, which she claims as Lanyer's poetic project) produces a community of good women around a set of assumptions, all of which are questionable: that all (hetero)sexual relations involve female victimization (that there can be no female agency in such relations, even if prostitution is involved); that female–female relations must necessarily not be sexual (since sex involves depradation) and thus would not involve any power differentials. However, it is precisely in order to praise the true inner beauty of the Countess of Cumberland that Lanyer launches her "*Invective against outward beuty*" (l. 185, marginal gloss) that includes the denigration of Lucrece: a contest between women is necessary to produce the category of good women, a contest involving invidious distinctions, including those of race, and one that, in its very vehemence, may also be sexually charged.

Just as Coiro insists upon considering how class/status differences between women will not deliver a unitary gender category, I would want to question the notion of gender identification by putting pressure on the assumption that the community of good women necessarily raises no questions of sexual relations. When, at the end of *Salve Deus*, a review of "famous women [of] elder times" (l. 1465) is undertaken in order to prove that none is comparable to the Countess of Cumberland, as Lanyer reiterates, telling each of these stories of good women (see ll. 1474, 1513, 1541, 1690), Lanyer concludes this section by declaring that "each desireth with his like to be" (l. 1600). The likeness she adduces is between the Queen of Sheba and Solomon, a likeness linking female goodness and male sovereignty. Even this is only a simile for the relationship of identification between the Countess of Cumberland and Jesus, a likeness that overcomes gendered difference. Likeness thus is not simply a matter of gender identification; moreover, likeness also expresses desire, precisely the desire of like for like. Through the sovereign male figure, female–female desire is intimated.

To rigorously pursue the conflicted question of classed, sexualized relationships in an anything but self-identical community of women in *Salve Deus* would involve a consideration of each of the patrons addressed by Lanyer since there is no reason to assume absolute uniformity in the volume. Such a project is well beyond the scope of this chapter. In the pages that follow, I use the dedicatory poem to Lucy, Countess of Bedford, as a focus to develop some of the terms for Lanyer's strategies of address; I choose this poem because the Countess of Bedford is a well-known patron and has received a fair amount of scholarly attention; as the Countess was the recipient of poems from Donne, Daniel, and Jonson, comparison between Lanyer's poem and those of her contemporary poets can be drawn. Although "To the Ladie *Lucie*, Countesse of Bedford" is only 28 lines long, and not much commented on, I am guided in my reading by Wendy Wall, who notes that the poem is "fraught with sexual overtones" (p. 327), something, as Wall points out, also true of other dedicatory addresses as well as in the long poem, especially when it offers the body of Christ up for the delectation of the Countess of Cumberland. This is not something much acknowledged by the critics whose volumes on Renaissance women writers best exemplify the kinds of strategies that Coiro identifies, Elaine Beilen and Barbara Lewalski.

Beilen's vision of sisterhood is tantamount to describing her good women as members of a monastic community, and the nine dedicatory poems are taken to unfold the gifts of the Holy Ghost, producing a composite "ideal Christian," a context in which the Countess of Bedford emblematizes "knowledge and understanding" (pp. 188–89). Lewalski makes much the same point in her chapter on Lanyer, "Imagining Female Community." Her summary of the poem to the Countess of Bedford paraphrases its message: it "identifies Knowledge, wielded by Virtue, as the key to her heart, and emphasizes (as does Jonson) her 'cleare Judgment' " (p. 224). Although Lewalski is intent upon female community, her mention of Jonson cannot fail to signal the fact that Lanyer's poem may be paralleled by male writers seeking patronage; indeed, her summary of Lanyer's poem echoes the one she provides for a poem addressed to Lucy by Samuel Daniel. "Especially pleasing," she opines of this poem, "was Daniel's recognition of her difficult situation as female courtier, and his judicious praise of her for qualities she apparently liked to be praised for—intelligence and learning" (p. 105).[14] If Lewalski, in this instance, hesitates slightly in granting the Countess of Bedford these qualities, it would seem that she does so to register a certain suspicion about Daniel (saying things to please his patron) as well as to note a certain amount of self-promotion on the part of the Countess (the latter, however, is an aspect of her self-fashioning that Lewalski seeks to endorse). No such hesitations are registered in the straightforward account of Lanyer's poem, and this presumably explains the difference in address between good women.

There is nonetheless reason to wonder whether or in what way the repetition by Lanyer of tropes used by Daniel involves their reconstitution within a sphere of exalted and exclusive femininity. Indeed, the very tropes that Wall indicates lend Lanyer's poem its sexual overtones are to be found in Daniel's. He too describes Virtue as the "key" (l. 39) to Lucy's interiority and also praises the "cleernesse of [her] heart" (l. 94]). Further consideration of Daniel's poem reveals something Lewalski conveniently overlooks: that his praise of female learning as the "key . . . T'unlocke that prison of your sex" (ll. 40–41) does not quite mean, as Lewalski argues, that she "has largely escaped the female role" and thus has expanded her possibilities as a woman. Rather, Daniel takes femininity to be itself a condition that must be overcome; when Lucy is unlocked, she assumes a position rightly hers as an aristocrat, in which she "may over-see / This rowling world" (ll. 44–45). Class position transcends gender limitation.

What Daniel—and Lanyer, perhaps—are up to in praising Lucy's learning and virtue can be glossed by way of an essay by Margaret Maurer on Donne's poems in praise of the Countess of Bedford. Maurer has no patience with the critical stance that takes Donne's exalted views of "a less than ideal Lady" (p. 206) at face value, and she places Lucy's patronage of poets in a context in which Lucy's religion seems highly artificial, and in which her financial profligacy, intriguing, power-brokering, even her masquing, allow Maurer to view her as a typical member of an exceedingly corrupt court.[15] Maurer's moralizing condemnation is as suspect as the prevailing pieticizing of the Countess of Bedford, but her main point is to describe the role of patronage poetry as part of a system in which she performed as a consummate courtier. Lewalski, in fact, adopts Maurer's point but mobilizes it to the conclusion that Lucy was "one Jacobean lady who laid claim to considerable political power and cultural status, and got away with it" (p. 123). Yet, Lucy's activities at court were not really exceptional; her power-brokering was well within the purview of well-placed aristocrats of either gender, whereas such things as marriage arrangements, which was one of her fortes, were normally in the hands of women.[16] That she often acted in accord with Queen Anne's interests against those of James I can hardly count as "subversion" in a court so intensely and unstably factionalized; "interest" hardly boiled down to queen versus king, or woman versus man.[17]

Nor were Lucy's alliances only with women, or even always with the queen (at least one of her letters explicitly registers her irritation at having to wait on the queen, and many of them make clear that she attended the king assiduously).[18] As Linda Levy Peck notes, "although the Countess of Bedford was both an important friend of Queen Anne and a member of her Household, equally important were her connections to three of the court's leading male officials [Buckingham, Hamilton, and Pembroke]; her patronage connections spanned council and household" (p. 72). I do not mean to suggest that Lucy's scope was equal to that of a male aristocrat; as Maurer points out, in detailing a moment when the Countess's marriage-brokering backfired, her gender could always be used against her as a way of pointing to the limits of her efficacy. Salisbury, against whose interests she had attempted to work, observes "that the 'noble and discreet parts of her mind' had temporarily been governed by faculties in which she 'more resembled her sex,' " thereby communicating, Maurer continues, "his displeasure in terms that remind her of her place" (p. 221). To succeed as a courtier, this exchange implies, meant to leave no trace of involvement—or of gender—behind. Reduced to "her place," Lucy is described as a woman. Properly herself, she is noble and discreet; or as Donne's poems so often suggest, she undergoes an alchemical process, a refinement and sublimation. In Daniel's poem, as we have seen, the trope for this involves locating the Countess as an unworldly overseer, making her social position tantamount to a transcendent one. As Maurer argues, consummate acts of courtiership successfully cover their material traces.

However much Lanyer's poem to Lucy participates in the kinds of idealizing and ideologizing of patronage that mask interest, gender does make a difference, but not in terms of the production of Lucy as "good" (learned, pious) woman. For that strategy is one Lanyer shares with Donne or Daniel. When Daniel, however, holds out the key of Virtue as that which separates Lucy from worldly sordidness, he deploys it in order to assert his gender. Emphasizing Lucy's class position is tantamount to granting her masculinity (as Jonson does explicitly in a poem praising her "manly soul"),[19] and the aim of this is to find a meeting point for poet and patron; Lucy is granted a self-possession located "in the minde" (l. 49), a site shared with the knowing poet, and named as "our royalties" (l. 60). This unworlding may serve Lucy's interest (in obscuring or aestheticizing courtly maneuvering), but it does not suggest that she has power as a woman in the world. That Daniel in effect lectures her on the aptness of her non-feminine choice as a way of unconfining her also implicitly makes her his subject.

When we compare how Lanyer uses the trope of Virtue "readie . . . T'unlocke the closet of your lovely breast, / Holding the key of Knowledge in her hand" (ll. 1–3) it is to allow the entrance of "him . . . by whom her youth was blest" (l. 5), a Christ who is immediately described as "the true-love of your soule, your hearts delight" (l. 6). Whereas Daniel's gesture to unconfine the sex of the Countess works immediately to produce an imaginary equalization of poet and patron—imaginary because it obscures and attempts to reverse status difference by the production of a "shared" masculinity—Lanyer's figuration insistently sexualizes the scene of Virtue's entrance. Indeed, what is remarkable, when one compares Lanyer's poem to Daniel's, is that the way in which he rhetorically overcomes his dependence upon her makes her more of a good woman than Lanyer's does; that is, the playing off of gender/social rank relations explicitly excludes any "worldliness" and thus any sexuality. In Lanyer's poem, it is entirely possible to regard Virtue's penetration of Lucy's heart as a same-sex encounter, indeed, even to regard the "proper" substitution of male lover for female key-holder as configuring Christ as a kind of supplementary instrument for penetration (as a dildo, in short);[20] at the very least, Virtue acts as a kind of pander in this triangular relationship, as she passes on to the Countess her former lover.

One could argue that Daniel's poem depends upon a familiar homosocial arrangement in which the Countess facilitates his relationship with a worldliness—with the patronage nexus—by acting as if he and his patron exist together on an exalted sphere of learning, detachment, and self-possession. It is a version of this homosocial scenario that, Hutson claims, Lanyer seeks to avoid, since it inevitably demeans women and makes them objects of exchange between men.[21] It is certainly true that nothing of Lucy's gender survives her exaltation, but it is not clear to me that when Daniel wields the key of Virtue, he sexually assaults the Countess or specularizes her body. Lanyer's poem would seem to be offering a kind of inverted homosociality, in which Jesus serves as go-between. Hutson has noted this, too, as a major component in the latter part of *Salve Deus*, where the worship of the Countess of Cumberland is couched in the imagery of Canticles. She seems to assume that the reverse blazoning of the male body of Christ and the substitution of male beauty safely allows for what she insistently refers to as a compassionate mutuality of women transacted across this body, rather than the typical male rivalry; however, as we have already seen, Lanyer can scarcely mention the excellence of the Countess of Cumberland without making invidious comparisons. It remains to be seen how same-sex relations are configured in Lanyer's poem to the Countess of Bedford.

As a figure "all stucke with pale deaths arrows" (l. 12), Jesus is offered for the Countess's embrace, to be received as a "dying lover" (l. 16). The humiliated, penetrated, and penetrating Christ of the poem to the Countess of Bedford bears resemblance, if only positionally, to the Countess herself (penetrated) and her female alter ego, Virtue the key-holder. Jesus is described as a "blessed Arke . . . /

Where your faire soule may sure and safely rest, / When he is sweetly seated in your breast" (ll. 19–21). The penetrator/penetrated situation is unstable and interchangeable here; moreover, not only is Jesus figured as a haven, but, as Woods's gloss reminds us, the ark also figures Lanyer's poem, which contains the passion as its central narrative. Indeed, Christ appears in the poem as one who "read" (l. 10) the story of earthly misery and took part in it by dying; so, too, it is his death wounds that the Countess is invited to "reade" (l. 13). Reader and read, again the boundary is crossed, and Lanyer's humble withdrawal before the Countess's penetrating gaze ("You whose cleare Judgement farre exceeds my skil, / Vouchsafe to entertaine this dying lover" [ll. 15–16]) also entails her leaving her book as that which may be lodged in the closet of her heart—or, at any rate, in her closet, accepted as a gift. But not one without returns, as the active/passive, male/female crossings must suggest. The poem ends with a ceremonial scene, in which Jesus—or the poem, or the poet—is now the guest in the bower of the Countess, bringing to her "Flowres of fresh comforts" that "decke that bed of rest" (l. 25). Lanyer's humble self-effacement is also her self-propelling as book and as Jesus. If there is here, as in Daniel, an idealizing and unworlding of the Countess as a figure of insistent privacy and piety, her bower of bliss is also repeatedly violated by a series of substitute figures: Virtue, Christ, the book, the writer. The pious scenario of a community of good women is thus coextensive with scenes of sexual intimacy and scenarios of sexual violence. These do not comfortably line up along the axis of gender difference.

Indeed, as Wall has emphasized, the Christ offered up by Lanyer is often feminized (in his suffering) and thus appears as a site of female-identification, which is to say, as Wall does not quite, of cross-gender identification.[22] Such is also the case in the address to the Countess of Cumberland toward the end of *Salve Deus*, and whatever the form of sharing between women that is imagined, it cannot quite be safeguarded, as Hutson would have it be. There is passion in this compassion:

> This is that Bridegroome that appeares so faire,
> So sweet, so lovely in his Spouses sight,
> That unto Snowe we may his face compare,
> His cheekes like skarlet, and his eyes so bright
> As purest Doves that in the rivers are,
> Washed with milke, to give the more delight;
> His head is likened to the finest gold,
> His curled lockes so beauteous to behold;
>
> Blacke as a Raven in her blackest hew;
> His lips like skarlet threeds, yet much more sweet
> Than is the sweetest hony dropping dew. . . .
>
> (*Salve Deus*, ll. 1305–15)

In the lines presenting the blazoned body of Christ, it is not merely the case that the most familiar terms of feminine beauty have been transported to his pale skin and scarlet lips; as Woods points out in her note to these lines, some of the similes used to describe him are those attached to the body of the bride in Canticles. Moreover, the lines liken the blackness of his hair to the raven "in her blackest hew" (l. 1313). The dark lady in this poem is Lanyer's Jesus. These deployments of Jesus as lover implicate a femininity that is not gender-bound; they imply heterosexual relations and religious passion that coincide with female–female eroticism.

There are several grounds for thinking about the aptness of these erotics for Lanyer's address to her would-be patrons. The piety of the Countess of Cumberland is not in doubt; yet, it also seems clear that her religious retreat, while she was married, had much to do with the abuses of a husband whose interests she continued to promote,[23] and, after his death, went hand-in-hand with the entirely worldly instigation of court proceedings to contest his will, and with the archival recovery of documents to substantiate Anne Clifford's hold on the patrimony.[24] In Lanyer's poem, sometimes rather bathetically, the pursuit of these claims against "evil men" is likened to Christ's treatment by his tormentors. If Christ's body performs the function of "subliming" property claims, it also serves to vehiculate Lanyer's desire. In this context, it seems worth recalling that it is not only the feminized body of Christ offered up to the Countess of Cumberland, but a morcellated body subject to the kind of violence that blazoning of the female body often involves. The account of the passion comes to this climax:

> His joynts dis-joynted, and his legges hang downe,
> His alablaster breast, his bloody side,
> His members torne, and on his head a Crowne
> Of sharpest Thorns, to satisfie for pride:
> Anguish and Paine doe all his Sences drowne,
> While they his holy garments do divide:
>   His bowells drie, his heart full fraught with griefe,
>   Crying to him that yeelds him no reliefe.
>
> (*Salve Deus*, ll. 1161–68)

This is followed immediately with an address to the Countess of Cumberland:

> This with the eie of Faith thou maist behold,
> Deere Spouse of Christ, and more than I can write;
> And here both Griefe and Joy thou maist unfold,
> To view thy Love in this most heavy plight.
>
> (*Salve Deus*, ll. 1169–72)

In this context it must be recalled that at the very end of the poem, the figures with whom the Countess is invited to identify are a group of male saints, ravished by the sweetness of Christ (forms of the word "sweet" are used repeatedly in ll. 1729 ff), the last of whom is the beheaded John the Baptist. Indeed, the poem ends on a highly ambiguous note:

His Head did pay the dearest rate of sin,
Yeelding it joyfully unto the Sword,
To be cut off as he had never bin,
For speaking truth according to Gods word,
Telling king *Herod* of incestuous sin,
The hatefull crime of God and man abhorr'd:
His brothers wife, that prowd licentious Dame,
Cut off his Head to take away his shame.

(*Salve Deus*, ll. 1817–24)

Whose shame? Is the sacrifice of John the Baptist—a beheading here clearly tantamount to a castration—meant to ensure the purity of his passion? And is the final alignment of the Countess with a group of males enamored of the sweetness of Christ meant somehow also to guarantee that her activities in pursuit of her daughter's inheritance be reread as spiritual, homosocial; not the work of a "prowd licentious Dame," but that of a male-identified woman—or, rather, of a woman identified with female-identified (suffering, beheaded) men?

In suggesting relationships between worldliness and spiritual retreat, between female goodness and male self-sacrifice, between passions of one kind and another (questions that also could be raised around the morbidity of the dying lover in the poem to the Countess of Bedford),[25] I do not seek to repeat the charges of sycophancy and of false religiosity that have been leveled at Lanyer (the same kinds of claims that a generation or two ago were regularly made about Donne's poems). As Lewalski aptly says, "Lanyer was a woman of her age, and her imagination was governed by its terms. At the time of this writing, she appears to have been sincerely, if not very profoundly, religious" (p. 219). What this suggests is that religion vehiculates many things, not all simply to be understood as religion: power relations, gender relations, patronage, and sex among them. In Lanyer's poem, it is not that sex is its deepest meaning, but that sexualized religious passion provides the mediating language to overcome social disparity and to put Lanyer on some kind of footing with her patrons. The textual/sexual body as go-between, as Wendy Wall has argued, is not unexpected in the period, and Lanyer, as she argues, goes about as far with the trope as any author does; but here, Lanyer seizes upon male prerogative both to vehiculate her desire (for patronage, etc.) and to imagine her place in the company of aristocratic women. To this extent, and in this highly mediated fashion, one could call this "community."

Lanyer may share with Donne or Daniel the ability to appreciate, as Maurer puts it, "the strategy of a disguise that makes its wearer's intentions plainer than common decency would allow" (p. 225). Maurer's generalization would seem to attach itself particularly to the Countess of Bedford's masquing appearances, appearing, according to Dudley Carleton, "too light and Curtizan-like" in the *Masque of Blackness*, for instance, or as Penthesiliea, Queen of the Amazons in *The Masque of Queens*, a guise Maurer describes as one in which "she abandons her identity as a discreet lady in the world's eye to claim a condition beyond discretion by virtue of her role . . . occupying the ground between some literally 'true' image of herself (in which case her costume would be indecorous) and some ideally 'true' status (in which case, it would transcend the requirement of civility)" (p. 216). Lanyer's poem, as I have been suggesting, comes close to the indecorous side of these revelations, masking female–female relations through the sublimity of Christian passion and the appropriate male figure of devotion. Yet, Maurer's remarks do insistently draw us to ask what it can have meant for Queen Anne's favorite—the Countess of Bedford—to have appeared as an Amazon, or why it is that the costumes for the queen's masques so often featured bare-breasted women. These are questions pertinent to Lanyer's address to her and the other patrons she seeks for her poem.

The possibility that female service of a patron could involve sexual services can be discerned as a subtext even in Lewalski's chapter on the Countess of Bedford. It begins by answering some sexually accusatory lines by Sir John Harington; "they pertain to the likes of Frances Howard, Cecilia Bulstrode, Penelope Rich and the Countess of Suffolk" (p. 96), Lewalski contends, not to the virtuous Lucy. Yet, Bulstrode was an intimate of Lucy's, and within a few pages, Lewalski is rescuing Lucy's "kinswoman and friend and the Queen's lady-in waiting" (p. 109) from Jonson's attack on her as the Court Pucelle (Ep. 49), the embodiment of "tribade lust" and "epicoene fury" (ll. 7–8; *Epicoene*, with its attack on learned ladies as a community of predatory Amazons, is in the wings). By the end of her chapter, when Lewalski unveils the one surviving poem by the Countess of Bedford, it turns out to be an elegy on Cecilia Bulstrode. Thus the chapter closes by joining Cecilia Bulstrode and Lucy in a proper spiritual relationship; all traces of impropriety have been sublimed. But it began by taking Jonson's position about Cecelia Bulstrode; if, finally, the Court Pucelle is metamorphosed into a virgin, the precedent can still be found in Jonson. In the elegy he wrote on Bulstrode's death, he ends by claiming (perhaps disingenuously) that she "might make the *Fable of Good Women* true" (Miscellaneous Poems 24).

One need not credit the misogynist motives for Jonson's attack on Bulstrode—an instance of his use of his gender as a weapon against aristocratic female patrons—in suggesting that there may be some truth in his tribade suggestions. Lanyer's poem to Lucy, Countess of Bedford, her addresses to the Countess of Cumberland—the insistent sexualization detailed in Wall's account of the poem—suggest as much. When, for instance, the poem to Lady Arbella Stuart discovers her in bed and asks her to "spare one looke" (l. 11) at the "humbled King" who offers his "dying armes" to her (ll. 12–13), one has to note that Stuart is initially described as the sun, so that the final embrace of Sun and Son could be viewed as male–male. But the "humbled King" is not merely the crucified Christ but also Lanyer's text, and indeed a site of authorial projection—she, like him, is one "who all forsooke," as she repeatedly reminds her would-be patrons. Indeed, Stuart is described as being in the all-female company of Pallas and the Muses as she emerges from her bed, and it is that company that Lanyer seeks to join by way of the book that she offers. Again, it is virtually impossible to separate hetero- and homoerotics in this bedroom scene; and, again, it seems clear that it is by way of these erotic crossings that Lanyer attempts to negotiate across the divide of class. That the potential scandal of same-sex sex might be appropriate for this patron is suggested by a 1605 letter of Anne Clifford's to her mother apologizing for being unable to fulfill "your Ladyship's desire," which was to have gone to Arbella Stuart "and to have slept in her chamber, which she much desired."[26] Although in this case, Clifford failed to do what her mother wanted, in her diary she records how after a quarrel with her mother when she was sent to sleep alone, her cousin Frances Bourchier "got the Key of my Chamber & lay with me which was the first time I loved her so well."[27] The point here is simply this: that just as male friendships in the period often cross over into a terrain that involves sexual relations, such, too, must have been the case among women, and especially among powerful aristocrats and those who served them, or whom they served.

This may be seen in the final poem on Cookham, that female paradise now accorded canonical status as the only complete poem by Lanyer in the most recent *Norton Anthology*, especially if we attend to a moment in it to which Coiro draws our attention. As the Countess of Cumberland is about to leave the estate, she and Lanyer proceed to the great tree that has shaded her, beneath which they, along with Anne Clifford "then a virgin faire" (l. 160), had read, and with whom Lanyer had sported:

> To this faire tree, taking me by the hand,
> You did repeat the pleasures which had past,
> Seeming to grieve they could no longer last,
> And with a chaste, yet loving kisse tooke leave
>
> ("Cooke-ham," ll. 162–65)

"We are moved by the act of sisterhood," Coiro comments. "By the next line, however, 'To Cooke-ham's' whole over-wrought, high art structure of ingratiating simile falls into a ludicrous joke: we realize that Lady Clifford has kissed the tree" (p. 373).

> Of which sweet kisse I did it soon bereave;
> Scorning a sencelesse creature should possesse
> So rare a favour.
>
> ("Cooke-ham," ll. 166–68)

For Coiro this intercepted kiss is not merely risible; it stages, once again, the distance between the aristocratic women and their dependent creature; the stolen kiss functions to break the world of similitude and of female community, an act of intrusion on the part of the upstart writer unhappy in her position and in being treated less well than even a "sencelesse creature."

There is, however, something to be added to this analysis, prompted in fact by Lewalski's observation that the tree "is almost the only element of nature gendered male" (p. 238). The vegetable love of this poem, like the insistence on her "alwaies beare[ing] a part" in the "beauteous *Dorsets* former sports, / So farre from beeing toucht by ill reports" (ll. 119–20), depends upon the exclusion of males from this female paradise and then on their reintroduction in the guise of similes of servitude and protection. This displacement of gender, so that the tree acts, as Lewalski comments, "as a kind of ideal lover, more dependable than her [the Countess's] own husband" (p. 238), functions in the same mediating way that the figure of Jesus does in *Salve Deus*—that is, ostensibly as a guarantee of the sanctity of female–female relations—or here, of their asexuality. The tree, it hardly needs to be said, is, however tamed and at their service, nonetheless a clear substitute for the phallus, and in several ways. It is a "stately Tree" (l. 53), a tree of state—it emblematizes sovereignty, and beneath it the Countess has a view that would "please the eyes of Kings" (l. 72). Although it is nominally an oak (Jupiter's tree), it appears "like a comely Cedar" (l. 57) and "like a Palme" (l. 61). This tree may be something like a family tree, but it is generative of other kinds of trees. It is the root of similitude, straight like a cedar, receptive as a spreading palm. From this male principle, that is, a genealogy of virtue arises, a principle that would equalize the aristocratic woman and her poet, who makes the similes. The Countess enters the tree, and it becomes a bower and her seat of state. In short: the tree is both male and female, natural and unnatural, a site of female phallic power due to aristocratic women and seized by their would-be poet.

The comedy and anger that Coiro reads in the scene of the farewell kiss as a sign of the class relationship is also legible in a sexual context. Kissing the rod, these women disavow a passion that the poet also declares when she "deceives" the tree, stealing a kiss she has no intention of returning, taking revenge on the tree by reducing it to an object even below her position. The tree, at the end, is just a tree, not the beautifully dissimulated image of female–female relationship. The "ingratefull Creature" (l. 171), as she terms herself, breaks the pretense of idyllic union, displaying not merely resentment, but also the desire for a kiss she has been denied. Not that a kiss is just a kiss, although Lanyer protests in the poem how much greater her love is than that of the Countess of Cumberland or her daughter; the lost kiss signals lost patronage and the loss of physical intimacy that went along with it. "And yet it grieves me," Lanyer laments, "that I cannot be / Neere unto her" (ll. 99–100). This lack of nearness, fully legible as the inevitable divide of class/status, also must be read as the loss of physical intimacies that served to cross the divide.

APHRA BEHN'S FEMALE PEN

In the concluding paragraph of an essay on Aphra Behn and sexual space, Jessica Munns takes up a possible objection to how Behn imagines and thematizes her relationship to writing.[1] Citing Sandra Gilbert and Susan Gubar's argument in *The Madwoman in the Attic*, that women's writing cannot be conceptualized through the equation of pen and penis, Munns counters provocatively: "Behn clearly feels quite comfortable with a pen/quill between her fingers." The hermaphrodite image that this description almost offers, and then displaces, is, however, the point that Munns wishes to make, claiming for Behn "a confident literary androgyny." This position entails Behn's refusal to remain marginal in relation to men and patriarchal powers of exclusion and signals her occupation of a utopic "third position." This space, Munns contends, "does not exist" except in Behn's assertions, which, although never denying her female gender, at the same time make a "claim to a male part," "my Masculine Part the Poet in me," as Behn put it in the preface to *The Lucky Chance*.[2] Munns ends her essay by issuing a stirring call to think about gender beyond stultifying binarisms, claiming Behn as a forerunner of Kristeva and as a thinker who can move feminism beyond an essentializing position "into the virgin territory of a new sexual space" (p. 207).

Men can be virgins, to be sure, yet this final figuration would seem to assure Behn's femininity, much as, in allying her with Kristeva, Munns attempts to give Behn credentials as a feminist foremother against arguments like Gilbert and Gubar's that would seem to exclude her. The feminist controversy here recalls a foundational moment in the criticism of Behn, that offered by Virginia Woolf (from whom Munns fetches the notion of androgyny), and the ambivalences lodged in Woolf's famous celebration of her: "All women together ought to let flowers fall upon the tomb of Aphra Behn . . . for it was she who earned them the right to speak their minds." As Woolf makes clear, it is less the content of Behn's work or Behn's character, "shady and amorous as she was," that she approves; rather, she applauds the fact that Behn existed and earned a living as a writer, the first English woman to do so, she claims.[3] It is easy enough to see the irony in Woolf's position; much as she praises Behn for leading the way for women authors "to speak their minds," she also censures Behn's life and writing for its unexemplary "shadiness." A similar irony can be found in Munns's defense of Behn, declaring her the inhabitant of a virginal space, or when she insists that whatever Behn's seizure of masculine prerogative involved it did not transform her into "a woman seducing a man" or "a woman pretending to be a man" (p. 206). This woman's pen/is is not phallically aggressive, nor does she wield it to assume a male position. Literary androgyny, it appears, is not even skin deep.[4] Munns's Behn is a woman—and a proper one—after all.

I open with this instance because it touches on many of the issues that can be found throughout the critical literature on Behn: questions of the propriety of her writing (worries about its complicity with a male-dominated literary tradition); doubts whether Behn can be called a feminist (a question heightened in the racialized context of *Oroonoko*, where Behn has been treated as another

Columbus, or as the first white feminist to ignore or contribute to the oppression of Blacks, and particularly to the erasure of the specificity of the experience of black women); questions about the nature of female desire. Munns is also not alone in gesturing toward Behn as a proto-modern or proto-post-modernist writer. As the "first" professional woman writer, Behn inhabits modernity in a presumably new way, and the claims that Munns makes are congruent with those like Ros Ballaster's argument that the history of the novel ought to begin with Behn rather than Defoe[5] or with those that treat *Oroonoko* as participating in and initiating an abolitionist discourse that prevailed a century or more later (Behn as Stowe).[6] Munns's insistence on the utopic non-existence of the position she advocates is perhaps a sign of how easily Behn can be transported to a future; it also has resonances with the characterization of the woman writer as a nobody—as disembodied—in Catherine Gallagher's *Nobody's Story*.[7]

Although these issues are undeniably urgent ones in any estimation of Behn and of her place in literary history, a review of the criticism could conclude that they also are intractable, that somewhere in Behn's voluminous, generically various output there is a basis for virtually all the contradictory views about her that have been expressed. Behn's affirmation of her "Masculine Part," for instance, could be juxtaposed to the phrase that titles this chapter, the "Female Pen" that Behn names as her instrument of writing in a well-known passage in *Oroonoko* in which her pen is ostensibly compared to and devalued in relationship to male writing. She writes of the hero of her tale that "his Mis-fortune was, to fall in an obscure World, that afforded only a Female Pen to celebrate his Fame" (3: 88).[8] Not only does Behn's insistence on her "Masculine Part" seem contradicted by this passage, "Female Pen" by itself would seem almost an oxymoron since the gendering of the pen signals its misgendering and dislocation—a heroic figure like Oroonoko should have enacted his history in some unobscure domain

(Europe, presumably, not Africa or Surinam), and have been written about by a metropolitan and male writer.

Behn's explanation why this did not occur, that the Dutch, who seized Surinam soon after the episodes upon which she based her tale, "kill'd, banish'd and dispers'd all those that were capable of giving the World this great Man's Life, much better than I have done" (3: 88), gives one indication how to proceed in reading the incipient contradiction. Behn points to a world historical setting and to the contingencies of the historical moment that determine how she came to author her text. Behn's historical narrative is by no means disinterested or merely factual; she laments the loss of Surinam and berates Charles II for its surrender. This fall—and the survival of the "Female Pen" as the impotent and inappropriate instrument of inscription—is part of (and reflective of) a royalist polemic/elegiac often motivating Behn's writing. The value of Behn's historicizing gesture, from which I take my cue in the pages that follow, is that it invites a reading of Behn in terms of shifting historical contingencies and the contradictions of the Restoration that is anything but reductive. "The political" cannot substitute for or provide a master code into which questions of gender and gendered practices of writing are to be folded. In the pages that follow, I seek to explore Behn's writing in terms that recognize the relationships among the historical, the political, and, therefore, the historicity of gender. Such attention might supply a sense of the enabling conditions for Behn's writing, rather than relegating her to an idealized utopian locus (as with Munns) or delegitimating her as a less than exemplary figure for feminist evaluation.

If one source of the complexity of Behn's writing has to do with the friction between her gender and her writing, much of the problem with understanding Behn comes from assuming that the female gender that she inhabited is transhistorically identical to a modern gender location. In fact, and quite obviously so, modern gender is by no means a stable category, as the acts of adjudication or debates within feminist thought about what constitutes proper femininity readily show. There is no reason to suppose that gender was any more stabilized in Behn's time than now, nor to imagine that the destabilizations of the late seventeenth century were the same as those currently operative. When Munns points to Behn as not endorsing a dichotomized view of gender, this need not be read as anticipating Bloomsburyian regimes of sexual ambiguity or as a utopian escape from the modern sex/gender system. Rather, what she sees in Behn (correctly, I believe) is something quite recognizable thanks to the work of Thomas Laqueur, who traces a history of gender from a one- to a two-gender model. Behn's texts are marked by this historical transition, and much that seems contradictory in them, and much of the difficulty in positioning her, has to do with the assumption that a modern gender system—a system of hierarchized and dichotomized gender difference—is fully in place in her texts.

In suggesting this, I must register a caveat immediately. Laqueur's work has some serious flaws, not least its assumption that the history of a biological understanding of gendered bodies is the same thing as a history of gender; many other discourses, institutional sites (e.g., the law or theology) not invested in the discourses Laqueur examines, were at work to define gender difference, and these are not governed by the shift that Laqueur delineates.[9] This means that the historical period during which Behn writes is not simply witnessing a shift in gender models. Rather, the shift Laqueur details is concurrent with and not always congruent to other definitional and institutionalized forms of gender, and it is the fraught relations between these that define the space of her writing, a space necessarily fractured and discontinuous.

Some domains more readily evince something like a modern oppositional definition of gender than others, but this resemblance is not always to be explained by Laqueur's narrative. There is, to take a crucial example, a continuity over a long durée of a traffic in women in support of male prerogatives involving property, inheritance, and title (the domain that Foucault calls "alliance").[10] Nonetheless, even this sphere underwent a transformation in the seventeenth century around gendered definitions of property rights, and the separation of public and private, domestic spheres. This domain of legal rights and territorial demarcations is largely governed by the institution of marriage, with which Behn personally seems to have had almost no contact (her husband may well have been a fiction that gave her the right to claim the privileges of a married woman or the independence of a widow), although it looms large in her plays and fiction, where it is often the most obvious site for proto-feminist statements lamenting the inequalities and reduction to chattel status that women occupy in this sphere.[11] Yet if these are proto-feminist sentiments, they could as easily be seen to be rooted in a past in which marital arrangements did not necessarily hook up to the emerging cult of domesticity; arguably, these sentiments arise from an identification with aristocratic freedom from proto-bourgeois norms.[12]

The two-gender model and the domestication of women are arguably the linchpins in an organization that points the way toward modern heterosexuality. Yet that term is something of a misnomer in the seventeenth century if one is to understand it as differentiated from (and presumptively the opposite to) homosexuality. The history of gender is not easily disentangled from the history of sexuality, one of whose landmarks in this period is the institution of the molly house, a site for men sexually interested in other men (not necessarily to the exclusion of their interest in women).[13] While the molly house has been taken as an early instance of a social form corresponding to an emergent male homosexual identity, no social equivalent for women has been identified.[14] As Valerie Traub has argued persuasively, the emerging heterosexual norm threw into high relief—and into suspicion—possibilities of same-gender female desire.[15] Nonetheless, as Emma Donoghue comments, there is no reason to suppose there should have been an equivalent to the molly house for women to meet women, considering the difference that gender made in access to public spheres; however, Donoghue amply demonstrates that various sites—especially textual ones—can be adduced to show that a recognition of female–female erotics existed in the period (Traub's evidence for an increased visibility of lesbian desire is also literary).[16] This evidence is not, I think, to be taken as merely literary. It suggests the distance between late seventeenth-century ideologies and practices of female domestication and the separate-sphere ideology articulated in the eighteenth and nineteenth centuries. Domains existed for women, forms of social intercourse not regulated by patriarchal disposal of female bodies.[17]

Behn refers to such a domain in her poem "Our Cabal," a social site of flirtation not confined to heterosexuality, of exchanges of wit and bawdy and of political intrigue. "Cabal" registers as a political term, but it also designates an expansive sexual terrain.[18] It is clear that such sites in a widening public sphere were not entirely inhospitable to women. The literary sphere was also increasingly available, as rates of female literacy and widening opportunities for publication suggest. Crucial, too, was the Restoration theater; the inclusion of actresses is often taken as the signal development here, but Behn was one of a number of women writing for the stage. Neither the press nor the stage was free of sexual suspicion, but they were also scarcely modeled on female domestication. If the theater was often thought to be a venue for the display of prostitutes and mistresses, the onstage use of cross-dressed women flirted continually with the display of same-sex desire. In that light, it seems fitting that so much of Traub's and Donoghue's evidence for protolesbian culture is literary; the restrictions on women's writing that will come to be allied to a sense of woman's place being in the home (and that proper writing for women must celebrate domestic virtue) has yet to take hold.[19]

The contexts sketched above, the political and literary axes for a historicized understanding of sex and gender, provide the frame for understanding how Behn locates the operations of her "Female Pen." Let us look closely at the passage in *Oroonoko* in which the phrase appears. It begins in a characteristically disarming way (characteristic of the narrative stance at several crucial junctures in this piece of writing): "I ought to tell you, that the *Christians* never buy any Slaves but they give 'em some Name of their own, their native ones being likely very barbarous, and hard to pronounce" (3: 88). This offhand remark, presented as if merely offering an afterthought, is crucially concerned with a writerly activity—naming—within the broadest global condition of Behn's authorship. Oroonoko has just put off his regal African attire, yet "the Royal Youth appear'd in spight of the Slave" (3: 88). So, too, renamed as Caesar, appropriated linguistically and physically by "the Christians," native royalty is inadvertently asserted. Insofar as "the Christians" give Oroonoko a Roman name, Behn dissociates their position from her own insistence on values in the royal youth continually betrayed by Christian double-dealing. Yet these values are anything but "barbarous," indeed they are repeatedly connected with Rome; however much Behn's narrator seems to position herself outside the Christian community, their translation of Oroonoko echoes her own. Caesar is, from this moment on, her name for Oroonoko. Moreover, as Behn declares in the prefatory letter to *Oroonoko*, she is in the position of "the Christians": she refers to her text as "*my Slave*" (3: 56). Much as the locution "Female Pen" retains the masculine association around that writing implement, so too the disavowed relationship between the narrator and "the Christians," between their name for Oroonoko and hers, provides the link of identification between the enslaved prince and the female writer.

These complicated movements of (dis)avowal and (dis)identification parallel the question of authorship in this paragraph as it works to suggest a matching inadequacy between the female narrator and the fettered prince who deserved another scene for his activities as well as a male author to celebrate them. This situation is furthered and specified, moreover, by the fact that Oroonoko is renamed by his owner, Trefry, and it is Trefry, who, at the end of the paragraph, serves as the very embodiment of the author who ought to have survived the Dutch takeover of Surinam to write the tale: "And Mr *Trefry*, who design'd it, dy'd before he began it; and bemoan'd himself for not having undertook it in time" (3: 89). The "Female Pen" interrupts the ideally seamless act of renaming and writing that should have been Trefry's doing (both of them set within the terms of slave ownership). Yet this is not quite an interruption, since the activity of the "Female Pen" is exactly what produces this narrative of (mis)authorship; Behn's staged interruption, as if her writing were merely inadvertent ("I ought to tell you . . ."), allows for a naming of the proper writer, Trefry, within a paragraph that also serves as elegiac memorialization of his ambitions. Even as the narrator is displaced by Trefry, she displaces him. Although the gesture to Trefry would seem to subordinate the writer, reducing her to an entirely secondary position, it is also upon Trefry and his demise that she depends. Through gestures of distance and of identification, the position of the "Female Pen" and the authority of Trefry are intertwined.

Trefry functions as the disavowed and yet specular instance of Behn's narrative procedures and position, not least because he, like the narrator, has promised Oroonoko his freedom, and for much the same reason, a recognition of his royalty. These parallels can be explained by way of the royalist politics that the narrator and Trefry share. Yet this identification also places the narrator in a "male" position, a gender position that has consequences for how one reads the erotic relationship between the narrator and Oroonoko; for she and Trefry parallel each other in this way as well. Here is Trefry's first sight of Oroonoko, worth citing at length because it echoes passages in *Oroonoko* that describe the female narrator's attachment and attraction to Oroonoko:

> he fix'd his Eyes on him; and finding something so extraordinary in his Face, his Shape and Mien, a Greatness of Look, and Haughtiness in his Air, and finding he spoke *English*, had

> a great mind to be enquiring into his Quality and Fortune; which, though *Oroonoko* endeavour'd to hide, by only confessing he was above the Rank of common Slaves, *Trefry* soon found he was yet something greater than he confess'd; and from that Moment began to conceive so vast an Esteem for him, that he ever after lov'd him as his dearest Brother, and shew'd him all the Civilities due to so great a Man. (3: 87)

Love at first sight: a penetration through the gaze that will come actually to be reciprocated, glance for glance, entrancing Trefry, "wholly vanquish'd . . . and subdu'd . . . to his Interest" (3: 87). The intensity of the male–male relationship here has its parallels elsewhere in the text (as in Oroonoko's relationship with Jamoan, the slave/prince he takes, or in the declaration of love offered by Tuscan as he attempts to save Oroonoko's life), and however safeguarded this love may be by terms of fraternity and friendship, its eroticization is all the more clear given that the narrator's relationship to Oroonoko, while ostensibly heterosexual, runs parallel to Trefry's relationship to him. Once again, these paths of (dis)identification are anything but simple, pointing as they do to the parallel emergence of what will come to be differentiated forms of desire. Furthermore, insofar as the writer's position has not entirely disavowed the masculine association of the pen, her relationship to her subject may be understood as a same-sex relationship. Conversely, since the narrator's position as Oroonoko's "*Great Mistress*" (3: 93) allies her with "the Christians," Oroonoko is in a devalued feminized position in relationship to his master/mistress. This finds its parallel in the relation to Trefry too; however much they are joined as "brothers," they remain master and slave. Gender as a relationship of power is not naturalized in terms of biological gender as understood under the two-gender model; its slipperiness is furthered by trajectories of identification opened across gender by way of hetero/homo reflection.[20] All these impinge upon—and facilitate—the position of the "Female Pen."

The root of the identification between the writer/narrator and Trefry is political, but the erotic space they inhabit cannot simply be reduced to their royalism. For even if royalist identification is the starting point, the effect, as Catherine Gallagher has argued (to somewhat different ends), of "embracing the absolute" as a writing position, is to dislocate gender binarisms.[21] The narrator may line up with Oroonoko as "feminine," as has been argued, if slavery is seen as structurally parallel to the oppression of women. But she also identifies with and as the royal slave. If her writing position is bi-gendered, so too is this instrument a fitting parallel to his devalued and exalted position. And insofar as the relationship is paralleled by Trefry's (as would-be writer, as slave owner, as the entranced recipient of Oroonoko's gaze and story), same-sex desire cannot be disentangled from heterosexuality.

To explicate further this complex set of gender identifications that enable Behn's writing position, I turn now to *The Rover*. Some of the labilities of the "Female Pen" are, arguably, tied to the narrator's unmarried position, and it thus seems worth attending to this play since it, as is typically the case in Behn's comedies, is driven by marriage plots and, as the critical consensus affirms, offers an extended critique of the barter paradigm that shapes the condition of women in marriage. Critics have ably shown how this critique is launched through the characters who, presumably, embody Behn's attempt to imagine alternatives to marital restrictions: the libertine figure of Hellena, who manages to contract a marriage with the rake Willmore that will allow for promiscuity in marriage (e.g., that will not result in her domestication); Angellica Bianca, the whore who attempts to manipulate the traffic in women by setting her own price.[22] Angellica's attempt fails, and this may be understood, as she understands it, as the impossibility of gaining the honor lost by having been a whore. If so, this may reflect upon Behn, whose relationship to the literary marketplace often is figured as a form of prostitution, and Angellica's failure thus could mark the limits upon the respectability of Behn's profession. However, Behn does not necessarily desire the respectability her character seeks, as is signaled when, in a gesture paralleling Angellica's, Behn hangs up "the Sign of Angellica (the only Stol'n Object)," as she puts it in the postscript to the play, making utterly visible her theft from her source, Thomas Killigrew's *Thomaso*.[23] This bravura admission of theft also acknowledges stealing from a male author, a gesture perhaps to be compared to the narrator's relationship to Trefry in *Oroonoko*. Behn's identification with the figure whose initials conjure up her name may not be due simply to the limited freedom of the whore in the market; it may also come from the recognition that the seller of her own body has access to a position properly only available to a man in the marriage market, or to a male author.

Although a fantasized/ideological solution to the problem of the traffic in women is offered in the marriage of Hellena and Willmore (marriage as a respectable cover for debauchery), the passionate energies in this play seem to gesture toward a union of whore and rake untrammeled by property and propriety and the rules of the marriage market that determine hierarchized gender positions.[24] Critics regularly note Behn's attraction to the rake figure, and take this as a sign of female desire—of Behn's desire—for a figure like Willmore. This explanation needs to be complicated, however; insofar as Willmore is a stand-in for John Wilmot, Earl of Rochester, it is easy enough to suppose that there is an authorial investment in the rake that does not simply reflect a desire for him, but a desire to be him. Indeed, it is worth considering that the characters in whom Behn is thought to be so invested—the female characters with whom she supposedly identifies—are rendered desirable precisely by being the object of Willmore's desire. By this I mean to suggest that the labilities of desire—the tracking of identification and desire as co-implicated—might well follow from the entanglements of same and other gendered desires in the period. There is, I would argue, a route from the rake's desire to female–female desire once one allows for Behn's investment in the male figure. This route is visible in *The Rover*, and even, as I will ultimately be suggesting, in *Oroonoko*. Before proceeding to make this case, however, this seems like the appropriate moment to pause over arguments made by Catherine Gallagher that bear upon those that have been advanced thus far.

In her study of Behn as "newfangled whore" (*Nobody's Story*, p. 14), Gallagher points acutely to the bind constituted for women by the whore / proper woman dichotomy. To be a proper woman in this formulation means entirely to hand over one's body to male possession; such dispossession constitutes a selling of the body for the sake of the proprieties, and thereby signals the dispossession (of body, of property, of juridical status) constitutive of the married woman. Yet, the whore's self-selling also is subject to denigration and her sold body doesn't gain anything from being marketed since, as Gallagher formulates this, it quickly becomes used and devalued. Behn's position, Gallagher argues, is to pose as whore but to make her writing a site in which she attempts self-possession by repeated acts of selling. Since she is not really sold, she is not really a whore, and thus behind the depradations of her dispossession is a self-possessed figure. "Her true self is the sold self's seller. She thus implies the existence of an unseeable selfhood through the flamboyant alienation of her language" (p. 22). Not only is this unseeable self incapable of materialization, it also makes Behn virginal, or at least places her in the same position as that of the woman who might be "single and never bartered her sexual favors" (p. 25). "Behn emerges as the heroine-victim of the marketplace," Gallagher writes, "utterly sold yet pristinely unsoiled because she is able to separate herself from her physical being" (p. 8). Her sold position is one that she manipulates but does not inhabit.

Gallagher's arguments bear on those I have been making about *The Rover* and the complex relations of (dis)identification between Behn and Angellica and Hellena. However, rather than opting for the unseen as the only possible real female self, it seems to me worth contemplating the possibility that the "seller" position that

Gallagher imagines behind the mask is a recognizable one. It takes nothing more than seeing it as a position normally marked male. Or, rather: one must recognize that it is "male" only within the patriarchal terrains of gender difference and gender hierarchy that Gallagher seems to assume constitute the entirety of the field of gender relations. Indeed, it is only if that is the case that a "vanishing act" coincident with the location of a viable female selfhood is necessitated.

Gallagher's argument, however, posits the woman writer as the extreme case of the writer of either gender, and, as she notes, the charges against Behn, of prostituting herself, were also made to male authors, an association of writing and prostitution that can be found well into the eighteenth century. Pointing to Dryden as one of these male authors so charged, Gallagher takes his pose of the sober critic behind the mask of self-selling as a piece of inalienable male property, much as in her reading of *The Lucky Chance*, male tumescence guarantees an unshatterable male identity. In the example of Dryden, this is too easily to accept his rhetoric as a truth guaranteed by the inequalities of gender, and to overlook the case made, for example, by Marcie Frank, that Dryden continually negotiates his social standing as a critic through perilous cross-gender identifications and disavowals that carry with them suggestions of other than heterosexual relationships.[25] So, too, it has to be noted that Gallagher's reading of the "success" of Julia in *The Lucky Chance*, which involves her making her dispossession work to her advantage, is facilitated by, if not dependent upon, a crisis in patriarchal control. These examples begin to suggest, then, that the woman's position Gallagher outlines might require comparison with the positioning of male authorship, as well as a more skeptical view of the solidifications of male power (although neither line of inquiry would necessitate abandoning a basic and undeniable understanding of gender difference as always advantageous to men). If these lines of inquiry do not seem available to Gallagher, it is because, as "heroine-victim of the marketplace," Behn is assumed to be in a position inevitably marked by hierarchies of gender. Whore and wife seem to be the only (unacceptable) alternatives; the market, in this instance, is a male monopoly to which a woman must answer. The pristine self that Gallagher constructs assumes not only that women are always placed in a subordinate relationship to men, but that they also seek to accommodate themselves to these demands and to acquire respectability in men's eyes.[26] The authorial Behn thus emerges as a proper woman—heterosexual, silent, obedient to the male voices that denigrate her, even chaste.

But what if Behn did not have Gallagher's investments in propriety? If she can't simply be seen as a forerunner of later women writers caught in the binds of domestication? From that perspective, one could argue that Behn challenges in advance the dichotomous notion of gender upon which Gallagher depends, precisely because it is not yet fully operative in the late seventeenth century. This "challenge" is therefore a mark of her place within an *older* system of gender. Behn, in this light, represents a continual challenge to heteronormative views of femininity, as well as to a *desexualization* that we have noted in Munns and is legible in Gallagher's preference for the elusive self rather than the "explicit sexuality" of self-presentation (p. 48), or in her nomination of Behn as the initial figure for female authorship, which subsequently undergoes what she terms "revirginization" (p. 87).

To pursue the possibility that Behn's femininity is not to be read through the axis of modern gender division, I return now to *The Rover* and to Behn's investments in Willmore and to his relationship to the third female lead in the play, Florinda.[27] Her situation is far more stereotypical than that of her sister Hellena or of Angellica Bianca. She simply loves a man whom neither her father nor her brother (who functions as the paternal surrogate throughout the play) approves as a marriage partner. Eventually, Florinda will be united to Belvile, but not until after her body undergoes continual assault. Arriving for an assignation with Belvile, she finds Willmore instead, who assumes her open gate means she is a whore. Fleeing in the streets, she falls into the apartments of the aptly named Blunt, the most abjected male character of the play, who decides to take his revenge on a whore who had earlier cheated him by raping Florinda. In the final act of the play, Blunt has her locked in a room, and all the male characters draw swords to see who will enter first to have his way with her. Florinda's brother, having the longest sword, beats Willmore, and incest is about to occur.

Why is this Florinda's course throughout the play? It is not, I think, that Willmore functions as an agent for the patriarchy against this rebellious woman (indeed, catastrophe is finally averted precisely by patriarchal accommodation). Rather, her utter conventionality as stage figure—and as a figure for "rebellion" based on a love-choice that recognizes Belvile's exemplary value—is being subjected to criticism rather than being held up as some kind of romantic/generic ideal (the fact that Belvile never recognizes Florinda in disguise is another way the play registers the folly of her choice). Florinda is forced into terrains of promiscuous desire that her more knowing sister, Hellena, negotiates (as did Angellica Bianca until she too fell in love). This forcing (always on the verge of rape) is engineered by Behn as a plot device and is often associated with Willmore as agent of rape. Nonetheless, Behn's desire may be invested in these scenarios. (Perhaps congruent here is the fact that Behn's plays represent women in dishabille more than those of any other playwright of the period.)[28] Willmore's attempt to argue Florinda out of resistance is worth quoting:

FLORINDA Heavens! what a filthy beast is this!

WILLMORE I am so, and thou oughtst the sooner to lie
with me for that reason,—for look you, Child,
there will be no Sin in't, because 'twas neither
design'd nor premeditated; 'tis pure Accident
on both sides—that's a certain thing now—Indeed should I make love to you, and you vow
Fidelity—and swear and lye till you believ'd

> and yielded—that were to make it wilful fornication—the crying sin of the nation—Thou art therefore (as thou art a good Christian) oblig'd in Conscience to deny me nothing. (3: 3)[29]

This argument is recognizable within those Restoration discourses Susan Staves has examined that are intent upon separating nature from custom.[30] Willmore attempts to disabuse Florinda of the usual social ties that accompany sexual activity and therefore produce categories of true love and of sin as mutually implicated. His recourse to the category of the accident is thus an attempt to resituate behavior in nature—a bestial nature that he embraces. What he exposes therefore is the confluence of that bestiality with human nature, and he seeks to strip off the disguises of social convention, as well as the stigmas of the social that attend sexual behavior.

This speech could instructively be compared to Gallagher's thesis about Behn because I believe it articulates the position Gallagher intuits as Behn's—one that has broken with the social binds upon female sexuality. Yet rather than producing a non-position or a reserve of propriety, it would precipitate promiscuity. To treat this speech simply as a piece of masculine aggression ignores the fact that aggression and desire are by no means mutually exclusive; to allow Behn to violate gender division opens the possibility that Willmore may be Behn's mouthpiece here toward a route of female willfulness ungrounded in the social conventions founded upon marriage. As in *Oroonoko*, the starting point for Behn's identification with Willmore is political; he is "the rover" and represents the exiled king during the Interregnum. His sexual position as rake stands in for Charles II. Behn lines up here as well.[31]

This male identification as a site for the enunciation of female–female desire is not a unique instance in Behn's writing. If we take as examples poems like "To the fair Clarinda, who made Love to me, imagin'd more than Woman" (no. 80) or "VERSES design'd by Mrs. A. Behn, to be sent to a fair Lady, that desir'd she would absent herself, to cure her Love" (no. 92), it is clear that the same-gender female desire that I take to be implicated in the heterosexual plotting of *The Rover* can be articulated more forthrightly.[32] The first of these poems is especially telling in the context we have been considering since it thinks same-sex relations in cross-gender terms.[33] These positions are not stable throughout the course of the poem. Behn calls the "fair lovely Maid" (l. 1) a "Lovely Charming Youth" (l. 4) since this cross-gendering legitimizes her response to her. But this response is not simply feminine submission to charms that Behn calls masculine, it is also pursuit, indeed, explicitly sexual pursuit. "No crime with thee we can commit" (l. 14), Behn affirms, as if female–female sex could not be sex. Because it is presumptively non-penetrative, thereby preserving virginity?[34] Because it is not generative and therefore could not result in the pregnancy that confirms promiscuity? If Behn entertains these views, it is only for the space of a single line, since she immediately takes them back: "Or if we shou'd—thy Form excuses it" (l. 15). But what form excuses and renders criminal sex uncriminal? The masculinization with which Behn restyles the maid, so that lesbian relations are recast as normative although simulated heterosexuality? Or because the poem seeks, as Willmore's arguments do too, to naturalize stigmatized desires? No definitive answer can be delivered about a poem in which the fair Clarinda inhabits a "deluding Form" (l. 10), except to say that that form cannot be understood within a normative definition of femininity. The sex act is similarly represented by the teasing question, "For who, that gathers fairest Flowers believes / A Snake lies hid beneath the Fragrant Leaves" (ll. 16–17). The answer to which is: anyone who believes in the single-sex model of biological gender, in which female genitals are male ones inverted, and in which the clitoris is the female penis, supposedly found in an enlarged state among tribades. Behn's poem traffics in that older model even as the cross-gender model is mobilized to allow the answer to the question to be "no one." If these lines seem to be legible as a piece of the modern wisdom that will prevail in the centuries that follow, of the impossibility of lesbian sexual relations, that hardly exhausts their meaning. As Emma Donoghue wryly comments, "Behn here cleverly takes society's ignorance and waves it in its face. . . . Behn is hinting that a sexual 'crime' is indeed being committed, but that society is too blind to see it."[35]

In this context it is worth recalling an elegantly instructive textual study offered by Bernard Duyfhuizen. Tracing the fortunes of a lyric of Behn's, "The Willing Mistress," he shows how, in one anthologized context, it may be read as an instance of Behn's male-identified libertinism and as a declaration of female sexual freedom; how, resituated in *The Dutch Lover*, the play in which the lyric appears, such libertinism is pointedly contrasted to the overriding terms of female subjugation dictated by marriage—in which a woman who has lost her virginity has no value; but how, in other anthologies and in slightly altered forms in which the poem appeared in Behn's lifetime and shortly after (in a version that may have authorial manuscript authority), the lyric undergoes a change in gender, so that the seduction involved may as easily be assumed to be lesbian as heterosexual. Interestingly enough, in that version the poem is titled "A Song for J. H.," J. H. being the initials of Behn's lover, John Hoyle, a man later accused of sodomy, and whose attractions to other men is no secret in Behn's writing.[36] The poem, as Duyfhuizen shows, is incapable of a single reading, and it is implicated in more than one possible gender configuration, and as testimony to possible hetero- and homosexual desires (in the latter instance male homosexuality may be implicated in female homosexuality).

Building on the teasing line in which the sexual act is described as "that which I dare not name," Duyfhuizen seeks to preserve lesbian desire as the great unspoken and therefore as the presumptive deep truth of the poem. Such a determination already supposes the necessity of lesbianism as a love that dare not speak its name; it assumes a hierarchy already in place in which homosexuality is inevitably oppositional to and the abjected other of heterosexuality. Yet, more to the point, and indeed what I take Duyfhuizen to have demonstrated, is that multiple sexual/gender possibilities exist simultaneously for Behn; contextualization of the lyric, rather than restoring it to a single determinative locus (as most contextualizations seem to suppose), proves exactly the opposite point. Duyfhuizen extrapolates from this poem to that addressed to the fair Clarinda that perhaps Behn's female speaker found in Clarinda "a satisfying and less threatening alternative to the sexual politics of the time" (p. 79). Yet, the poem to Clarinda, by juxtaposing homo- and heterosexual desire, participates in just those politics, and the transformability of hetero- and homosexual desiring positions one into the other does not mark either as a site free of danger. Female–female erotics, as Behn conceives them, are not necessarily benign (criminality looms over the relationship with Clarinda); indeed, it is by assuming that the only way to express power differences is by way of gender difference that the sameness of gender is thought to guarantee an absence of force or danger—or excitement.[37] In effect, this understanding desexualizes same-gender relations, or, at best, makes them the site of utopic longings that must necessarily be radically decontextualized, nonexistent at the time of anyone's writing. Once again Behn comes to disembody nobody's story.

These complex articulations of the desiring position of Behn's "Female Pen" enable us to return to *Oroonoko* and to the example that will occupy the remainder of this chapter, that found in the relationship of the narrator to Imoinda. Countering what was, until recently, a dominant trend in feminist criticism of *Oroonoko*, which argued for an identification between the female narrator and Oroonoko (based on the parallel between patriarchal oppression of women and the institution of slavery), Moira Ferguson points to two problems in this line of argument: first, she notes (as have other critics) the limits of Behn's opposition to slavery (Oroonoko is a royal exception to an institution that Behn otherwise supports); second, she argues that Oroonoko is also critiqued for his masculinist behavior.[38] For Ferguson, the narrator and Imoinda emerge as joint heroines of the text, and Imoinda is the exemplary figure for the representation of female disempowerment and victimization at the hands of Oroonoko. Ferguson has in mind the death of Imoinda, of course, but also the scene in the harem when Oroonoko finally possesses her body. This is represented as tantamount to a rape—Oroonoko is said to have "ravish'd in a Moment, what his old Grand-father had been endeavouring for so many Months" (3: 75). In this, Imoinda's condition in the text bears more than a passing resemblance to Florinda's in *The Rover*; she is under continual threat of rape (by Oronooko, by the king of Cormantien, by Trefry, and by the rest of the Englishmen in Surinam); indeed, Oroonoko recommends that Trefry rape the slave whom he desires (3: 90), a suggestion overcome only when the slave Clemene turns out to be Imoinda. Rape is averted, but only to be transformed into another legitimating version of rape, not that of the slaveholder but that of the husband. Any number of Behn's plays could be called upon to provide examples of her awareness of such a parallel. Yet, to assume that Behn's critique of forced marriage extends to all marriages (or to all heterosexual couplings) seems to me questionable. Behind it would seem to be the assumption that Behn opposes all forms of sexual behavior, or that she dreams of some form of union that would not entail force or submission. Her deployments of romance would suggest otherwise. This genre, to twentieth-century readers, can be a suspect cover for the ideological work of reinforcing gender difference. But it is often for Behn a form through which she works toward possibilities of female sexual fulfillment.[39]

Ferguson's argument necessarily ignores something quite evident in the text, the narrator's romantic investment in Oroonoko himself. As even she points out, the scenes in which Imoinda's body is violated are told "seemingly from the vantage point of Oroonoko," although Ferguson would have it that they nonetheless convey "Imoinda's perspective" as well as the narrator's and thus extend to a female readership the possibility of contemplating "their own disempowerment" and of resisting "patriarchal power" (p. 45). The sleight of hand here is suspect in a number of ways, not least in collapsing the difference between the narrator and Imoinda (only the latter is ravished and executed, after all). But the argument also entails what Ferguson seems to want to deny: a coincidence between Oroonoko and the narrator insofar as his vantage point gives access to hers. Critics who make this assumption frequently analogize Oroonoko's treatment of his wife to the narrator's complicity with it. "The white woman speaks in the novel literally over the dead body of the black woman," Charlotte Sussman, for one, concludes, and similar arguments are made by Stephanie Athey and Daniel Cooper Alarcon, who find the "metaphysical" privilege of the white female narrator to be determined by this relationship to the embodied Imoinda; or by Margaret Ferguson, who further claims that because the narrator is so entranced by Oroonoko, Imoinda functions as her rival in the text.[40]

There is, of course, something to be said for these latter arguments, and it might therefore seem as if the problems posed by *Oroonoko* are simply intractable if the narrator's relationship to Imoinda can be read as both lethally antagonistic and sympathetically identificatory. It seems clear that there is no way out of this impasse, moreover, if the text is held up to more modern and therefore supposedly more enlightened positions about race and gender and their interrelations. As Margaret Ferguson suggests, what is required is "more attention to modalities of identification and difference" than most critical practices afford (p. 223). The historical terrains of sex and gender that I have been mapping would seem to offer some answers here. One further route might be to follow Duyfhuizen and to regard *Oroonoko* as, in itself, a kind of palimpsest; it might be the case that multiple contextualizations will "explain" (without simplifying) the complex and contradictory positions, the textual-sexual spaces of the tale.

These are reflected in the generic overloading of *Oroonoko*, a text composed of everything from a fact-based narrative to the extravagancy of an orientalist tale, with a good measure of Shakespearian tragedy and Renaissance travel narrative thrown in as well. The intelligibility of *Oroonoko*, while not to be reduced to the multiple generic codes of its writing, is nonetheless in some measure a product of these conflicting genres.[41] These are not, however, simply literary matters, for these codes are ways of handling and representing the very issues that trouble criticism, primarily those concerned with the political (especially colonialist and imperialist politics, but also the local politics involving the Stuart succession in crisis at the time of Behn's writing), with gender relations, and with racial relations. Arguably, these conflicting codes, meant to manage domains not necessarily thought of together, can have some salience when one recognizes their potential usefulness for disentangling questions of race and gender. It is perhaps the critical need to collapse one into the other, or to treat them as fully parallel, that has led to some of the impasses in the discussion.

Oroonoko is composed of incommensurable discourses. Taking stock of the different registers in which the text operates simultaneously and the uneven relations among textual strands (and the cultural domains to which they relate) would be a formidably complicated task, but it would at least reveal that what seem like singular demarcations (woman, Black, etc.) are not. The black woman in the orientalist tale should not be the same figure as the black female slave,[42] and part of what is difficult in Behn's text is that when it operates in the new world and offers a fair amount of historically convincing detail, it does not cease to operate as well within the codes of the harem fantasy used in the scenes in Africa. Behn's historical knowledge about the African slave trade seems less engaged than her denunciations of local politics in the colonies and their metropolitan ramifications. The conventions of romance, not the realities of slavery, allow her depiction of the special treatment of the royal couple (exempted from labor), as well as their reunion. There is scarcely a page in *Oroonoko* that fails to offer such dilemmas.

Areas of knowledge and modes of representation that we expect to be coordinated (and in the case of this text, that we would desire to be of use to go on thinking progressively about relations of gender and race) may well not be. In ways that hardly need further comment, it is true enough that Behn's text is racist: orientalism exoticizes; royalism indulges in an exceptionalism that condemns the remainder of the slaves to their "rightful" condition. Yet the kind of moral condemnation that the tale now provokes critically (a response, of course, to a body of criticism that had taken Behn's celebration of the royal couple as a warrant for a thoroughgoing antiracism, and that has grown suspicious of the analogy between white women and black men) may also be somewhat out of place.[43] Behn is not exactly responsible for the blindnesses of the critics who once applauded her. My point is not that *Oroonoko* should be exonerated from its participation in racialized discourses; nor can one claim that no one in the seventeenth century could have been any more enlightened. It is simply that the intelligibility (and some of the pleasures) of Behn's tale are sacrificed for the sake of the moralizing gesture.

As a small piece of this complex situation, I return now to the question of sexual relations between racially differentiated women in *Oroonoko*. The either/or that criticism offers—in which the narrator wants Oroonoko and therefore abjects Imoinda, or in which the narrator allies herself with Imoinda against Oroonoko—depends, in both cases, on the same notion of sexual desire, a heterosexuality that is based on the opposition between the sexes, effecting rivalry between women or alliances between them. Such structures do have a place in the novel: the old king of Cormantien's cast-off wife is part of a system of harem rivalry, and her aid to Oroonoko is based on it. In treating this as the only sexual system in the text, other possibilities affecting both cross-gender as well as same-gender attractions/repulsions are ignored. Imoinda's virtual rape in the harem can be read as a critique of patriarchal marital arrangements. But just as surely a libertine perspective also operates, and the description of the ravishment of Imoinda, including her slight resistances and hesitations, are arguably titillating:

> The Prince Softly waken'd *Imoinda*, who was not a little surpriz'd with Joy to find him there; and yet she trembl'd with a thousand Fears. I believe, he omitted saying nothing to this young Maid, that might perswade her to suffer him to seize his own, and take the Rights of Love; and I believe she was not long resisting those Arms, where she so long'd to be; and having Opportunity, Night and Silence, Youth, Love and Desire, he soon prevail'd; and ravish'd in a Moment, what his old Grand-father had been endeavouring for so many Months.
>
> 'Tis not to be imagin'd the Satisfaction of these two young Lovers. (3: 75)

Where is Behn in this moment? I think the answer is anything but straightforward. The description is punctuated by the locution "I believe . . . I believe," and in these authorial transports, the positions of both Oroonoko and Imoinda are assumed. The narrator, at once, participates in the scene from both perspectives, vicariously the object as well as the subject of desires that cannot be reduced along singular, and opposing, positions of desire and identification. Included, then, in the unimaginable satisfactions of this scene—in their imagined satisfactions—are the narrator's enunciation of "male" desire as her own, an identification across gender that allows for the vicarious enjoyment of Imoinda. Lest this claim seem far-fetched, it might be worth recalling that there is a figure in the tale who occupies just such a position vis-à-vis Imoinda, the impotent king of Cormantien. The narrator with her "Female Pen" may be in a parallel position of rivalry.

Criticism of *Oroonoko* is governed by the supposedly transparent logic of modern desire, which assumes that identification and desire run on opposing tracks. (The little boy child, in the foundational narrative for this thinking, wants to be its father and have its mother; therefore wants to kill its father; therefore comes to take another female as substitute for the mother, and thus resolves the dilemma, stabilizing a masculine identity through this heterosexual resolution.) This Freudian wisdom, certainly disputed in recent feminist analysis, is also disputed by Behn's text, but not because it has arrived at some post-Freudian perspective (not because Behn is Kristeva, as Munns argued).[44] Rather, the mechanisms of identification and desire must function differently under an aegis in which heterosexual object choice and its institutionalization in marriage do not preclude other forms of desire. If it is the case that Imoinda's ravished body is a site of protest on Behn's part, it may serve to register the depradations of marriage in which women's bodies are disposable property. But its ravishment could also signal Behn's writing position, her narrator's desire for the "masculinist" privilege of Oroonoko, although she finds herself more in the position of the impotent king.

Perhaps this line of thought could be rendered more cogent when one recalls how often Behn nominates as a sign of male desirability masculine softness (and how, in *Oroonoko*, the sign of Oroonoko's attachment to Imoinda is what critics often refer to as his feminization). Behn still operates within the frame of reference in which male desire for women could result in male effeminacy. But she also operates in a culture in which male desire for other males is institutionalized in sites of cross-dressing (it is that feature of the molly house that is always highlighted). That is, Behn writes at a moment in which male effeminacy signifies doubly. That the lability of male desire is signaled by a female form must mean something about female desire, and, of course, there is a widespread cultural belief in innate female promiscuity.[45] Marriage and its overestimation of chastity is bent on the control of female sexuality, its channeling into a single legitimate and legitimating path. It is no surprise, therefore, that one cannot point easily to institutionalized sites for such female self-expression (beyond the theater and the whorehouse), but there is no reason to assume that Behn's literary practice is on the side of institutionalized repression of female sexuality, especially if its most visible form is marriage. Moreover, although this will not win Behn awards for political progressiveness, the possibility that lesbian desire might attach itself to a black woman's body traffics in notions of the heightened sexuality of non-western females that Valerie Traub has detailed.[46] What perhaps keeps this from being merely a projective site, however, is the fact that "black ace" was a seventeenth-century slang term for female genitals; this sexual/racial nomination is potentially self-referential.[47]

Ros Ballaster has pointed, rightly I think, to the attractions of incest for Behn (*Love Letters Between a Nobleman and His Sister* confirms this; recall that Florinda ends *The Rover* about to be raped by her brother).[48] Yet, the question arises: what would incest look like if psychosexuality were not governed by the heterosexualizing Oedipal model? As Ballaster observes, Behn's incestuous couples (and particularly in *Oroonoko* where Imoinda is "Female to the noble Male; the beautiful *Black Venus*, to our young *Mars*" [3: 63]) tend also to be twins. Incest for Behn is not usually parent-child, but brother-sister. However much incest would seem to conform to a system of gendered opposition, locating it between siblings/twins pushes hard on the notion of difference as what is being overcome, and in the direction of identification and substitution, so that both logics are at work. It is easy enough in the text to see how much Oroonoko's desire for Imoinda is a deflection from and enactment of male desire (she substitutes for his dead foster father; the king and Oroonoko are rivals for Imoinda; so too is Trefry). What is less visible because it is not the subject of narration is that such overlays of homosocial and heterosexual desire also determine the narrator's relation to the couple. Imoinda is often presented in the text as a ravishing object; whose gaze is assumed as she is described as erotically alluring? Only a male reader's? As Moira Ferguson claimed, one gaze can implicate the other.

The argument against such a bi-gendering would be that the gaze in *Oroonoko* is lethal and therefore must be masculine, but to so argue involves an endorsement of the oppositional model of gender, which, I have been arguing, only partially governs Behn's writing. In "News from the New World: Miscegenous Romance in Aphra Behn's *Oroonoko* and *The Widow Ranter*," Margaret Ferguson notes, in the context of the narrative violence unleashed upon Imoinda's body, the possibility of lesbian desire (Ferguson credits Michele Barale for the point): "the narrator's lavish description of Imoinda's 'carved' body suggests, of course, the possibility of female homoerotic pleasure as yet another alternative to procreative sexuality."[49] Although Barale's observation is not really integrated into Ferguson's arguments, it is undeniable that the description of Imoinda's body carries a strong erotic charge. It occurs in another of those paragraphs marked by a parenthetical locution:

> I had forgot to tell you, that those who are Nobly born of that country, are so delicately Cut and Rac'd all over the fore-part of the Trunk of their Bodies, that it looks as if it were Japan'd; the Works being raised like high Poynt round the Edges of the Flowers: Some are only Carv'd with a little Flower, or Bird, at the Sides of the Temples, as was *Caesar*; and those who are so Carv'd over the Body, resemble our Ancient *Picts*, that are figur'd in the Chronicles, but these Carvings are more delicate. (3: 92)

Just when Oroonoko has reclaimed Imoinda, the narrator interrupts their reunion in order to tell us something she has supposedly forgotten until then, that Imoinda's body is covered with elaborate tracery, marks of scarification. What can this interruption mean if not the narrator's own claim to bodily possession? The marks that she traces run all over and cut into Imoinda's body; the narrator thereby reveals her intimacy with it at the very moment it is handed over to Oroonoko. Moreover, the marks are obviously signs of possession, brands. And in their insistent artistry, they obviously too are writer's marks. The narrator penetrates Imoinda with her "Female Pen." Although Ferguson has argued that *Oroonoko* involves competition between the narrator and Imoinda for Oroonoko and what can be made of him, a dangerous baby or a book as a "safe-sex" substitute for miscegenous coupling, the scene of inscription of Imoinda's body, its cutting, reveals a rivalry between the narrator and Oroonoko for Imoinda's body. It reveals, too, the violence of desire, violence here perhaps a sign of a desire to wrest the woman away from the man. But such might even be the case in the supposed complicity between Oroonoko and the narrator at the moment of the decapitation of Imoinda, a final marking and slicing of the body. If she is made to "pay" in this horrendous way for being a dutiful wife, Behn may then be exposing the cost to women of such subjugation and enslavement. If, in part, this perspective can still be chalked up to rivalry for the body of Imoinda, one violence answers another. Although this may not be a very utopian conclusion to come to, since it implicates same-sex desire in the violence of hetero desire, it nonetheless gives material existence to lesbian desire in the text.

It suggests the degree to which Behn invests bodily in Imoinda and in her writing. I emphasize this point to take issue with Catherine Gallagher's argument that *Oroonoko* offers a kind of allegory about print culture in which the black bodies figure the ink that marks the narrator's estrangement and veiling. Such a reading effectively disembodies the materiality of print as much as it reduces black bodies to merely metaphorical status (Gallagher's argument could thus be seen as perfectly in line with Behn's supposed appropriation of black female bodies and the "metaphysical status" she thereby acquires). To see Imoinda's body as a site of inscription, as a body that bears the marks, is not to make the same argument as Gallagher's (even if it supposes that the black bodies in the text also function as sites of textuality): Gallagher assumes that print could be only a locus of alienation; I am arguing that these are bodies in which the writer is invested and her desire is enunciated. In the passage about scarification, the markings on Oroonoko stay comfortably visible and on his forehead, whereas Imoinda's body is entirely covered with them. (This differentiation cannot be reduced to the analogy public : male :: private : female since Behn is making public the entirety of Imoinda's body, but only a bit of Oroonoko's flesh is seen.) The woman's body is the privileged site of representation. Throughout the text, Imoinda's desire itself is represented as enslaving; when most under her sway, Oroonoko is most impotent and inactive. Of course, it would be absurd to suggest that such female empowerment is really comparable to the depradations of the slave system even though Behn uses the language of slavery here and elsewhere to describe erotic subjection. But it does suggest what power looks like to Behn and what as a woman she desires. This is, of course, politically suspect. But it is intelligible through the historical matrix that this chapter has sought to provide. However much Behn's politics (by which I mean not only her royalism but her sexual politics as well) may be inassimilable to modern liberal or post-liberal feminisms or to projects that aim at redemptive readings of texts by women, my point is not to end by endorsing the kind of condemnation of Behn against which such redemptive readings have been launched. It is rather to keep open that sexual space this chapter has sought to describe.

Ravished and ravishing Imoinda: the reversability also figures a transgendering effect. There is perhaps a parallel in a scene in the second part of *Love Letters Between a Nobleman and His Sister* in which Antonet, the maid who was to substitute for the heroine Sylvia in a sexual assignation with Octavio, seems to have failed, and in which it seems that his anger at Sylvia means that he has seen through the plot and found the maid a less than adequate substitute for her mistress. Sylvia tests this hypothesis by trying out the maid herself, putting herself in her thwarted lover's position to see what he would have found wanting in the maid. She finds nothing lacking, finds the maid, that is, a version of herself: "she embraced her, she kissed her bosom, and found her touches soft, her breath and bosom sweet as any thing in nature could be."[50] Autoeroticism, twinship, and homoeroticism are to be found here, yet Sylvia also identifies with the male as she has her way with her maid, and the maid is abjected, treated as an object of Sylvia's pleasure just as her part in the substitution plot renders her nothing more than an instrument. None of this is very edifying as a spectacle of proper female behavior. My point in short: Aphra Behn's "Female Pen" is (to use Woolf's adjective) a "shady" instrument. All puns intended. Rather than trying to exonerate her, it is time to give up the project of making her a good woman or a good feminist. Or rather to see that in her depictions of the pleasures and dangers of sex, and in the inability of her texts to settle the question of desire simply in terms of object choice, Behn's writing allows for ways of thinking about gender—and for a feminist politics—that has no need for the legend of good women.[51]

Two TRANSLATING WOMEN

INTRODUCTION

"All translations are reputed femalls, delivered at second hand": John Florio's statement in the dedicatory epistle to his translation of Montaigne has been taken as definitive in its equation of translation as female and in its implications for the woman translator.[1] "Degraded activity" is Margaret Hannay's (p. 9) summation of what translation is in this equation, depending too on Florio's characterization of such work as a "defective edition" (A2r). Or, rather, Hannay's phrase is mere citation of Mary Ellen Lamb, who also characterizes translation, thanks to its association with women, as "degraded activity" (p. 116). Hannay's phrase appears, in fact, in her summary of Lamb's arguments; quotation marks abound, except in the case of "degraded activity." But perhaps no quotation marks are needed, for, to cite Lamb, it could be said that "the dynamics underlying this way of thinking are transparent" (p. 116). This echo of "degraded activity" from Lamb to Hannay might be likened to the relationship of original to an (un)defective translation, "the parthenogenic ideal of an otherwise perfect copying" (p. 139), to quote Patricia Parker's description of what the humanist ideal of male–male transmission would be were no women—or translators—to intervene.

For Parker, as for Hannay and Lamb, women are defined by Florio's definition, barred from a place in the humanist regimes of copy: "Women were associated in the early modern period with translation in the sense of adulteration or contamination" (p. 139), Parker writes. She continues: "Translation and the female—seen as secondary, accessory, or defective—are thus . . . linked . . . even without recourse to reminders that the activity of translation in the Renaissance was often the only sphere of writing open to women (and hence, perhaps, characterized as a feminine activity even when male writers like Florio engaged in it)."[2] No recourse to reminders here, no need to look at an example of women translating. Once again, the sentences are so commonplace as not to require quotation marks. Here is Mary Ellen Lamb: "Translations were 'defective' and therefore appropriate to women; this low opinion of translating perhaps accounts for why women were allowed to translate at all" (p. 116). Not exact citation, from Lamb to Parker, to be sure: varying a commmonplace, something transparently true, no doubt? "Translation as bearing away," as Parker might say: as filching. "Falling away from the integrity of the original" (p. 140). Or reproducing it literally, if not quite word-for-word? Could one say that Parker here translates Hannay who translates Lamb? Not literally: but what is translation literally? Latin *translatio* translates Greek *metapherein*. Translation: literally metaphor.

Florio, to be sure, contrasts translation with a "masculine" form of writing in which "all mens conceipts . . . are their owne" (A2r) and does represent translation as female, defective, and secondary; my point in drawing attention to the unanimity of a critical consensus that repeats Florio, that echoes him, sometimes directly quoting, sometimes not, means only to call into question the critical point of such reproduction, such assent to Florio. For Florio is taken as an authoritative—because male?—articulation of the plight of the female translator; so authoritative, indeed, that one might suppose *he* were the female translator embodied. Critics seeking to describe the conditions for female translators translate women as Florio does, translating them into Florio and reproducing as critique Florio's description of his own translation. If Florio represents translation so invidiously, why assume that he therefore speaks the truth about women as translators? Why assume that a translator's pronouncements about translation render translation devalued, degraded? No doubt, Florio's remarks have a long progeny, extending to George Steiner or Harold Bloom, as Lori Chamberlain demonstrates in her exacting study "Gender and the Metaphorics of Translation." But, as Chamberlain goes on to note, depending, too, on Hannay's claim that women were allowed to translate because the activity was regarded as degraded, "Our task as scholars . . . is to learn to listen to the 'silent' discourse—of women, as translators—in order to better articulate the relationship between what has been coded as 'authoritative' discourse and what is silenced in the fear of disruption or subversion" (p. 470). At the very least, then, Chamberlain assumes that there is something to be heard in translation that is not governed by the prescriptions that seek to guarantee its entirely docile, secondary, effaced, and degraded condition.

Parker proceeds from Florio's "second hand" delivery to the first woman, Eve, created second—and from Adam, as the ur-myth of such refusals of origin and primacy to women. This is not quite the mythic scene that Florio himself invokes, although his—the birth of Minerva "from that *Iupiters* bigge braine" (A2r)—shares with the biblical narrative a scene of male delivery, the collapse into the male origin of a biological feat only women are capable of performing. Yet, although the biblical narrative invidiously answers "man" to the question where women come from, the story Florio is telling, about where translation comes from, does not quite map, point-for-point, onto the narrative in Genesis. Perhaps we need to measure a difference in translation rather than assume that one story says exactly the same as the other. Where, moreover, is Florio, the translator, in this scenario of the birth of Minerva? Neither Jupiter nor Minerva, he plays the role, he says, of Vulcan, delivering Minerva. The translation may be gendered female, but the translator is not. Moreover, what is being born here is not woman, although Minerva is female, but the goddess of wisdom. The classical myth is an allegory about the origin of ideas. Unlike the Bible, Florio is not narrating the origin of gender difference, however much his myth shares elements with that narrative. If these two foundational western myths (would it be possible to say which translates the other?) share a misogynist plot by imagining male originality in each instance, there may still be something to be said for the difference between the woman made responsible for the fall and the goddess that embodies wisdom. This could be argued even though both of these may be read as masculine projections, attempts, on the one hand, to taint forbidden knowledge as female, and, on the other, to control valued knowledge as the female offspring of a male mind.

Neither of these may allow for female originality, but before shutting the book, there is another question to be posed. It is raised when Florio describes what male originality looks like. Here, too, Florio posits a scene of male birth, this time of Bacchus "closed in, or loosed from his great *Iupiters* thigh" (A2r). This analogy is meant both to describe Florio in his "last Birth" (as the author/compiler of a *Worlde of Wordes* [1598], a dictionary) as well as Montaigne: "and this was to *Montaigne* like *Bacchus*, closed in, or loosed from his great *Iupiters* thigh." In these analogies, Montaigne or Florio is in the position of Bacchus, while in the analogy describing secondhand delivery, Montaigne is presumably in the position of Jupiter, Florio's book is Minerva, and he is Vulcan. Who, then, is Jupiter in the first analogy? Not the author or the originator of the text, but the origin of that origin. Hence, when secondhand delivery is described, the author originally, secondarily, delivered by Jupiter steps into the place of origin. Only in this seconding is authorial primacy even achieved.

One need not do more than invoke Irigaray to see that the feminine affirmed in the second case is a support for a masculinity that can name itself as primary only through this positing of a second. But one can go beyond Irigaray to ask what the doubling achieved in the first instance: that is, why masculine origination is first thought of as male–male parthenogenesis—without women, to be sure, and this is to be noted: but also without being able to secure the author's originality except through his origin elsewhere—in Jupiter. These two scenes could be compared to the humanist dream of male–male copy and to the denigrations of women/translation, but they also suggest that the latter invidious scene—which nonetheless allows a place for the female—is also the one that creates—retrospectively, secondarily—human male origination.

The non-identification of apparently analogous scenarios of male birth to explain the difference between "masculine" and "femalls," between what is men's "owne" and what is "second hand" falters, and on several counts: the male author can be in the position of Jupiter only by the wisdom / the translation produced from him; the original male author is born of a male god, but in an act in which not only is he not the origin but the god himself is a surrogate: Bacchus was sewed into and released from Jupiter's thigh after the baby was taken from the womb of his dead mother, Semele. Jupiter, in this instance, may give birth, but he is not, as when he delivers Minerva, fully in the female biological position of reproduction.

What, then, is to be made of these complicated scenarios of masculine birth? Lamb insists, in her reading of these scenarios in Florio, that women were allowed to translate precisely because translation "did not threaten" men (the phrase is used three times in successive sentences, p. 116). But she also says that the figuration of male birth, especially the violence in Florio's image of Vulcan "hatcheting" Minerva from Jupiter's brain, "suggest[s] anxieties based in the fundamental differences between the sexes, women's abilities to bear children and men's role of getting and maintaining an erection" (p. 116). The point of the passage, thus, is an expression of hostility toward intellectual women (the very women first said unthreateningly to do the degraded work of translation), a "subconscious" message, to be sure, Lamb adds, since Florio addressed his dedicatory epistle to the Countess of Bedford and her mother, Lady Harington, seeking patronage.[3] "One wonders how the intellectual Countess of Bedford and her mother reacted" (p. 117).

One wonders several things more about this reading: would the intellectual and childless Lucy have associated her femininity with reproduction? Does the fact that most women can bear children, and that most who can, do, mean that women as a whole—even those statistically counted here—associate their gender solely with this biological function? (I won't even ask how male erection is parallel to female childbearing, or why erection should only be thought of in that conjunction.) If, as Lamb says, brainwork is often metaphorized/translated as childbirth, does this then necessarily mean that the metaphor works actually to "deprive" childbearing women of their biological capacity, as she claims? If there is anxiety here, what happened to the supposed complacency? If this passage is to be read as a collapse of women into the female translator position, what happens to Florio in this passage?

Florio *is* anxious in this letter—to secure Lucy's patronage and her favor, not least because she set him the task of translating Montaigne, and was, he claims, a cruel taskmaster too (overt hostility is registered). Where do such commands fit within the supposition of female secondhandedness when an aristocratic woman is in question? He worries, too, whether this girlchild of his is fitting to his patrons and suggests that just as Montaigne's address to "the Lady of *Estissac*," on the affection of fathers for their children, may reflect on and be legible as Lady Harington's relationship to her daughter, so Florio's "fine-witted Daughter" (A2r), his translation, may be esteemed. The book is offered into the service of these commanding women, and so offered, Florio seeks to do for it what Montaigne did for "his other selfe, his peerlesse paire *Steven de*

Boetie . . . and thinke," Florio urges the Countess, "hee speakes to you my praise-surmounting Countesse of *Bedford*" (A2v)—that is, Lucy is to read herself where Boetie is. These analogies (of fathers and mothers, sons and daughters, male friends and female patrons) are as riotous as those involving male birth and gendered difference; in reading the original as/in the translation, gendered positions are refused any stabilization. Similarly, at the end of Florio's letter, his ability to perform the cruel task imposed upon him is made possible only by the aid he has received from his friends, Theodore Diodati and Matthew Gwinne, the latter also—that is, as had been the Countess of Bedford—described as identical to Montaigne's "second-selve," Etienne de la Boétie (A3r).[4] Add then to the second hand, this male–male seconding, this humanist copy. Add to the instability of originality these complex paths of crossed—gender-crossed—destination. Can translation really be secured and invidiously demeaned as female? True, these crossings may be in the service of Florio—of his gender, even of his mastery of his unmastered, gender-crossed, socially subservient position. Nonetheless, they suggest paths of possibility—for women, for translators—foreclosed if the difference between original and translation, male and female, is unbreachably maintained. And, as this reading of Florio has been aiming to suggest: these paths in Florio's letter are paths of translation. Bywords for translation: *belles infidèles*, false friends, *faux amis*, names that cross gender.[5] *Traduttore traditore*.

My aim in posing these questions is to affirm, in Chamberlain's words, that "translating is like writing" (p. 466), that is, that translation is a kind of writing, and to register a caveat against, for instance, the subtitle of Tina Krontiris's *Oppositional Voices: Women as Writers and Translators of Literature in the English Renaissance*, where the diacritical difference between writer and translator rather than a likeness seems to be indicated, thus affirming a hierarchy between original and second, between real writing and something else. Krontiris summarizes her project: "my focus has been on those women who wrote or translated," she begins (p. 23). Translation may be an "oppositional" strategy, but it is conceptualized as other-than-writing, as "relatively passive" (p. 20). "A woman translator could thus hide behind another author (usually male)" (p. 21). Yet, as Krontiris also affirms, "in the Renaissance translation was much more highly ranked than it has been since" (p. 20), which is rather an understatement. When one thinks, for instance, of Luther, one cannot ignore his making the Bible German; is it possible to consider the Reformation and fail to mention translation in conjunction with the vernacularization of culture? To forget those burned as heretics for their translations?[6] Sidney was honored by Sir John Harington by being dubbed the "English Petrarke." Could not "Renaissance" translate *translatio studii*?[7] There should be no need to go on suggesting the ways in which humanist culture and the rise of vernacular literatures depend upon translation, nor to start making a list of translators: Ficino, Erasmus, North, Golding . . . ; where would it stop? Jonson, Shakespeare, Marlowe, Spenser, Wyatt, Surrey. Or, to recall a title like R. F. Jones's *Triumph of the English Language*, to situate translation within the history of the English language and the nation (with all the attendant misgivings one would want to register conveyed by Jones's imperial/colonial assertion, and certainly with no aim simply to celebrate the "accomplishments" of the Renaissance).[8]

Women translators are part of this "Renaissance," too. Lamb laments, in her essay on the Cooke sisters as learned women: "The narrowness of the intellectual boundaries within which educated women were allowed to exercise their learning undoubtedly accounts at least in part for the amount and nature of the Cooke sisters' translating. They fit their work neatly within the constraints of the time. They confined themselves to religious texts and they published only those translations which were of some public benefit. These publications were almost against their will" (p. 119). This summary sentence alludes to, among other works of theirs, Anne Cooke's translation of Bishop Jewell's *Apologia Ecclesia Anglicanae*, a book ordered to be in every church and home, as Lamb details

(p. 109). Yet, she also claims that women were barred from the public life promised by humanism to its pupils. Cooke's translation became the standard translation of this important book: it *was* that book for those who could not read Latin. Why call this demeaning and forced work? What is being assumed about what Cooke would have chosen to write? Perhaps what Valerie Wayne assumes as she castigates Vives for his less than egalitarian views on women's education, and transfers his insistence on limitations to one of the authors considered below, Margaret Roper: "Better to translate Erasmus. . . . Better still to do the embroidery."[9]

Florio's invidious mobilization of gender difference does not automatically attach itself to translation; as Wendy Wall notes, commenting on Florio, "humanistic education encouraged translation and imitation as important modes of discursive learning. In fact, the opposition between original and secondary or imitative works is a categorical opposition largely absent in the Renaissance; the notion of original writing became valorized only later."[10] As Wayne argues, Vives's program of imitation for boy students assumes a progress toward a kind of stylistic appropriation/individuation denied to girls. But: the education offered was in large measure, programmatically, the same. Injunctions about use do not determine what will be done.[11] The critics who repeat Florio also assume that the limitations prescribed always took effect, assume it even when texts of great importance were produced, texts that then get characterized as virtually valueless forced labor. Who reduces Roper's *Pater Noster* to the status of embroidery? Why argue that in choosing to translate Garnier's anti-authoritarian *Antonie* one cannot be sure that the Countess of Pembroke knew what she was doing?[12] Who, in pointing to how "literal" women's translations were, is taking them literally—as not their own, as simply the invisible conduit for the reproduction of the original male text?[13] Can translation be taken so literally? Is there no more to say, after detailing the skill of Mary Sidney's translation of Philipe de Mornay's *Discours de la vie et de la mort*, than to "regret that the countess limited herself to the silent art of translation and did not write her own meditations"?[14]

What is one's own? Wayne claims that humanists would as soon have had women do their sewing as reading or writing. Vives, as translated by Richard Hyrde, writes:

> Woman's thought is swift, and for the most part, unstable, walking and wandering out from home, and some will slide by reason of it [her] own slipperiness, I wot not how far. Therefore reading were the best, and thereunto I give them counsel specially. But yet when she is weary of reading, I cannot see her idle as were the women of Perseland drowned in voluptuousness and pleasures. St. Jerome would have Paula to handle wool. (p. 44)

My point is not simply that Wayne ups the ante and makes Vives seem even more repressive than he means to be. Is this Vives's "own" thought? Sewing enters by way of St. Jerome. But, beyond this, consider the following:

> Two things are of the greatest peril to the virtue of a young woman, idleness and lascivious games, and the love of letters prevents both. Nothing else better protects a spotless reputation and unsullied morals: for they are more securely chaste who are chaste from conscious choice. I do not necessarily reject the advice of those who would provide for their daughter's virtue through handiwork. Yet there is nothing that more occupies the attention of a young girl than study. Hence this is the occupation that best protects the mind from dangerous idleness, from which the best precepts are derived, the mind trained and attracted to virtue.

This is Erasmus in a 1521 letter to Guillaume Budé—or, rather, a modern translation of that text.[15] Who copies whom here, is it Vives or Erasmus who put reading and sewing in this conjunction? (Dates of publication will hardly answer such a question in a manuscript culture in which letters circulate.) Or here:

> redying and studyeng of bokes so occupieth the mynde that it can have no leyser to muse or delyte in other fantasies whan in all handywerkes that men saye be more mete for a woman the body may be busy in one place and the mynde walkyng in another: and while they syt sowing and spinning with their fyngers maye caste and compasse many peuysshe fantasyes in their myndes whiche must nedes be occupyd outher with good or badde so long as the[y] be wakynge.[16]

This is Richard Hyrde, defending classical education for women, in the preface to Margaret Roper's translation of the *Precatio Dominica* of Erasmus. Or, is this Hyrde, the translator of Vives, translating Erasmus? Or Vives, Englished by Hyrde, and thus Hyrde? "For I never herde tell nor reed of any woman well lerned that ever was (as plentuous as yvell tonges be) spotted or inflamed as vicious."[17] "And truly if we would call the old world to remembrance, and rehearse their time, we shall find no learned woman that ever was ill."[18] The first citation here is Hyrde, the second, Hyrde's Vives. Both would seem to be translating some lost original, or each other.

There is no surprise in finding original and translation trading places: this is nothing but the educational program recommended by humanist study, the variation upon commonplaces, double translation in a bilingual culture aiming to be English by means of the classics, to be European and Latin by means of the passage through English. These national and international pretenses weave women in and out of these scenarios, learned, but domestic, ambulatory and confined, near and far. Women here embody what Barbara Correll calls a "woman function," one not confined to bodies of a single gender although continually marshaled differentially in the attempt to secure and hierarchize gendered difference.[19] The f these passages on women could be set beside the 's with which we began, and its reading program, in gne's essays are continually translated for the Count- and her mother as mirroring texts in which they will find themselves—as fathers and friends, and in which Florio is reflected, too, subordinated to their demands, to Montaigne's text, as author of a "femall" translation.

To move beyond the impasse that lies in assuming the truth of Florio's equation and to begin to see the complex paths of (limited) affordance afforded by translation to women, one needs, perhaps, to go in the direction indicated by Lori Chamberlain, who, after pointing to the persistence of the ordinary view of translation with its maintenance of male/patriarchal privilege, summons up "the most influential revisionist theory of translation" (p. 468), that represented by the work of Jacques Derrida. Clearly the Derridean critique of origin, the insistence on an insuperable originary *différance*, a doubleness at the start, opens the way for a reconceptualization of the hierarchy of original and translation (Derridean protocols have guided my reading of Florio above, much as they play a part in the readings elsewhere in this book).[20] Chamberlain points especially to Derrida's "Living On / Border Lines" as a text about translation that does not fail to expose the ordinary premises of gender difference underpinning the original/translation couple.[21] Although I will return to what I see as the limits of that claim, the Derridean text to which Chamberlain directs us has important connections to the arguments offered in the chapters that follow.

Not quite expressed in "Living On / Border Lines" is the fact, acknowledged elsewhere by Derrida, that the problematic of "living on"—that is, of survival—is derived from Walter Benjamin's "The Task of the Translator," a crucial text for reconceptualizing what that work is.[22] Fundamentally, for Benjamin, translation is how the "original" text acquires its afterlife; indeed, there is the strongest sense in Benjamin that the original needs its translation, and not simply so that the latter text confirms the greatness of the former. Rather, the demand issued from the text gestures toward that which exceeds the text itself; the translation does not capture this—and the problem of the translation thus does not lie in its faithfulness to an original; rather, translation exposes the untranslatable core of the work, which is also the guarantee of a futurity.[23] The life of survival—of living on—is not biological life, but history; the connection and kinship between original and translation is thus not based in resemblance or a genetic tie, Benjamin argues, but in the ways in which the texts together point beyond themselves—beyond the confines of a border, the assured integrity of the difference between original and translation.

This thematic, and indeed its specification in Derrida's "Living On / Border Lines," is richly suggestive for the chapter that follows on the Countess of Pembroke. Derrida reads the unheard of conjunction/ translatability of Shelley's "Triumph of Life" and Blanchot's *L'Arrêt de Mort*. Behind Shelley, as Derrida briefly indicates, are "all the 'triumphs of death' of the Italian *quattrocento*" (p. 82)—of which, of course, Mary Sidney's translation of Petrarch's *Triumphus Mortis* is one. This is the case, Derrida argues, because it is forever indeterminable whether the triumph of life is the triumph over life—that is, the triumph of death—or a triumph of life-beyond-life; by the latter, Derrida would not appear to mean the immortality that the textual tradition familiarly declares for itself, but the life-beyond-life represented in the structure of translation. Shelley can be read beside Blanchot because his *récit* has a title which either delivers a death sentence (this is what *l'arrêt de mort* means idiomatically) or stops it from ever being delivered ("literally," *arrêt* means "stop").

But, to follow the protocol of Derrida's reading, what is uncanny in the Blanchot text is that it seems also to read/translate Sidney. Blanchot's *récit* is indeterminably one or two narratives, in which an "I" in each of its two parts is either the same or not, and in which, in each part, a woman, initialed in the first instance, named, but with a name that starts with a different initial, in the second part, is/are involved with the narrator. The woman of the first part, J., dies and is reborn; the woman of the second part is a translator whose name, Nathalie, suggests birth, is perhaps J. born anew, translated. In Sidney's "Triumph of Death," also in two parts, the "I" is indeterminate, even in terms of gender; a woman dies and dies again in part I; in part II she speaks to tell the "I" that "he" is dead and that she lives. These strange translations are also the relationship of a translator to her original, Petrarch's "Trionfo," but also, as Mary Sidney makes clear elsewhere, to the "original" of her writing—Sir Philip Sidney, her dead brother.[24]

What is uncanny is not merely the thematization of writing/translating, but that the violation of and suspension of the border life/death is not to be taken in Sidney, or in Derrida, as simply something about texts. It is rather, at the very least, the question of how Mary Sidney lives on—in her life and in her writing, beyond the death of her brother. But these questions of what it means to live beyond the death of the other, beyond the writing of a text—one's own or not—are also questions about life and what it means, about history and memory, and, more narrowly, about literary history and cultural memory. Questions related to the task of translation.

I would not want what I have just written to be read as simply a reversal of the value of translation, from "degraded activity" to exalted activity, nor simply now to put the translator where the original was, the woman where the man was. This is, indeed, I think something that happens with Derrida, when, in the roundtable about translation recorded in *The Ear of the Other*, asked by Monique Bosco to confront the political situation of the translating woman, he attempts to translate the woman out of the binarism: "from a perspective that would see translation as something other than a secondary operation, at that moment the position of the woman translator would be something else, even though it would still be marked sexually" (p. 152). This "something else" rather quickly succumbs to a reversal of the kind also to be found in

Florio, in the very figure of Minerva, for Derrida puts woman in the place of the law. So, too, in Blanchot, where the final, untranslatable "elle" of *L'arrêt de mort* is either the woman or "la pensée," a point Derrida recalls as the final answer to Bosco's intervention.

Moreover, in reconceptualizing the relationship of original and translation, Derrida substitutes a love relationship for the hierarchizing master/servant relationship: the translator is "the one who is loved by the author and on whose basis alone writing is possible. Translation is writing. . . . It is a productive writing called forth by the original text" (p. 153). As Derrida formulates this in "Les Tours de Babel," his essay on Benjamin, as well as in "Living On / Border Lines," the relationship solicited is the urge to form a couple that cannot ever quite be consummated. The figure for this coupling is the hymen, the marriage band that also is the sign of virginal intactness. That is, the "sacred alliance" (*Ear of the Other*, p. 125) that Derrida offers in place of the hierarchy of master/slave, writer/secretary is the marital contract.[25] There is warrant for this, to be sure, in Blanchot's text. But there is also reason to suspect this as a relationship entirely "something other" than the hierarchical one. Here, Sidney offers a corrective, for the coupling/decoupling of Petrarch and Laura—or of the Countess and her brother—refuses to privilege the norm of heterosexual marriage. Derrida, to be sure, does point, in his reading of Blanchot in "Living On," beyond hetero union to what he thinks of as virtually unspeakable, "something even worse" (p. 169) than the couplings between the narrator and the women in *L'arrêt de mort*—a union between the two women, J. and N., "the *hymen* between the two women" (p. 169). Yet this fantasy is one that supports and shatters the narrator, a lesbian fantasy for the male "I."

Derrida's speculations so displace the feminine, so override difference, as to subsume woman in a gesture at best utopic (this is what Chamberlain seeks to affirm on the basis of Derrida's troubling of difference), at worst, once more erasing sexual difference into a masculine same. In the readings that follow, that a woman is writing does make a difference, and the sexual domains toward which these translations point, the strange couplings they imagine—for which incest is too easy but nonetheless a useful starting term—may be said to be true to the historicity toward which Benjamin glances—one not rooted in nature or biological reproduction. Unnatural translation.

Rooted, let us say, in citationality, with this Derridean caveat in mind: "Once quotation marks demand to appear, they don't know where to stop" ("Living On," p. 76). Or where to start: and thus how to stabilize the difference between original and translator. This is the logic of the *récit*, the re-cited. How to maintain the priority and privilege of a writer one wishes to celebrate? How, but to provide a list, begin a series: "she was our Sappho, our Aspasia, our Hypathia, our Damo, our Cornelia. But what speak I of these, though learned, yet infidels? Nay, rather, she was our Christian Fabiola, our Marcella, our Paula, our Eustochium." So Thomas Stapleton celebrates the *unique* accomplishment and life of Margaret Roper (p. 98). Intertwined with the life of her father and her father's friend, Erasmus, there is more to say about Roper than that she hid behind a male textual tradition. Translate women into that male position and, one might say, she was our Sappho.

"Translate" "women" into that "male" position and, one might say, "she was our Sappho."

MARGARET ROPER'S DAUGHTERLY DEVOTIONS: UNNATURAL TRANSLATIONS

Margaret Roper's claims for consideration as a writer rest mainly on her *A devout treatise upon the Pater noster* (1524), a translation of Erasmus's *Precatio Dominica* of the year before.[1] The accomplishment of this work of a nineteen-year old—judged as "mature" in a 1937 essay on her skills as a translator—is not its only qualification for consideration.[2] For it is the presence of selections from the treatise on the Pater noster and some of her letters to her father, Sir Thomas More, in *Women Writers of the Renaissance and Reformation*, that has guaranteed attention to Roper for the present generation of critics and students evaluating the accomplishments of women as writers in the sixteenth and seventeenth centuries.[3] Of the twenty-nine large pages allotted to her in this collection, only eleven contain her own writing; the rest are given over to bibliography (certainly valuable for those who wish to extend their scope of study), to selections from the preface to the tract provided by Richard Hyrde, a member in all likelihood of the educational establishment in More's home, and to the sixteen-page-long introduction by Elizabeth McCutcheon to, as she calls Margaret More

Roper, "the learned woman in Tudor England." McCutcheon's introduction thus serves as the first entry for most current readers of Roper. The ways in which she frames the enterprise of a critical consideration of Roper's writing is therefore worth attention.

McCutcheon conjures Roper into existence in her opening paragraph by recalling Hans Holbein's 1527/28 pen and ink drawing of the More family, still extant, "which More sent to Erasmus, his fellow humanist and longtime friend." Thanks to it, McCutcheon continues, "we can still see Margaret Roper, then twenty-two years old." What we can see as well, she argues, are two fundamental images offered in the drawing, "Margaret with books and Margaret with family," images whose value McCutcheon takes to be "proleptic" since they shape how Roper has come to be seen: "Margaret Roper has continued to be admired for her erudition and loved for her devotion to her father" (p. 449).

Holbein's sketch is certainly the image of Margaret Roper that is best known (there is also a later less well known portrait miniature). McCutcheon does little more than describe the drawing, listing the members of More's household assembled in it and stressing the dominating presence of Roper on the right side of the image, and of More "magisterially" sitting in the center, surrounded by his father and son, another daughter, wards, and his fool. From this image of an extended, if undeniably patriarchal family, McCutcheon reduces "Margaret with family" into an image of "her devotion to her father."[4] The image, however, cannot so easily be collapsed into that relationship. Margaret Roper, an immense figure on the right side of the sketch (if she stood up, she would be twice as tall as the other standing figures) holds an open book on her lap; her sister Cicely, beside her, turns toward her with an animated expression on her face, and her stepmother, Alice, behind her, also seems emotively responding to the text that engages her eyes. Margaret Roper is thus positioned among female relatives; that would seem to be her family location. And although this is an image of "Margaret with books," it must be noted that she is neither reading nor writing.

Hans Holbein the Younger (1497?–1543), "Sir Thomas More and His Family." Margaret Roper is the second figure from the right side of the drawing. Oeffentliche Kunstsammlung Basel, Kupferstichkabinett Inv. 1662.31 (reproduced by permission; photo by Martin Bühler, courtesy Oeffentliche Kunstsammlung Basel).

Her implacable gaze, however, does distinguish her from her sister and stepmother; it links her to two other figures in the image who also display this kind of void stare: the fool, Henry Pattenson, the sole figure in the drawing who seems to solicit the gaze of the viewer, and Thomas More, whose head, like Roper's, is at an angle, and who, like her, looks vacantly into space. Everyone else in the image exhibits a gaze of attention—to books, to each other, or even as a sign of some internal state (as is the case of the elder John More and of Anne Cresacre, More's ward and the future wife of his son). If "Margaret with family" can be reduced to the figure of the "devoted daughter," as McCutcheon claims (p. 449), the relationship of father and daughter in this depiction would suggest that it has to do with the ways in which their devotion would seem to locate them elsewhere. Insofar as the fool is there too (and the handwritten annotation on the drawing identifying him—"Henricus Patensonus Thomae Mori morio"—does not fail to solicit the expected pun on More's [im]proper Latin name), it is perhaps overhasty to collapse the dynamics of Holbein's image into a picture of daughterly devotion. Shared folly as well as the fact that the image was destined for Erasmus might locate Roper in a sphere that cannot quite be reduced either to family or to the exclusive father-daughter pairing.

What More, his eldest daughter, and the fool share in this image is, arguably, a certain distraction, gazing at cross-purposes. More is, indeed, almost literally magisterially central to the image; he wears his chain of office, yet he seems elsewhere, not with the family or occupying his worldly position; Roper, confined to a certain proper femininity—it is undoubtedly a prayerbook she holds on her lap, since her stepmother is kneeling at a prayer stool behind her, and her sister Cicely fingers her rosary—a femininity that amounts to a potential gender separatism, nonetheless also seems detached from the female devotional sphere in which she has been located; she is not praying, nor interacting with her sister or stepmother (nor is she interacting with any of the male figures, in sharp contrast to the insistent figure of Margaret Giggs, pointing to a passage in a text and attempting to get John More's attention). One could call this detachment a sign of unworldliness, or of oblivion (as it may be in the fool's face), or of studied oblivion (which may also be Henry Pattenson's pose). Or one could call it the stance of the humanist, with its pretensions to a disembodied sphere of letters (of *bonae litterae*, learning), belying all worldly ambition; to a Christian humanism, to bring together the gendered spheres represented by the chancellor and his daughter.

This detachment is, of course, a recognizable feature of early humanism and central to its rhetoric, in which the worldly ambitions of humanists, new men on the rise in the increasingly bureaucratized world of centralizing monarchies, were clothed in the assurance (not entirely suspect, of course) of their promotion of traditional aristocratic privilege or royal prerogative. And just as it was a goal of humanists to encroach unthreateningly upon traditional spheres of power, the subordination, domestication, pietización of women—Margaret Roper on the floor, her stepmother on her knees—was an aim, indeed, as Barbara Correll has convincingly argued, a necessary corollary for male ambition in humanist representation.[5] But, as Correll has also shown, this image of the docile woman as counterpart to the docile humanist counselor of kings was always capable of destabilization, precisely because the role of "woman" in humanist texts was also a cover for humanist ambition. Hence, to return to the Holbein drawing, it is possible to read in the very similarity of their abstraction a relationship between daughter and father not only in which each serves to simulate and "tame" the other, but also in which the tension between humanist ambition and the relegation of women to a privatized domestic sphere—and this cloistration also includes the "learned woman"—may be manifest.

To establish the latter point, McCutcheon cites from a 1523 letter of More to Margaret Roper reminding her of the limited audience she could expect for her learned endeavors, naming "your husband and myself—as a sufficiently large circle of readers for all that you write" (p. 460); she cites as well the passages in that letter and in another in which More tells of the surprise he produced on two occasions when he displayed pieces of Margaret's writing (conveniently to hand) for other learned men to admire.[6] Although these episodes would seem to confirm Roper's confinement within a domestic sphere and to allow her script to travel only inside her father's pocket, they also insistently produce her as confined. McCutcheon assumes these lamentable limitations; indeed, she reproduces them when she describes the Holbein drawing as conveyed by More to Erasmus, ignoring the fact that, whoever sent it, Erasmus acknowledged its receipt in a letter to Margaret Roper.[7]

Erasmus's letter expresses his delight in the lifelikeness of the Holbein drawing, and especially in its depiction of Margaret: "I recognize all of you, but no one more than you Margaret. I seem to see shining through its lovely exterior, the yet lovelier spirit within" (p. 37). Erasmus thus is also "proleptic," in this case of McCutcheon's own effort to find the image of Margaret in Holbein. His ability to read her interiority from her exteriority is legible as another familiar trope that serves in the production of humanist self-effacement. That this focus on Margaret as the dominant figure in the group and as the (dis)embodiment of humanist aspiration might potentially disrupt the requisite subordination of women may be suggested by the fact that Erasmus turns from the compliment to Margaret Roper to praise her father in the very next sentence: "Surely, I congratulate all of you, happy as you are, but no one so especially as your dear father" (p. 37). This is virtually a non sequitur unless one takes Margaret's interiority to be somehow her inheritance from her father. Much as McCutcheon quickly transports Margaret from books and family to daughterly submission, so, too, Erasmus cannot pause over the image of Margaret Roper without somehow making what he sees in her become a reflection of and upon her father, without imagining, as it were, her father reading the letter over his daughter's shoulder.

There is extant only a single holograph manuscript of Margaret Roper's, and it is, in fact, the letter she wrote replying to this one from Erasmus. Remarkably, McCutcheon does not anthologize it, nor is it or the correspondence with Erasmus even mentioned in her introduction (the letter's existence is only discernible through one article listed in the three-page-long bibliography). This exclusion keeps Roper within the sphere of Sir Thomas More. Not that the letter is much more than a well-turned piece of epistolarity. And yet in complimenting Erasmus, thanking him for his letter (that paradigmatic scene of writing reproduced a hundredfold in *De copia*),[8] which Roper represents as an unprecedented and unforeseen event, her evaluation of his letter suggests its uses beyond the compliment she claims to have been paid, "raised by the favour of your letter." "As often as I show it to anyone," she continues, "I realize that from it no small praise will accrue to my reputation, which cannot be made more notable in any other way than by your letter" (p. 43). The receipt of his letter has not been taken merely as a private compliment; much as More displayed his daughter's writing, Margaret has shown others the letter from Erasmus. Thanks to it, Roper can make claims upon a public and an enhanced reputation. Roper uses the letter from Erasmus as a passport beyond the domestic sphere.

Roper goes further as she ends her letter, closing with the hope that Erasmus will once again return to England so that she might "some time be able to speak face to face and see our teacher, by whose learned labours we have received whatever of good letters we have imbibed" (p. 43). Erasmus, of course, never literally tutored Margaret More, and that is not her point; rather, she makes Erasmian texts foundational for her own. Instead of her father or her husband or the teachers More provided for her (the sphere in which Sir Thomas insistently locates her, in which McCutcheon does too), Roper names Erasmus in her father's place. That this revision of her educational history functions as a kind of challenge to her relegation to the paternal/domesticated sphere may be suggested by the way Roper ends the sentence wishing for Erasmus's visit; she refers to him as "one who is the old and faithful friend of our father." That is, if Margaret Roper appears to be staking a claim to her own interpenetration of the world of humanist letters, her final gesture is a belated attempt to sanction that move by way of the friendship of More and Erasmus, by subordinating herself within a circuit of male friendship. If so, Roper herself deploys a version of the "woman function" as Correll describes it, but for her own ends.

Judging by Roper's insistence on her surprise at its receipt, Erasmus's 1529 letter could seem to be an entirely unprecedented event: "I have never dared to hope or to expect that you, so fully occupied with so much important work . . . should ever deem me worthy of the honour to which I have been raised by the favour of your letter" (p. 43). It was not. Several years before—around Christmas of 1523, just a few months after More had consigned his daughter to an audience of father and husband—Erasmus had sent her a quite public letter, the dedicatory epistle to his commentary on Prudentius's Christmas and Epiphany hymns (Allen and Allen, no. 1404). McCutcheon mentions the letter this way: "The Ropers' first child was born in 1523, an occasion that Erasmus commemorated by dedicating his commentary on Prudentius's Christmas and Epiphany hymns to Margaret. We do not know how many children Margaret gave birth to, but two sons and three daughters are known by name" (p. 450). McCutcheon is accurate enough; midway in his dedicatory letter, Erasmus mentions the birth of the Roper child. But that is by no means the only reason he gives for his dedication. Rather, the letter opens by acknowledging how often he has received letters from Margaret and her sisters and expresses the hope that his "little gift" will be an adequate response to their letters. For he says he has been "challenged by your letters," and the Prudentius commentary is a response to the challenge.[9] In this way, Erasmus writes the letters of Margaret Roper and her sisters into a recognizable scene of humanist emulation. Not surprisingly, then, between the acknowledgment of the challenge and the possibly inadequate response of the commentary (more tropes of humanist humility/assertion), Erasmus reroutes the letters of the sisters: they are, he writes, "even if someone should remove the signatures," recognizable images of their father (the compliment is turned in Greek). Extraordinarily, Erasmus takes their signatures to be their father's or, rather, attempts to move their epistolary exchange into the proper all-male sphere of humanist letters. It is easy enough to see that this rerouting functions as a kind of defense against the impingement of the women's letters that Erasmus has nonetheless acknowledged.

The sense of challenge continues, however, when Erasmus links his gift to the child that Roper has given his wife. My paraphrase simply follows Erasmus, and the situation is immediately refigured; "Or, if you prefer, you have given them [the 'first-fruits' of the marriage] to him—or, more precisely—each has given to the other the *paidos* [in Greek], to be kissed and caressed" (p. 33). If for a moment Erasmus subordinates Margaret Roper to an entirely passive maternal function (a gesture that has its echo when McCutcheon's mention of the letter serves only to raise the question of how many children Margaret Roper had), he remodels her "delivery" of Roper's child into an epistolary exchange, a scene of emulation. Or so it seems when he proceeds from this refiguration of mutual giving to announce that what he sends Roper is "another Child," his text on the Christmas birthday boy. What began as a letter expressing rivalry has become a scene in which Margaret's letters and her baby are interchangeable, in which Erasmus' text is *his* baby. Indeed, and this is perhaps the most remarkable thing in the letter, and quite at odds with reading it as simply concerned with Roper's fulfillment of her maternal function, when Erasmus mentions William Roper, and the first fruits he has given Margaret, he praises him this way: "if he were not your husband, he could pass for your brother." This insistence upon similitude, of husband and wife as twins, of marriage as a sibling relationship, makes sense in terms of the ways in which Erasmus seeks to position his writing in relationship to Margaret Roper's. When he goes on to praise the Roper marriage as excelling even the state of virginity, it is presumably because the fruits of this marriage include a great deal beyond babies. They include or can be included in the baby books that brother humanists make together in the emulation and imitation crucial to their friendships.

Erasmus's translation of Margaret Roper into a worthy humanist rival matches the account of the learning of the More daughters in his oft-cited 1521 letter to Guillaume Budé (Allen and Allen, no. 1233). E. E. Reynolds, in his study of Margaret Roper, translates the crucial passage: "A year ago it occurred to More to send me a specimen of their progress in learning. . . . Believe me, my dear Budé, I never was more surprised; there was nothing whatever silly or girlish in what they said."[10] It is in this letter that Erasmus reports how he once did not believe "that letters are of value to the virtue and general reputation of women," and how "More completely converted" him to the opposite opinion.[11] If female letters are folded back into the paternal script here, the effect nonetheless is also to make More's daughters, who produce "nothing . . . girlish" ("nihil . . . puellaere"), into honorary sons. This is a translation regularly attempted: to preserve learning as male, the learned woman must be refigured as masculine, as when Guarino praised his immensely learned former pupil Isotta Nogarola and urged her "to create a man within the woman,"[12] or when the More hagiographer Thomas Stapleton opened a chapter on Margaret Roper by citing scripture to the effect that "a wise son maketh his father glad," and proceeded to declare Roper's accomplishments such that they "would scarcely be believed in a woman."[13] This position of "more than" woman can be used to elide Roper with her father. But it can also provoke the possibility of an equalization of man and woman that Erasmus will represent as a threat and attempt to contain.[14]

Containment of Roper within her maternal function is not the main point of Erasmus's letter, however; rather, numerous paths of identification are opened, possibilities that a woman's letters might come to occupy the same position as a man's. If William Roper is Margaret's brother, the baby they make together is at once incestuous and the kind of male baby that Erasmus can deliver. Indeed, Erasmus's birthday letter can be compared to the wish More expressed just before Margaret delivered the child that Erasmus acknowledged as a rival: "May God and our Blessed Lady grant you happily and safely to increase your family by a little one like his mother in everything except sex" (Rogers, *Selected Letters*, no. 128).

More takes back the wish for a boy if Margaret can give birth to a girl who "will make up for the inferiority of her sex" as Margaret had, by her virtue and learning. The point is that such a girl would be the boy More wants.

Although it is true, as McCutcheon says, that "we know nothing about the actual circumstances surrounding Margaret Roper's translation of Erasmus's treatise" (p. 462; the kind of evidence that McCutcheon wants would seem to be some kind of private record or document), I believe it is possible not merely to find Roper's 1524 *Pater noster* returning the compliment of Erasmus's dedication of the Prudentius commentary of the year before, but to regard her translation of the *Precatio Dominica* as her way of delivering a boy/girl child in response to the challenge offered by Erasmus's rivalry. I take it, too, that her translation serves to further Roper's identification with this chosen teacher and thus possibly to challenge the confinement and submission mandated by her father. For its publication moves Roper's writing into spheres of male—male rivalry and imitation.[15] For these reasons, I would argue that however much a tract expanding the meaning of a prayer directed to "our Father" could appear to be an exemplary instance of daughterly devotion, it might nonetheless be read as an unnatural translation. To make good on these claims, I turn now to Roper's *Devout Treatise*.

Commentary on the skill of her translation has focused, unsurprisingly, on the ways in which Roper manages to turn Latin into fluent English, and on the changes made in so doing that might reflect Roper's take on the treatise.[16] Although these are important considerations, to be sure, the question of what differences might be found even at those moments when the English seems merely to reproduce the Latin with fidelity has not been broached. Rather, it has been assumed that Margaret's proper female piety and daughterly devotion simply resonated with Erasmian aims. Yet, in the context I have been sketching, it seems important to note that the initial petition of *A devout treatise upon the Pater noster* takes up the question of filiation, strikingly differentiating how the petitioner may be thought to be God's child as opposed to the child of an earthly father. "Here O father in hevyn the petycions of thy children," the treatise opens, and soon declares the nature of this filiation to have occurred when God "by adoptyon receyved us in to the great honour of this name" (p. 11). The speaker of the petition thus is an adopted child, not a natural one. Moreover, the natural father is denounced in the most explicit terms: "The tyme was when we were servauntes to wyckednesse and synne by the miserable generacion of Adam: we were also children of the fende" (p. 11); becoming God's adopted child, the petitioner has "renounced and forsaken our father ye devyll and had begon to have no father in erthe" (p. 13).

The petitioner thus can be called "child" because the name has been given; this is not a natural act of generativity but one performed by adoption. That is to say, nomination here occurs through an entirely artificial route: by means of a naming that is also a fiat. Like calling your book your baby. The violent separation from the generation of Adam, from the devil, from an earthly father could be likened to the stance of the humanist in the Holbein image: a bodily distraction and dispossession. It makes it possible to read the thematic of spiritual regeneration as akin to the rebirth of and in *bonae litterae*. This is, in fact, how humanism often justified itself—that only through letters is a human subject produced.

This thematic of adoption remains insistent throughout the *Pater noster*. It undergoes a significant rewriting in the third petition when those "called children" though divine nomination can in fact be further renamed, "wherby y^u father mayst aknowledge us as thy children naturall and nat out of kynde" (p. 43). Roper's phrasing significantly expands and reunderstands Erasmus here— ut & tu pater agnoscas filios non degeneres" (p. 42)—by insisting on the etymological significance of "degeneres," and thereby entirely overturning the distinction between natural and unnatural, between biological and nonbiological reproduction. The adopted child becomes the natural one; the replacement of the earthly by the spiritual father is also the absolute effacement of the earthly father. The earthly father is, to use Roper's translation of "sublatus," "fully quenched & wyped away" (p. 27).

It is in the course of the third petition that a trajectory is mapped from adopted to natural child, to the sublation of the distinction between them, and the route is by way of letters. To be a child one must labor to be one: "onely they whiche with busye studye whyle they lyve here labour to be such as ther must be" (p. 37). No better way than *imitatio Christi*, especially by hearkening to what "he sayd for our lernyng and instruction" (p. 39). Just as Erasmus presents his commentary on Prudentius as his baby Jesus, so here the imitation of Christ falls under the sway of humanist *imitatio*. Jesus is "a very kynde and naturall childe for he is a very full and perfite ymage & similitude of [God]" (p. 21). Equating the natural with the simulation equalizes procreation and imitation. Not surprisingly, then, when the tract moves on to the fourth petition, "give us this day our daily bread," the bread is the word. But there, as in the third petition, earthly and heavenly food are regarded as equivalents to each other. "It is all one realme bothe of heven and erthe" ("sicut in celo et in terra" [p. 37]) and hence "it is one breed that indifferently belongeth to us all" (p. 47). Roper's "indifferent" translation is an equalizing one: effacing and rewriting earth into and as equivalent to heaven, it equivocates upon the materiality of the letter, dissembling in humanist style worldliness as an otherworldliness, equalizing the realms of "kynde" (nature) and "ymage & similitude" (*imitatio/translatio*). Jesus is the crucial mediating figure here, for his mode of being God's child is that upon which all of God's children seize: an equivalence "indifferently" available to all believers.

So, too, the Lord's Prayer is an infinitely repeatable text, a closeted, secret, private declaration that is nonetheless "indifferently" the same text for any believer, a disowned and repossessable script. It circulates like the humanist letter as Roper receives it and makes it public, as Erasmus publishes his own and others' letters in the editions of "his" epistles. Roper inserts herself into this sphere of exchange through her translation, and finds her script in these prescripts (the Lord's Prayer, Erasmus's *Precatio Dominica*) through a crucial anglicization. Where Roper insists on the adopted name "child," Erasmus's Latin has no word for what she renders as "child" except "filius," son. But when she contemplates her "indifferent" relationship with the model child, God's son, she claims brotherhood, much as Erasmus had turned her husband into her brother. On the one hand, Roper degenders "filius" by translating it "child"; on the other hand, she embraces her nomination as "frater." The word she uses throughout to express the petitioner's relationship to Jesus is that they are "brethren." Are brethren brothers? Has a fraternity in which all are indifferently "brothers" replaced a kinship relationship of natural brotherhood? It would seem likely. If so, it is in this "fraternal" position that Roper writes as one among equals in the generation of similitudes.

In her determination to read Roper as her father's daughter, McCutcheon (who, of course, is not singular in this respect; Reynolds's life of Margaret Roper is subtitled, *Eldest daughter of St. Thomas More*) claims that the *Pater noster* gave Margaret Roper another chance "to reflect upon a relationship between child and father" (p. 462). What the reading I have offered thus far means to suggest is that Roper found in Erasmian reproduction a way to swerve from and to rewrite her relationship to her earthly father. Unlike More, Erasmus neither married nor had children; his deepest passions seem to have been pederastic (More was himself an early object of affection), and their translation was effected in the realm of letters, into pedagogy, the regimes of making boys.[17] It is thus not surprising that Erasmus rewrites the Pater noster in pedagogic terms, nor that Roper would seize upon that "unnatural" mode of reproduction as her means of entering the world of letters. In the mid-seventeenth century, Roper was praised as the embodiment of her father in precisely these terms: "one may well say that this Daughter was the most learned and polished Book which issued from the Minde of Sir *Thomas Moor*," and the encomium certainly resonates with the strategies of Roper's *Devout treatise*.[18] But nothing in Roper's embrace of imitation guarantees the paternal position of the later encomium. The fraternal relationship makes it impossible to establish paternal priority; the natural relationship of parent and child is superseded by this unnatural brotherhood.

Thomas Stapleton, in the chapter on Margaret Roper in his life of More, not only describes her as the "wise son," or as a daughter whose superlative learning "would scarcely be believed in a woman," but also insists on the resemblance of father and daughter: "More than all the rest of the children, she resembled her father, as well in stature, appearance, and voice, as in mind and in general character" (p. 103). Resemblance can work in two directions, however; whereas Stapleton means to make Roper the image of her father, Roper's tropes remake him in the image of the heavenly father who has, in turn, made her an (ungendered) child, a (regendered) brother. The switching point in these procedures is the figure of Jesus, the child who is also a manifestation of the father; the switching point, I have been suggesting, is thus, too, Erasmus's Jesus, the child who rivals the one the Roper "brothers," Margaret and William, make. The Erasmian text comes between father and daughter.

These procedures can point us back to how Roper used the *Pater noster* as a way to reflect on father-child relationships, and, not least of all on her relationship to Sir Thomas More. For it is not difficult to recognize in this otherworldly troping the very habits of More himself, whose renunciation of the world was cast in identical terms. Roper's petitioner who moves "to forsake our naturall affections and that whiche we have moost dere as our fathers and mothers wyves chyldren and kynsefolke" (p. 31) would seem to anticipate her father's path to the scaffold; indeed, this is one of the few passages in her *Pater noster* where the petitioner seems, by having a wife, not a husband, to be gendered explicitly male. But the treatise also continually worries the analogical relationship, as in earth so in heaven, and, as we have seen, works hard to turn renunciation into a refigured, sublated mode of repossession of what has been lost. More, too, uses these tropes, especially in the conversations he is reported to have had with Margaret Roper in his final imprisonment. "Me thinketh God maketh me a wanton, and setteth me on His lap and dandleth me," he tells his daughter, a rescripting of his confinement and imminent death in which More not only becomes a baby on the lap of his heavenly father, but also a favorite, petted creature in an erotic scenario.[19] Or a bit later, watching Richard Reynolds and three monks on the way to execution, "Lo, dost thou not see, Meg," he comments, "that these blessed fathers be now as cheerfully going to their deaths as bridegrooms to their marriage?" (p. 242). In other words, if More and Roper share these techniques of translation, it may serve as a way of rescripting their devotion to each other, perhaps to make acceptable an intensity that Jonathan Crewe has characterized as incestuous.[20]

This is a question to which I will return, but I would pause for a moment over this question of imitation for the possibility that it might solve what has been a prevailing problem in establishing the canon of Roper's works. I refer to the very long letter, briefly excerpted by McCutcheon, and there labeled "As Written to the Lady Alington."[21] From its first printing in the 1557 edition of More's English writings, the authorship of this letter, seemingly written by Margaret Roper, has been put into question. There, an alternative for its authorship is tilted in the direction of More: "But whether this answere were writen by Sir Thomas More in his doughter Ropers name, or by hym self it is not certainely knowen" (Rogers, *Correspondence*, no. 206). Rogers prints the letter as Margaret Roper's, but in her headnote to it she cites the opinion of R. W. Chambers, that in the dialogue of the letter, "the speeches of More are absolute More; and the speeches of Margaret are absolute Margaret." Authorship of the letter, Chambers opines, is therefore undecidable, and it has remained so. (McCutcheon opts for Richard Marius's characterization of it as a piece of joint authorship.) The assumption seems to be that "absolute" presentation must be self-presentation. Yet if father and daughter so resembled each other, and if it was part of the aim of Roper's writing to rewrite her father in terms of the shared image, it seems fully believable that Roper herself could produce so convincing a version of her father that his worshipers (and their numbers are legion) would want the text in which he speaks to be his own.

This letter has proved difficult in one further respect; in it, Roper attempts over and again to get More to agree to swear the oath and thus to save his life. From the earliest biographers, it has been assumed that the daughter used as a ploy her promise to attempt to convince her father to change his mind as a means of winning access to him in prison. Yet, at a crucial moment in their dialogue in the letter, Roper reveals what we know to have been the case, that she (along with all of More's family) took the oath. She attempts to persuade More to do so too by pointing to yet another family figure who had sworn allegiance to the king:

> sith thensaumple of so many wise men can not in this matter move you, I see not what to say more, but if I shoulde loke to perswade you with the reason that Master Harry Patenson made. For he met one day one of our men, and when he asked where you were, and heard that you wer in the Towre still, he waxed even angry with you and said, "Why? What aileth hym that he wilnot swere? Wherfore sholde he sticke to swere? I have sworne the oth my self." And so I can in good faith go no ferther neither, after so many wise men whom ye take for no saumple, but if I should say lyke M. Harry, Why should you refuse to swere, Father? for I have sworne my self.
>
> (Rogers, *Correspondence*, no. 206, p. 529)

The intermediary figure through whom she speaks her part is the fool, Henry Pattenson, whose words she repeats verbatim. In this scene, we return to the shared blank gazes in the Holbein image, and to the shared folly of More and his daughter. But we also encounter here in these reflections Roper's attempts to turn the tables upon her father.

This is visible too in one of the letters Margaret Roper wrote to More during his final days in prison (Rogers, *Correspondence*, no. 203). Commenting on his lamentable absence, she constitutes their relationship through letters—those she writes to him, the one she has from him: "your most fruteful and delectable letter, the faith-full messenger of your very vertuous and gostly minde, rid from all corrupt love of worldly thinges" (Rogers, *Correspondence*, p. 510). More's letter is sublated—absorbed as food, relocated as heavenly, expelled from corruption. Within a few sentences, More is transported where the letter carries him: "Father, what thinke you hath ben our comfort sins your departinge from us?," she asks, and the answer lies in the example of his "lyfe past" and the assurance of his heavenly destination, where she hopes to "mete" him again (p. 511). The comfort she takes thus involves turning More into an exemplary figure for imitation and devotion. She performs a heavenly translation; he is as good as dead. We might recall in this context the eerie, paranoid response More made to his wife's plea that he stop all the foolishness, swear the oath, and come home, More's insistence that were he to return from the grave, he would find his family happily rid of him.[22]

If this scenario suggests a Roper less piously devout, less simply a worshiper of her father, further plausibility to this argument is provided if we return to the *Pater noster* to register one further implication of the choice of the Erasmian text as the site for her public appearance. It has been assumed that the *Precatio Dominica* is fully unexceptionable, an expression of piety fitting for a woman, and fitting too as a demonstration of humanist learning in the service of universal Christianity.[23] In this context we must recall the difficulty that the English text encountered when it first appeared in print. Thomas Berthelet, the printer of the *Devout treatise*, was summoned (in the context of the suppression of heretical [i.e., Protestant] books) to explain his publication of Roper's book. (Indeed, we know for sure that Roper was the author because Berthelet named her in this inquest.) A. W. Reed's discussion of this case has been taken as authoritative, and his claim that it was merely a technicality that was involved—"he had neglected to exhibit his copy" (p. 167)—has been repeated. Yet, as Reed notes, Erasmus's biblical scholarship certainly irked some English Catholics. Moreover, immediately upon the appearance of a French translation of the *Precatio Dominica*, it was condemned for impiety by the Sorbonne.[24] This was not the fate of its English translation, but the English were one with the French in condemning the *Colloquies* in 1526. This must remind us that in the early and mid-1520s, especially in his religious works or in his pronouncements about the subsumption of religion within a lay Christian humanism, Erasmus could be suspect, and not least because it was not so clear to many that he and Luther held opposing positions on a number of "heretical" issues. Although it is not evident to me that anything in the content of Roper's translation might have been viewed as suspect, I do mean to suggest that the choice of text was not quite as neutral as has been supposed. It is not difficult to see that Erasmian lay piety could lead to Protestant practices.

The "gostly lernyng of the gospell" (p. 31) and Erasmian imitation provide Roper with a writing position in which she can both claim (spiritual) equalization and undermine female subordination; in which her alliance to a spiritual father can relegate her earthly father to a demonic position (the old Adam of the letter to Lady Alington) or elevate him to spiritual equality, that is, to a brotherly position that is her own; or simply kick him upstairs.[25] Such spiritualization makes the natural unnatural; or, rather, it allows us to see how unnatural the relationship of Roper and More may have been. It raises, moreover, the distinct possibility that the terms of their relationship were not simply dictated by More.

Consider, for example, that it was Margaret alone who knew of her father's hairshirt; she washed it for him, and he sent it to her from the Tower. Likely, too, she knew of (witnessed?) his self-flagellations. Mortified flesh is nonetheless flesh. If, as Crewe claims, the telling instance of their relationship in William Roper's life of his father-in-law is the moment of Margaret's final kiss after More was condemned to death, this is a kiss compulsively reiterated in Roper's narration, a public scene that, as Crewe underlines, constitutes making a scene.[26] More's final letter comments on this moment, and praises Margaret for it precisely as if her passion were a token of unworldliness: "I never liked your maner towarde me better then when you kissed me laste for I love when doughterly love and deere charitie hath no laisor to looke to worldely curtesye" (Rogers, *Selected Letters*, no. 218). This sublation of passion may have been a shared understanding.[27]

It certainly marks Roper's *Pater noster*. As Rita Verbrugge has stressed, Roper often intensifies Erasmus's text to further abject the body, to represent it as even more vile and more to be expunged than Erasmus does. The passage about sublation cited earlier from the second petition, in which "all malycious and yvell desyres [are] fully quenched & wyped away" (p. 27), names a repeated subject; "corrupt & unclene affections" (p. 27), "noyous and wicked spirites" (p. 29) are an object of continual loathing; "innocency and purenesse" (p. 29) a constant goal. Repeatedly, Roper puns on the double meaning of salvation, seeking to be made "clene" (p. 33) and healthy, to arrive in "thy hevenly and celestiall company whiche is defouled with no maner spotte of yvell" (p. 37). The desired trajectory, summed up in the final petition, is from "our moost foule and unclene father the devyll" to "everlastyng helthe" (p. 61). That even these pious desires could be fueled by Roper's humanist education is suggested in the letter to More in prison from which we cited earlier (Rogers, *Correspondence*, no. 203), when Roper imagines More's salvation "body and soule" by citing Juvenal, "Ut sit mens sana in corpore sano." Here Roper adopts the Erasmian stance that so scandalized his contemporaries, equating classical text with holy scripture.

In the *Devout treatise*, this unworlding takes material form under the pediatric tutelage of Jesus, textual examplar of the salvific mortifications that produce the exemplary text.[28] But it is also legible in the one miracle More is credited with: when sweating sickness seemed about to claim Margaret Roper's life, More proposed the administration of an enema, and she was saved.[29] Roper's *Pater noster* imagines salvation in these terms too; to be made one with the body of Christ is to become "one spirite"; that is the way that God "purgest and makest clene" this new body joined in "the clerenesse of brotherly love" (p. 51; I cite from the fifth petition, on the clearing and equalizing of debts, recalling too the extraordinary fact that only Roper and her husband managed to inherit from Thomas More. What they received from him was a house named "Butclose"). This anal connection reminds us of the secrets shared by Roper and More (More's supposed final words to her began: "Ye know the very bottom and secrets of my heart," or, in another version, "You have long known the secret of my heart").[30] Roper's miraculous rebirth is an anal birth. But this form of relationship is fully congruent with, if not determined by, Roper's writing. Just as Roper entered the contest with Erasmus in terms of male reproduction—textual reproduction—so this secret anal connection points to an alternative to heterosexual intercourse and reproduction.

> verily thy sonne while he lyved here in erthe was wont to call his gospell the hevenly kyngdome & the realme of god: whose knowlege yet he sayde to be hydde and kepte secrete from us but nat withstandyng thy children humbly require and with fervente desyre beseke the[e] that this realme . . . myght daylye more and more be disclosed and opyned here in erth. (p. 27)

Opened is the "bowell of the soule," which the petitioner would have fed with the bread that is at once bread and the word (p. 47).

This enema is not just a laxative, it also feeds even as it sublates the body.[31] It operates like the letters of More, as Roper describes the effect of their receipt.

When William Roper tells the story of the miraculous clyster, he represents it as something "ministered unto her sleeping, which she could by no means have been brought unto waking" (p. 213). It is difficult to know whether this means to guard that orifice—the devil's path—from any penetration and to keep it off-limits, or whether this admits to an intimate knowledge of bodily resistance—that the anus was off-limits to her husband—and to the virtually unspeakable possibility of its availability to her father. If this is the imaginary, unconscious bodily site of father-daughter incest, and of the most deep-seated fantasies of origin and of reproduction that are not gender specific, it is then the seat and site of a brotherly relationship, a configuration of incest outside the oedipal terrain.[32] It suggests why and how Margaret Roper and More's relationship might be so fully unavailable and impenetrable to the husband's gaze in William Roper's account of his father-in-law.[33] In More's fantasmatic recourse to the clyster as a means of restoring his daughter, Margaret Roper is a boy penetrated anally; the fantasy is legible within humanist pedagogy and pederasty. And it is legible, too, in Margaret Roper's self-identification as a humanist writer and in her interpenetration of the humanist sphere of letters accomplished in her translation of Erasmus.

The scandal of the clyster, finally, lies in its representation as something done to Margaret Roper's unconscious body, as a final rape of the submissive woman, the devoted daughter. Rather, as I have been wanting to suggest, Roper rewrites the body along the routes of just such a mortification, and this revision is the active path for her as a writer and a humanist. At the moment of her near death, More seizes upon her in a way that can only remind us of the uses Margaret More Roper made of his body—and his letters—during his final imprisonment. Then, at last, the tables had turned. William Roper's representation of this scene, or any pious attempt to treat the clyster as an antibody miracle, all too easily grants to More's agency something that, by now, should also (if not primarily) be recognized as Margaret Roper's desire; this is how she imagines taking in the body of Christ—the word and the food; that "thou good father shuldest prively and invisibly reache it forthe unto" her (*Devout treatise*, p. 49). Hence, she should have the last word; here is the opening of the final extant letter to More:

> I thinke my self never able to geve you sufficient thankes, for the inestimable coumforte my poore heart receyved in the reading of your most lovinge and godly letter, representing to me the cleare shynynge brightenesse of your soule, the pure temple of the Holy Spirite of God, which I doubte not shall perpetually rest in you and you in hym. Father, if all the worlde had be geven to me, as I be saved it hadde ben a small pleasure, in comparison of the pleasure I conceyved of the treasure of your letter, which though it were writen with a cole, is worthy in mine opinion to be written in letters of golde. (Rogers, *Correspondence*, no. 209)

Who gives the clyster to whom? This is a black letter that is nonetheless golden, and twiceover so; it circles from God to her father, in a round of interpenetration; she receives it in all its shining brightness, once again imbibing a delectable letter that sustains her. And she declares this a pleasure beyond anything the world could offer, a pleasure nonetheless to be rewritten in letters of gold. What pleasures are these if not those that constitute Margaret Roper as a woman of letters?

THE COUNTESS OF PEMBROKE'S LITERAL TRANSLATION

Mary Sidney, Countess of Pembroke, has received high marks for her translation of Petrarch's *Trionfo della Morte*. Robert Coogan, for example, in an essay surveying and assessing the role of the *Trionfi* in the English Renaissance, notes that although hers was the last translation undertaken in the period—it was done sometime in the 1590s, in all likelihood—it is, he writes, "the finest translation of this triumph in the English language." By finest, Coogan means that it excels in "accuracy"; "each *terzina* in Mary Sidney literally translates the corresponding *terzina* in Petrarch," he goes on to say.[1] Coogan depends in his essay on judgments reached earlier by D. G. Rees, who, in a consideration of translations of the *Triumph of Death* from the Renaissance through the nineteenth century, had found Mary Sidney's superior to all others. "Hers is in fact an exceedingly literal translation," Rees wrote, going on to praise its "close adherence to the original."[2] These are views shared by Gary Waller, the contemporary critic who has often praised the *Triumph of Death*; endorsing Coogan's description of the poem as "the most triumphant poem of the early Renaissance," adherence to the original is also what Waller finds remarkable, so much so that he both cites Rees and then repeats the same words without putting quotation marks around them; he too claims, to quote him, that "the most outstanding technical feature of the Countess's translation is her reproducing Petrarch's original stanzaic pattern."[3]

These views of the countess's accomplishment could seem unexceptionable, yet they raise questions that I would address here. Indeed, the questions perhaps have begun to suggest themselves simply in the account that I have been giving, for there is, among the critics of the poem, an uncanny sense of *deja lu*, as if, that is, they were reading each other, and not Mary Sidney's poem. Echoes, inside and outside quotation marks, seem to recycle the same words and thoughts, to have decided on criteria that need only be restated, in whomever's words, for their truth to be apparent. In reading these critics, the chronology I have offered—in which Rees has priority of place—is virtually supplanted by the recirculation of the terms of praise that makes such priority a secondary question: what matters is the fact that the countess excels at translation, excels thanks to her literality, her accuracy, her adherence to a great original. This matters so much that Waller can both quote Rees and then use the same words outside quotation marks, making them his own. So much, in fact, that Waller's sentences are repeated, word for word, in three different locales, in the introduction to his edition of Mary Sidney's poems, in his biography of her, and in his pages on her in his volume entitled *English Poetry of the Sixteenth Century*. Of course his reuse of the same words—letter for letter—does not come with quotation marks around them; they are his words after all—and Coogan's and Rees's too, as we've seen.[4]

The sign of propriety in Waller's recirculation of the same words is precisely what is denied Mary Sidney, a troubling fact when one adds that Waller's work on her behalf has been done, increasingly so in the last decade, in the name of feminism. Yet there is not even a moment in which the gendered suppositions governing the praise of literal translation have been noted, that the original is placed in the paternal position—as if there could be no question but that Petrarch's words were his own, no reason to question his originality or priority—whereas the translator is a dutiful daughter or wife, faithfully adhering, and tied to a role that Waller calls *reproduction*. Yet, as I've been hinting already, chasing the round robin of critical estimations and echoes, reproduction—even faithful reproduction—could evacuate the terms of priority, opening possibilities of ownership precisely in the lack of self-sameness that citation—even literal citation—makes possible. Where even the issue of technical mastery of interlinked *terza rima*, with its imbrication of rhymes, might speak not so much to the matching of Petrarch as to the intertangled effects to which I have been alluding. Effects, I would hasten to add, that cannot be thought of in the hierarchies that invidiously characterize the relation of original and translation, of adherence and reproduction.

Literal translation supposes that there is something literally there in Petrarch, something so self-identical that it could simply be faithfully reproduced. In that light, it is worth noticing two quite different assessments of what Mary Sidney sought in Petrarch's triumph. For Margaret Hannay, in her recent biography, *Philip's Phoenix*, Mary Sidney, by translating the *Triumph of Death*, could place her voice in Laura's and find strength in Laura's declaration in the poem that the relation that had seemed to exhibit Petrarch's mastery had, in fact, been mastered by Laura, whose withdrawals and refusals, whose very silences, had produced their effects in him. "In delightful irony," Hannay writes, "the passive mistress proves to have been in control of her ardent lover";[5] Hannay reads Petrarch's poem to find it giving voice to a voice that displaces the poet's, presenting, as she puts it, "the Petrarchan situation from Laura's point of view" (p. 108). Virtually the opposite conclusion is reached by Mary Ellen Lamb in her study, *Gender and Authorship in the Sidney Circle*; she finds the poem frankly "disturbing" for embracing a voice that speaks its own destruction: it is, after all, the dead Laura that Petrarch gives a voice to speak a self-abnegation empowered by an almost suicidal passivity.[6] The refusals that tell in Hannay's account are strikes against her in Lamb's. This may be how women found a voice in the period, Lamb contends, and for that reason it is worth recognizing the strategy of speech *in articulo mortis*, but no woman would want to endorse that speaking position. Indeed, it might be said that, in some measure, Hannay agrees; her discussion of the poem occurs at the opening of a chapter devoted to how those who sought the countess's patronage wrote about her. The *Triumph* is taken as a kind of paradigmatic version of those encounters, in which men are given voice to write the countess by the power she has—a power that does not entail the kinds of entitlements within the written sphere that her would-be suitors had. The countess's patronage was, after all, highly circumscribed; wealthy and powerful as she was, much depended on her position as wife to the Earl of Pembroke; after his death, poets stopped importuning her. Hannay is able to construe her life as a series of heroic encounters in part because she is far less troubled by what Lamb sees: the cost of such success.

Seeing that, however, Lamb's account of the poem enacts the very erasure that she finds so disturbing, and, in that respect, her argument echoes Hannay's, but now from the opposite direction, for whereas Hannay ultimately treats the poem as an instance of how the countess empowered others, Lamb empties the poem of the countess by arguing that the countess subscribed to the lethal effects of the effacements of a petrarchan poetics that only simulates, at best, any sphere for female subjectivity. Either way, the poem, and the countess, disappear. But into what? One answer that might trouble these suppositions: into a Petrarch whose *Trionfo della Morte* either simulates his mastery or achieves it, into an original, that is, whose self-sameness is split by the representation of the relationship between lover and beloved. But what then would it mean literally to translate this divided text? Would the only access to the text lie along the gendered lines in which the countess is in the position of Laura? Can she simply be in that position when she is writing the poem? Must one conclude, as Waller does balefully in his most recent account of the countess, that "she was a woman, written by men," a death sentence if there ever was one.[7] Or that if she was a woman writing as a man, that must mean some fundamental betrayal of and to her gender? Wouldn't such conclusions ascribe to the original a determinate power that might itself fall into question even in this most literal of translations, if, that is, one were to argue that even literally to rewrite the poem could locate the countess's hand at a site of original duplication? And if, in Petrarch, the effect of displacement, of giving voice to Laura, serves to enhance only the poet's power, can one deny that Mary Sidney is the poet—is the author—of her *Triumph of Death*?

In asking these questions, I follow Ann Rosalind Jones, who has argued in *The Currency of Eros* for a difference that would inevitably be there even in the most faithful adherence to an original, the difference that gender will make. However powerful the discourses of gender in the Renaissance were in their attempts to keep women chaste, silent, and obedient (to cite the usual formula), they were not all-powerful, and the very existence of writing by women is one sign of that fact. To make the woman and her writing disappear into the male text or into male-dominated society involves giving more power to men than they had. "Women were interpellated by the Nom/Non du Pere," Jones writes, "but they were not interpellated into a tragic female speechlessness," and one reason for that, as Jones argues, was that the texts on which they modeled their own were not themselves seamless; nor was the social imperative to silence women without a contradictory element: to solicit the participation of women in the construction of the social, the hegemonic process described by Gramsci.[8] Even were Petrarch's poem the very monument to male accomplishment and mastery that it is taken to be, for Mary Sidney to rewrite it faithfully word for word would mean for her to have rewritten it. Still, to take up the position of writing her own demise, to find voice only at the point of death, might call these arguments into question. Here one can turn to Wendy Wall's account of how that rhetorical position could empower, for as Wall suggests, in a close examination of Isabella Whitney's "Wyll and Testament" and a tradition of women's writing to which it can be allied, the representation of oneself in that state of dispossession could be just that: a site of representation rather than one of identification, and a site moreover so riven with contradictions about person, place, and time—since one speaks, and yet is dead, since one takes possession at a moment of dispossession, since one occupies a temporality split between a future that one will never occupy and a present one is evacuating—that the contradictions, rather than being annihilative, are productive.[9] Among other things, as Wall suggests, these contradictions occasioned by speech at the last moment can serve to reflect upon and to critique the limits of women's speech and therefore to transgress them. The very extremity of the situation of writing as a woman is enacted and, in some measure at least, overcome. Isabella Whitney writes a last will and testament and does not die; Mary Sidney writes in the voice of a Laura who can claim power after death, but Mary Sidney goes on living.

If we grant these arguments, it would then be possible to distinguish Petrarch's assumption of his own dispossession by the voice of Laura and Mary Sidney's occupation of that voice, to measure thereby the ruses of power as well as the enablements that occur on either side of the divide of gender. So doing, one might still be in the position of assuming that the only site of identification—of identification and disidentification, at one and the same time—was determined by gender, that it was to Laura that the countess looked to find her voice. Yet she writes "I" in the poem not only there but also when she assumes the voice of the mourner, the voice inscribing the loss of another. And that position, the assumption of the voice of mourning, as everyone who has written about the Countess of Pembroke agrees, impels all her writing. In 1586, and within the space of some six months, Mary Sidney's father, mother, and brother died. It was especially the death of Sir Philip Sidney that mobilized her: her major projects were the completion of the psalm translation left unfinished at his death and the piecing together of the two versions of the *Arcadia* and their publication. (She also oversaw the publication of *Astrophil and Stella* and the *Defense*.) Hannay's description of the stance taken in the *Triumph of Death* also governs her thesis about Mary Sidney's career as a whole: that she occupied vis-à-vis her brother the position that Laura takes up in relation to Petrarch in the poem. Nonetheless, her *Triumph of Death* must also be a poem of mourning for Philip Sidney. This places the countess in the position of Petrarch.

Gary Waller comes to something like this point; having argued for the faithful adherence of translator and original, he continues by extending that relationship to the adherence of brother and sister; for him it is inescapable that the power and pathos of Mary Sidney's triumph represents her continued act of mourning for the brother with whom she so insistently identified.[10] Waller follows the countess literally when he represents her as the dutiful follower making whole what Sidney had left maimed, and Hannay's rewriting of that claim is a powerful one; she counters that such signs of devotion and subservience mask the very creation of Sir Philip Sidney that was the Countess of Pembroke's accomplishment. Hannay balks, as well, at the identifications for which Waller argues, and not surprisingly, for his arguments recirculate the late seventeenth-century suppositions of John Aubrey, that the relationship of brother and sister was incestuous. "Given the Sidneys' piety and their unembarrassed affection for all members of their family, the charge of incest is preposterous," Hannay disposes of the claim in a note.[11] Preposterous is a nice word; it suggests some of the unstated anxieties in Hannay's quick rebuttal: it mixes up before and behind in ways that might render gender identification indeterminate; it mixes before and after, the very work of incest, but also of all retrospective constructions, which is as much as to say, all the activities of consciousness; it also makes guilty what was at first innocent. Which is to say: the charge is preposterous because it is true.[12]

To think about the identification of the countess and her brother—without, I hasten to add, endorsing Aubrey *literally*—one might follow the theorization of how one comes to have a gender position that Judith Butler argues in *Gender Trouble*, that the assumption of gender is troubled at the start since it rests upon identifications with lost objects, and that the presumption of a single and determinate and self-identical gender position only testifies to the impossibility of such an acquisition, gender resting upon and mourning the loss of that singularity, founded upon desires for and identifications with those not necessarily of the gender to which one is assigned.[13] Mary Sidney's empowerment as a writer seems to have been coincident with the death of Sir Philip Sidney; moreover, the choice of Petrarch would seem in some measure to acknowledge the role of her brother, the English Petrarke, upon her. Which is not to voice again the notion of her faithful subservience to him or to the literary model he represented; rather, it is to suggest that in her *Triumph of Death*, Mary Sidney occupies both positions, as Petrarch and as Laura, and that Sir Philip Sidney is written into the poem in both parts as well. Indeed, the poem could be said also to be rewriting *Astrophil and Stella*, much as Petrarch's triumph rewrites his *canzoniere*. If the countess's poem is a faithful translation, it faithfully translates these complex routes of identification, across literary texts, across sites of imitation, across sites of identification that cross gender identification as well, or that, more finely, relocate gender as an unstable and less fully determined site.

To make this point, as I have said, is not to endorse Aubrey's salaciousness, and not, I hope, to echo Waller, for whom, too, incest turns out to be a secret (even from the countess herself, Waller opines) that reflects upon Mary Sidney's "disturbing" female sexuality.[14] Yet, to criticize these positions is not to take up Hannay's portrait of a pious and desexualized countess either. Indeed, I would argue that I follow Hannay, if not literally, in reading the countess's active piecing and putting together of her brother as an act of phallic enhancement that becomes further legible within the preposterous logic of incestuous, cross-gender identification. Something like this has been argued by Jonathan Crewe in his suggestion in *Hidden Designs* that the secret that historicism has failed to uncover in *Astrophil and Stella* is the love of Philip and Mary Sidney.[15] As Crewe argues, once one grants that Stella is a screen, numerous possibilities of dissimulation are put in place. Indeed, as Crewe suggests, the absolutely unspeakable might involve a host of desires, including the possibility that Stella stands in for a man.

Crewe's point here finds an odd echo in a throwaway line of Mary Ellen Lamb, who suggests that one could theorize the possibility of women finding voice in the sixteenth century in much the way that Foucault describes the emergence of homosexual identity in the nineteenth century; that just as the sites of disempowerment gave discursive space to the newly emergent homosexual identity, so, too, one might find women's voices emerging from what was said in the attempt to silence them and keep them in their place.[16] As Lamb argues, although it is a point she wishes to repudiate, much as does Hannay, the site involves an identification of women's voices with their sexuality. This is, admittedly, undeniably, misogynist and projective in many instances; yet here it seems to me that the response made by Hannay and Lamb—which is to deny sexuality because it has been so written—is arguably mistaken. And not least if the sexuality involved does not support normative and regulatory regimes, indeed could be sites that undermine the mechanisms aimed at producing normality. Incest violates the taboo that maintains the proprieties of reproduction. If one were to read the emergence of Mary Sidney's voice as transgressing the proprieties of gender, as occupying the territory of, and indeed even inventing the site of male (dis)empowerment, then her faithful and literal translation I would argue reproduces the social and the literary precisely by evacuating the linchpin that ties those things together. Hers is a reproduction outside the domain of compulsory heterosexuality, and it makes legible a range of desires lodged within and also on the surface of the social. As Crewe suggests in *Trials of Authorship*, incest is not to be read as the "dirty secret" (p. 98) but as co-extensive with the constitutiveness of the social; such a point continues the line of argument that Jones offers: we are dealing here with the most active solicitation of women for the construction of the social, the fullest engagement of desire, the transgression of the boundary between licit and illicit that founds and troubles the licit and the normative and that renders it *preposterous*.

For, as Kenneth Thorpe Rowe suggested, despite himself, in the classic 1939 article supposed to have laid Aubrey's claims forever to rest, incest is the most ordinary story one can tell. Aubrey, to recall the passage, recounts that he had "heard old gentlemen say that they [Philip and Mary Sidney] lay together" and that "the first Philip earle of Pembroke was begot by him, but he inherited not the witt of either brother or sister." Rowe contends that such storytelling reflects upon Aubrey as "innocent—but also salacious" (p. 592). Thus, Rowe continues, it took little more than some wine and the "process of association" to put together his tale: "Philip Sidney dearly loved his sister and was much at Wilton; perhaps he lay with her there. Someone remarked, from the association of names, and thinking loosely of family resemblance, not of direct descent, that Philip Herbert inherited not the wit of his mother nor of his uncle Philip; shortly, Philip Herbert was begot by his mother's brother" (p. 593). In following his processes of association, producing the startling conjunction of the preposterous and the obvious, Rowe forgets to mention one further piece of evidence that might lead in the same direction, and along the same trajectory of disidentification, the possibility of reading literally the letter prefacing the *Arcadia*;[17] there, to recall the passage, a text written only for the countess, only to her, is taken also to be the maimed child that she and her brother have produced together, she, as it happens, in the more active position, soliciting and desiring—"you desired me to do it, and your desire to my heart is an absolute commandment," he at first the reluctant father and then a kind of male mother who has delivered a child that is characterized by its "deformities," indeed is called a "monster," not merely for what it is as it came out but as much for what "came in"; this monstrosity bears her name and wears her livery. The letter traffics in gender crossing, unnatural desires, and their offspring, crossing boundaries that hint at (if they do not explicitly name) incest, sodomy, and bestiality. The work Sidney characterizes as that of an "offender" he nonetheless also offers as a token of the writer's love; indeed, of one "who doth exceedingly love you," and it is a question whether the excesses of the letter are not precisely of the kind that makes impossible the kind of argument against Aubrey that Rowe seeks to marshal.

Not, as we have seen, that Rowe disbelieves everything; indeed he has no trouble believing another story Aubrey tells: "She was very salacious, and she had a Contrivance that in the spring of the yeare when the stallions were to leape the mares, they were to be brought before such a part of the house, where she had a vidette to looke on them and please herself with their Sport; and then shee would act the like sport with *her* stallions. One of her great gallants was crooke-backt't Cecill, earle of Salisbury." "What is recorded in the first part of the passage," Rowe writes, "does not appear to be unconsonant with the frank Renaissance attitude toward nature and beauty"; Aubrey's age was less frank—"therefore," Rowe concludes, "the conclusion by way of inference" (p. 594). The conclusion about the countess and her brother, however, is rather more literal when Aubrey moves from the voyeuristic scene to endorse what old men have said. The missing connection is there in the slip from her stallions to her gallants, or it is as soon as we supply the missing signifier; as Michael Moon has suggested to me, all one needs to get from the horses to Philip is the Greek etymology of his name. Cross-species sex, sex between brother and sister; joined in the signifier, put into the mouths of old men—is this Socrates lecturing Phaedrus on the horses of the passions, or are these the old men that, as Katherine Duncan-Jones suggests in her recent biography, Philip Sidney was so good at pleasing?[18] When Aubrey proceeds from the horses to Sir Philip by way of imagining the countess having sex with the aged Cecil, we need only recall how assiduously Philip sucked up to Leicester and to Walsingham, not to mention his mentor Languet. It is then within the normative and scandalous routes of the homosocial, along the lines of power and patronage, that one might begin to locate the love that dares not speak its name in Mary Sidney's writing, and not least so when she does nothing more than faithfully insert herself into these circles.[19]

One more testimony might be added here, and with it we return to the terms of the relation of original and translation with which I began, John Donne's poem on the Sidneian psalms, which points to the union that Mary and Philip achieved as their way of reproducing a division and doubling in the source.[20] David's psalms, Donne writes, were already a double and divided text, written by a "cloven tongue" (l. 9) and it was only through a further "cleft" (l. 12) that the spirit of divided and doubled David met in brother and sister, "Two, by their bloods, and by thy Spirit one" (l. 14). As Crewe reminds us, "spirit" is a perfectly equivocal term, and the attempt to translate this union to an elsewhere, to a dephysicalized site—much like the site of the phoenix and the position of spiritual unity beyond gender for which Hannay argues—is belied by the choice of the word.[21] The "two that make one" (l. 17) in Donne is a union in spirit and blood, in spirit that is the efflorescence of blood that has not been expended in vain; it makes, Donne, says, an "Organ" (l. 16), and more than a musical instrument is meant, more than the toy that brother and sister traded across the Arcadian pages. Like the Nom/Non du Pere, or the Phallus that is its signifier, it goes on beyond their deaths. So, Donne concludes, have the translators been translated. Literally; for however etherealized Sir Philip and Mary Sidney are now, they exist in the only site in which we can be certain that they ever were coupled, here, now, where ink is their blood and spirit and the page their making.[22] Literally, materially, translated, reproduced. On those triumphant pages that we must, at last, however briefly, open.[23]

To notice, for instance, that the speaker of *The Triumph*, the "I," is never gendered; true, in Petrarch's version as well, there is no mark of gender throughout the first part of the *Trionfo*; but, as the second section begins, the speaker is, insistently, a man, *uomo* (II, ll. 3, 20); as insistently, the speaker in the countess's triumph remains simply an "I," its gender never marked. And the effects of this? In the first part, the speaker who bears no mark of gender—and, since this is the countess's poem, is therefore implicitly marked as female—begins by describing a "gallant Ladie" (l. 1) and "hir chosen mates" (l. 14), and it is within this entirely female world that an "I" first appears, noting yet another woman on the horizon, one in black "such as I scarcelie knowe" (l. 32), who arrives and seems to address the speaker of the poem:

> Thow Dame, quoth she, that doeth so proudlie goe,
> Standing upon thy youth, and beauties state,
> And of thy life, the limits doest not knowe.
>
> (I, ll. 34–36)

The effects of this address are multiple: the lines identify the speaker of the poem as the about to be dead lady or as the one who desires that condition—a few lines down an "I" in the poem reports that she will "thank who shall me hence assoile" (l. 54). One effect of this, then, when we return to Petrarch's version of the poem, is that the speaker is put in the position of Laura. That this crossing is possible has something to do with how Laura appears in the poem, for instance when one notices that she dies at least three times in the first part of the poem—she seems to be dead when the poem starts, seems to be dead after the woman in black appears, seems to be dead again when her company can do nothing for her at the end of the first part of the poem, when she ascends to heaven—which is, one might have thought, where we were to begin with. When she returns in part II, it is to announce that the speaker of the poem, not she, is dead (a point to which I will return shortly). These prevarications make her the very site of that passage across limits that are continuously being violated, transgressed, crossed beforehand and afterward in ways that can only be re-marked rather than marked once. All of this, I would suggest, helps the countess cross the line as well as she comes from the start to occupy the position both of Petrarch and of Laura, and to occupy them in the unmarked "I." This is not the only direction in which the cross-identification works, however, for at the end of the poem, the last question the speaker poses to the dead beloved is to ask when they will be united. The answer is, devastatingly, "Thow without me long time on earth shalt staie" (II, l. 190). The limits remain, therefore, unknown, the desired transgression of part I refused. Yet in her identification with that still-living speaker, the countess identifies herself, and this remains transgressive, if not a violation of the ultimate ontological border; for the final crossing by way of identification with Petrarch cannot fail to position Sir Philip at the site of the dead lady.

The labilities of cross-identifications, of marks that are remarked and yet remain indeterminate and unmarked, can be seen at the close of the address to the "Dame," or rather can be seen precisely because where the address closes and where it is responded to are impossible to tell. Twenty-odd lines after the speech begins, the line that announces "replide then she" (l. 51) could as easily be referring to the line that comes before as to the one that comes after. What comes before, in fact, is a line that says "To this, thow right or interrest hast none" (l. 48), and it is exactly the case that the question which of the two—the lover or the beloved, the one alive or the one dead—is in this state of dispossession is only furthered when one cannot tell who says the line, whether it begins the reply or ends the speech. And the line, of course, only makes this situation all the more dizzying by itself announcing the very state of dispossession. Thus one cannot know whether it is the speaker or the one spoken to who is so dispossessed. Moreover, if it is the lines that follow that constitute the reply—"This charge of woe on others will recoyle" (l. 52), they begin—those lines recoil even further when one notes, following Rees, and therefore following everyone who has commented on the faithful literalness of the countess's translation, that here the translation errs: what is translated as "others" is, in Petrarch, a reference to the speaker himself.[24] And the effect of this so-called mistranslation? A further displacement along the lines of gender; for the others on whom this death recoils are the host of ladies that form the squadron around this doubled figure of the dead, the wished-for dead, the over and again and not yet dead—a figure, who, I would add, also is at moments in the poem inextricable from the very figure of Death, the woman in black first sighted and not recognized. Lines of cathexis are opened here that heighten a female–female erotics to be found from the very opening lines of the poem in which the "I" of the poem may be read as a woman speaking of and to other women as her "chosen mates" (I, l. 14). This displacement along the lines of same-sex identification furthers the scandal of crossing and of cross-identification that the poem undertakes.

It gets marked again, insistently so, as the second part opens, when the "I" of the poem refuses to call itself man, but is insistently and only "I."

> That night, which did the dreadfull happ ensue
>   That quite eclips't; naie rather did replace
>   The Sunne in skyes, and me bereave of view.
>
> (II, ll. 1–3)

"And me" bereaves the poem of the line describing the "I" as "come uom cieco" (II, l. 3). The blind man blinded, eclipsed, replaced. "Replace" is not in Petrarch's version, and it marks the site of translation, as the blind man becomes this visionary. This marks and remarks the crossings of the second section, when Laura appears to Petrarch to tell him that she lives, and he is dead, when she takes over the mastering function of passively leading him to the revelation of their shared love. Read as his writing, these crossings dissimulate his occupation of every writing position; but read as the countess's crossing out of and replacement of the speaker position so that she is both him and her, another "strange passion"—to recall the phrase the countess uses elsewhere to characterize her relationship to her brother—is revealed.[25] It is there perhaps even more palpably in the first part of the poem, when the speaker stops a digression that seems to have gotten out of hand, one about the futility of heroic lives wasted. Read in Petrarch's poem, voiced in his voice, the digression is, at best, a self-pitying gesture, but word-for-word when it is in hers, the digression comes all too close to revealing whose futilely heroic death is covered by the figure of the dead lady, especially if one notes that, unlike Petrarch, the countess attributes courtesy (I, l. 146) as well as beauty to the figure; the mourned beloved can only be her brother, wasted in the wars, and the pained stop to the digression is the virtual announcement that what seems out of place in the poem is all too literally its subject.

These lines could be placed beside the other place where the countess, it is claimed, mistranslates; not surprisingly, it is a moment when she speaks of her own desires when she should be speaking of his:

> If lyking in myne eyes the world did see
> I saie not, now, of this, right faine I am,
> Those cheines that tyde my heart well lyked me.
> (II, ll. 127–29)

Where she says "my heart," Petrarch puts his.[26] The chains around her heart are the ones she tied and ties around his. This crossing occurs at the end of a particularly dense and complex section of the poem, one in which the lines between speakers is continually crossed, so much so that when "silence foulde[s] / Those rosie lips" (ll. 41–42) they seem to go on speaking, and when "I" reports "my eare possest" (l. 54) with the desire to cross the line, "with spirit readie prest, / Now at the furthest of my living wayes" (ll. 52–53), that "I" is then compared to another who is marked as male, as if the "I" were not—that is, if he speaks the lines in which the "happless he" is described, but it might be that his ear is possessed with her unmarked voice. For, as usual, after that speech, an "I" appears, and, as usual, it renders retrospectively impossible the determination of voice, even as it renders indeterminate who speaks in the position of that "I." Moreover, it is in this possessed state that the speaker's "failing-sight" (l. 61), dying or going blind, gives access to a voice that belongs to a woman who seems just to have appeared: "Well, I hir face, and well hir voice I knewe," this blinded, ear-possessed speaker declares, "who oft did thee restraining, me encyte" (II, l. 63), and the woman so entirely known either is or is not the woman to whom he has been speaking all the while, or is the woman who has never stopped speaking, no matter whose voice we think we hear or see. So apprehended, she appears to be another woman or, at any rate, a site of new recognition. Yet who is this other woman, this screen? Is it Stella, and is the countess now declaring that her refusals only produced the countess's further incitements to refuse and grant at once? It should be noted that twice during the speech of the recognized, unnamed woman, she insistently compares herself to a man who has come to the end of his life and embraces it with as much joy as a man who returns home from exile. She is that man (II, ll. 72, 74), and the pathos of his/her "onelie ruth" (l. 75) is that the return home does not include the one spoken to.

This change in gender identification is something that does not happen in Petrarch's version, and something that further allows the cross-identification of the dead woman in the poem with Astrophil / Philip. That is, if it does not occur a bit later in faithfully translated lines—in which the other woman seems to have become Laura, or to have become the countess without a screen, and in which the male beloved now has her brother's name, or at least the name that insisted itself—the insistence of the letter—in Aubrey's account.

That is to say, he is called a "wanton steede" (l. 98), she the brake; he runs a "race" guided by the alternating current of "kinde acceptance" and "sharp disdaine," the application of the spur and bit. In Petrarch's poem, the usual dynamics that are called petrarchan are split between the speaker and his dead lady; and in the countess's they are reunited:

Never were
Our hearts but one, nor never two shall be:
Onelie thy flame I tempred with my cheere;
This onelie way could save both thee and me.
(II, ll. 88–91)

The one-ly way of the poem is its truth, and the point of arrival of this section of the poem is that moment of so-called mistranslation with which I began, and which might now be seen to be as faithful as anything else in the poem. "Through fiction, Truth will neither ebbe nor flowe" (II, l. 147), the countess writes, "my love dares speake no more" (l. 150), and having said that, goes on speaking, crossing all the lines.

It only remains to be said that the lines to be crossed are ones we put there—I think, for instance, of the quotation marks around speeches that modern editors attempt in Petrarch's text, but to little avail.[27] If his indeterminations of voice may be signs of a desired masculine appropriation, the countess's unmarking of ownership of voice, her occupation of and crossing over of the marks of identification, carries the same but utterly different meaning. Such is the triumph of the Countess of Pembroke's literal translation. It comes without quotation marks.

Three WRITING AS A WOMAN

INTRODUCTION

"To be, or not to be, 'a woman'; to write or not 'as a woman' ": Denise Riley's question resonates with this project.[1] For although it is certainly the case that even at the material level of manuscript production, a female hand can be detected at work in sixteenth- and seventeenth-century texts, this fact in no way guarantees the category of the woman writer (for one thing, the hand marked as "female" is often an italic hand, which also marks class whatever the gender of the writer).[2] As Riley argues—and does so in the name of feminism—there are important reasons to resist not merely the already suspect idealizations housed in the category "woman," but even to question the more neutral sounding, seemingly empirical designation "women." And on several grounds: first, in that it assumes a collectivity pre-existing the nomination; second, because those who are so designated, or choose to affirm themselves as "women," may be caught inside networks that they may also seek to resist, and precisely as women; finally, that no one is once and for all and at every moment a woman. These caveats lead Riley at once to suspend the category and to affirm it, for however problematically or intermittently the category takes hold, it does do that, and to refuse it would be tantamount to a withdrawal from the inevitable scenes of interpellative nomination. So, too, in this project, the aim has been to affirm the gendered difference of writing in the period, but not without recognizing that there are massive problems in so doing. The phrase, "writing as a woman," registers this. While "as" could—and means to—register gendered difference, it also suggests—and means to—that writing as a woman does not guarantee the gender of the author.[3]

For this latter point, I have in mind not only the fact that much writing-as-a-woman is male-authored (Ovid's *Heroides*, as Elizabeth Harvey has demonstrated, is one crucial model for this practice)[4]—and it is to this problem I will turn in "Mary Shelton's Hand." But there is also the fact that much writing written by women acknowledges gender precisely as constraint—indeed as a virtual impossibility—for writing. Negotiations of this dilemma must engage a contestatory definition; if there are injunctions against a woman writing (injunctions that mandate silence and privacy and restrictions to domestic domains), the assertion of the possibility of women writing must either reformulate gender or refuse it. (It is to a version of that dilemma as found in the work of Elizabeth Cary that I turn in "Graphina's Mark.") Riley's work, in its careful attention to the grounds of defenses of women in the seventeenth century and earlier, reminds us how often these tracts must dislocate definitions of women, or how they must seize upon aspects of personhood not saturated by gender in order to launch their claims. One such ground is an intellectual and spiritual capacity arguably not the property of either gender (humanist cultivations of female literacy, for instance, start with a premise of equal educability, even as they attempt to ensure that women's educations should have no consequences). But to seize upon terrains that are not marked by gender must also mean either vacating the category of "women," or, at least, to score or overstep its limits. For a woman to write, it may be that she cannot write as a woman, or that "woman" must be transported to registers or territories usually not thought of as women's, but not necessarily barred either. For a woman to write as a woman must involve the revelation that woman is not a self-evident or tautological category, indeed, that it may have no ontological ground.

Hence, a problematization of the question "to write or not 'as a woman' " need not foreclose possibilities for women writers, much as the solution to the dilemma might seem caught in a bind of simulation that will forestall a definitive notion of "woman." The problem of venturing a notion of the woman writer *tout court* lies in the ways in which "woman" may remain not merely an unexamined category, but in the danger that its affirmation will repeat limitations that require consideration. On the other hand, any understanding of women-as-constructed poses the danger of the erasure of women and of gendered difference. This is not least the case if this problematic is posed within the familiar terms of the essentialism/constructionism debate, and especially when that binarism genders essentialism as female; construction, male. This double bind has, of course, often motivated the repudiation of theory in feminist criticism in the hope of clearing a space for women.[5] Yet, as Riley describes her motive, "in no way does it aim to vault over the stubborn harshness of lived gender while it queries sexual categorisation" (p. 3). That is, what is needed is first of all to break the deadlock between construction understood as an evaporation of lived reality and essentialism as rooted in the supposition of a transhistorical and universalization of gendered inequity and female suffering. To do so, one must recognize how the theoretical division is maintained by the division of the sexes.

As Riley suggests, to affirm the eternal, transhistorical opposition of men and women too quickly loses sight of the historical differences in gender. Moreover, as she notes, pointing to the work of Ian Maclean, gender difference is not in every instance couched in oppositional terms.[6] That is to say, the difference of gender is a set of different differences, sometimes marked with negative/positive valences, sometimes on a scale of more or less, sometimes simply as differences that can be mobilized in various directions, and that will even throw up such phenomena as "masculine women" or "effeminate men" (the former often valued positively, however much that might trouble a critic bent on securing "women" as an utterly differentiated category, feminine to the core), or produce an author like Margaret Cavendish, who, as Riley details, offers both views of women in her *Femal Orations*. As Riley cautions, the specter of difference could lead toward a dissolution of gender as a category or to a celebration of earlier regimes as times of greater possibilities lost as bodies become more and more saturated with and sutured to gendered identities. It seems important therefore to stress that any inquiry into the category of "women" or of the woman writer does not aim at dissolving the category into some third term or third sex, an indeterminate middle or divine androgyne. Gendered difference is real, and real not least because of the massive work that social discourses and regulations do to maintain it, that somatic and psychological inhabitation of these categories enforces. Nonetheless, it is only by questioning the divide that one can also understand its own regulatory effect—and our contribution to it by insisting upon it; for by so doing, the categories male and female that are thereby maintained also are impoverished.

This impoverishment, as Riley argues, depends upon a reduction to gendered difference that may make sense for our own times, as the linking of personhood to gender has come to seem more inexorable. But, even in modernity, there remain questions of what is being mobilized when gendered categories are invoked, and how fully they operate in any instance and in relationship to other categories—those of race or class, for example. More broadly, as Riley asserts, for earlier periods, the imbrications of gender in discussions about the relations of soul and body, for example, in notions of personhood, nature, reason, and the like, may easily override gender difference, or make it possible to find the category of gender continually resignified in less than absolute kinds of ways. The emergence of women writers in the period—despite all the injunctions—is made possible, Riley's arguments would suggest, because of the ways in which intellectual activity is capable of limited detachment from gendered determination. There are costs to this, of course, and not least that women writers may not recognize their activity as part of a gendered collectivity, that no progressive political agenda may follow from the existence of women writers, that it may be difficult finally to label Renaissance defenses of women "feminist."

Riley's arguments are compatible with the most formidable of recent contributions to a theory of gender—those offered in the work of Eve Kosofsky Sedgwick and Judith Butler. Butler's *Gender Trouble*, for instance, worries the question of "women" in ways that echo Riley's, and Sedgwick's exploration of the instabilities of sexual designation in *Epistemology of the Closet* likewise calls into question a syntax of gendered difference tied to heteronormativity. Indeed, one of the refreshing things about Riley's work lies in its suspension of sexual difference as the operative term for analysis. That is, in refusing the opposition of gender as some foundational instance, she thereby calls into question whether gender difference exists prior to categorization, and therefore whether gender difference can be assumed in advance. Although questions of sexuality are not significantly formulated in Riley's work, as they are in Butler's and Sedgwick's, it cannot be entirely accidental that her discussion of "the indeterminancy of sexual positionings" cites as exemplary anthropological discourse "with its berdache, androgynous and unsettling shamanistic figures" (p. 5) and articulates a desire for such data to be treated as not merely exotic. That is, the figure of the berdache serves to suggest cultural organizations of gender that do not assume an easy correspondence between genitalia and gender. Such figures must not only complicate a naturalized version of gender difference, but also suggest that historical and cultural differences are far more determinate of gender categories than is biology or psychology.

Riley's berdache is instanced in the context of a refusal to allow indeterminacy simply to lead to a celebration of other supposedly more liberatory regimes of gender; it means rather to point to the constellations of consolidations that are historically differentiated. But history, too, for Riley is not some once and for all ground, but rather sites of multiplicities and of incommensurable temporalities. Although at times a certain suspect voluntarism can be felt in Riley's arguments (as if one could simply choose when to be or not to be a woman) as well as an impatience with gender difference as if that alone could suspend its work, she nonetheless poses possibilities for agency and self-determination as coexisting with social designations; moreover, how and when one is interpellated as a woman depends upon social/ideological formations that must necessarily be striated institutionally, locally, and in terms of the long and short durées of various gendered understandings. It is in that context that it seems crucial to recognize that one of these matrices for the production of gender is the history of sexuality, for the modern sex/gender system has everything to do with the regimes of heteronormativity (regimes to be resisted and whose proclamations to control the social entirely must be contested, but whose massive work is also undeniable), whereas the early modern period cannot be read easily under the modern aegises of the hetero/homo divide. Again, to say that is not to appeal to some supposed earlier moments of sexual freedom, for the mappings of sexual possibility in the early modern period must constantly negotiate normatizations and routinizations as well: the assumption of marriage as every Protestant woman's lot, for example; sites of the unspeakable, legally codified in sodomy laws, for instance; manifestations of behavior capable of unleashing lethal energies (against sodomites, tribades, etc.). But it is also because of certain labilities in the structures of desire that some possibilities for "women" emerge that may prove especially intractable to any definition of women that also seeks to assure their femininity.

When Joan Kelly denied that women had a Renaissance, she wrote without much sense of the sheer amount of women's writing in the period. But it is doubtful whether literary activity would have led her, as it has led some more recent critics and historians, to affirm that women did have a Renaissance.[7] To the point here, moreover, would still remain the nagging question whether women writers are writing as "women," that is, whether their intellectual activity easily aligns them with the restrictions and regulations that the term "women" is meant to secure. (It must also be stressed that certain forms of literary activity—manuscription especially—were allowable to women writers and preferred by aristocrats of both sexes.) Nonetheless, Kelly also notes certain ruses in the representation of women, certain transitive occupations of gendered positions, and although she reads these as always supporting male power, she also demonstrates (in her reading of Castiglione) that male consolidations of power at the expense of women negotiate power differentials between men precisely by using gender difference as a means to represent power differences. That is to say, however much Kelly preserves the category of women as a site of oppression, she also gestures to ways in which men and women can share social positions and gendered identifications. Without leaping from this to any but the most restricted sense of female empowerment that might follow, it still seems possible to affirm both that women did not have a Renaissance and that some women, precisely by not being fully caught by the disenablements of gender—by virtue of the fact of aristocratic birth, let us say, or by assumptions of literate skills reserved to a minuscule portion of the population—did participate in "the Renaissance." Obviously, such enablements can in no way be taken to represent instances generalizable to all women. This fact bears upon the manuscript that I examine in "Mary Shelton's Hand"; however, it is also arguable that print culture shares some features with manuscript culture, more than is allowed when the two forms of publication are treated, as they usually are, as radically incompatible. That is to say, if one can recognize that manuscript culture presumes certain affordances for some women, that is also the case with some forms of publication.[8]

To pick up from Kelly, and to exert some pressure on her examples of gender transitivity by insisting on the ways in which the history of gender is fully imbricated in the history of sexuality, is to provide the further historical and theoretical grounds for the two instances of writing considered in the chapters that follow. Indeed, the instance of women's writing that is the subject of "Mary Shelton's Hand" was touched on briefly in *Sodometries*.[9] In the chapter "The Making of Courtly Makers," I argued, based in part on an anecdote from Puttenham's *Arte of English Poesie*, that a consideration of gender transitivity—of cross-gender identifications—in the sixteenth century might enlarge our sense of the range and possibilities for cultural activity in the period. Puttenham's anecdote centered on an ambiguous word, "weemen," that could as easily be read as an affirmation of the solidity of male identification (but which also thereby entailed the real possibility of male–male desire) or as an endorsement of cross-gender desire, of the desire of men for women. One consequence of this, I suggested, was that "women" could move into the position of "we men" without simply being erased in so doing, since Puttenham's term "wee men" refused the absolute closure of gender difference or, more to the point, was not bound to a syntax of heteronormativity since the opening for women represented by Puttenham followed from the presumption that male desire might as easily be satisfied by men or by women. Although it must be stressed that, in Puttenham's account, "women" remained in a subservient position to men and to male desire, it need not be assumed that such would always be the situation, and I offered some examples to that effect.

One instance to make the case that I summoned up in a cursory fashion in *Sodometries*, and to which I return in "Mary Shelton's Hand," had to do with a poem assigned to the authorship of Henry Howard, styled Earl of Surrey, in its first printing in the 1557 volume of *Songs and Sonnets* that has come to be called *Tottel's Miscellany.*[10] There, Tottel titled the poem "Complaint of the absence of her lover being upon the sea" (Tottel, no. 17), and the presumption that the speaker of the poem is a woman has been repeated ever since. For the argument in *Sodometries*, what was of crucial importance to me was the fact that a manuscript version of the poem exists in a hand that had been identified as Mary Shelton's. It is the possibility that that hand was authorial that I explore further below. And, as I shall argue, to pursue that possibility means, on the one hand, to be taking stock of an instance of manuscript culture that did not necessarily bar the woman writer—indeed, that represents a site of significant enablements. But, on the other hand, it also means that the question of the woman writer is tied to questions of desire that cannot be stabilized by heteronormative presumptions. This means, finally, that the woman writer does not necessarily inhabit a normative definition of gender, if being a real woman necessarily implies the articulation of hetero desire or, even more to the point, a subscription to a femininity that assumes gender subordination, "women" as those defined entirely in their relationship to the institution of marriage. That institution, however, and its relationship to the problem of writing as a woman is more fully considered in "Graphina's Mark," a discussion of the work of Elizabeth Cary—especially of *Mariam*—that attends to the ways in which Cary's thematization of "writing as a woman" (including its embodiment in the character she names Graphina) involves complex paths of identification striated by race, class, and gender. These detach the writing woman from the usual constraints of the marital bond and implicate her in quite other forms of social relations.

MARY SHELTON'S HAND

The poem that begins "O Happy dames, that may embrace / The frute of your delight," assigned to the authorship of Henry Howard, styled Earl of Surrey, in its first printing in *Tottel's Miscellany*,[1] first circulated in manuscript. This chapter is concerned with the sole extant manuscript copy of the poem, that entered in Mary Shelton's hand into what is usually called the Devonshire manuscript (BL Add.17492) in all likelihood in the 1530s, perhaps early in the 1540s, but at any rate sometime before Surrey's execution in 1547, that is, at least ten years before the poem was printed. Differences between the manuscript and the printed text make it likely that Tottel did not set the poem from the Devonshire manuscript but from another manuscript, perhaps one like the contemporary Arundel Harington manuscript, a collection of poems compiled as a self-conscious anthology, in which groups of works by the same author are gathered on sequential leaves. *Tottel's Miscellany* looks like that: its first printing includes groups of poems by Surrey, Wyatt, and Nicholas Grimald, followed by a long section of poems by uncertain authors. However, manuscript ascriptions are not always reliable; even the Arundel Harington manuscript is rather vexing in regard to some poems supposedly by Surrey, a point that bears upon the argument I wish to advance here.

In *Sodometries*, I argued—or rather, held open as a possibility—that "O Happy dames," a poem seemingly spoken by a woman (as indicated by the title Tottel provided for the poem, "Complaint of the absence of her lover being upon the sea" [Tottel, no. 17], and the subsequent consensus that takes the female speaker of the poem to represent an act of male ventriloquism) might be a poem *written* by a woman, by Mary Shelton in fact. No one has ever entertained that supposition, I assume because of the authority of Tottel's attribution of the poem to Surrey. But although her authorship of the poem has never been suggested, the ways in which Shelton's hand in the Devonshire manuscript has been described has virtually precluded such a consideration. In *Sodometries*, I quoted S. P. Zitner's description of her hand as a "scrawl," and noted that Zitner was simply repeating Richard Harrier's characterization in his study, *The Canon of Sir Thomas Wyatt's Poetry*.[2] I pointed out, however, that Mary Shelton had more than one hand: her italic signature can be found on the torn page that now serves as the front leaf of the Devonshire manuscript. This signature meant, very simply, that Mary Shelton was an extremely literate person; the fact that she used italic for her formal signature aligns her with the most progressive humanistic educational programs of the period and provides an indicative mark of the kind of high literacy that must also be related to poetic production in the Tudor period. That her ordinary hand was a "scrawl" would not distinguish her from many other writers of the period, who reserved italic for signatures or for writing in Latin. Indeed, one sign of high literacy in the period was precisely the ability to manage several hands. In short, once the scrawl in which "O Happy dames" appears in the Devonshire manuscript is recognized as *one* of the several hands of Mary Shelton, it is not, as "scrawl" would seem to imply, an indication of minimal literacy.

In the Devonshire manuscript, "O Happy dames" is untitled, and no authorship for it is provided. This is not unusual for manuscripts of the period, and indeed the fullest systematic study of the manuscript that has been undertaken (Richard Harrier's) has precisely to do with this fact. The Devonshire manuscript contains a number of poems that are attributed to Wyatt elsewhere, and Harrier sought to establish which other poems in the manuscript might safely be ascribed to him as well. This scholarly activity, which clearly has a place, accounts for most of the work that has been done on the Devonshire manuscript, indeed on most early manuscripts. There is no need for me to elaborate the conditions of modern scholarship that have dictated the assignment of authorship as the main protocol in the study of manuscripts, in part because it has been the subject of recent work by Arthur Marotti, who has frequently remarked that its effect has been to slight other social significances that such materials have. Although I do not believe that the desire to name Mary Shelton as the author of a poem supposedly by Surrey is identical to Harrier's efforts to sort out which poems in the manuscript deserve to be considered Wyatt's, my argument and his are sufficiently alike to raise the necessary and uncomfortable question whether the discovery of women writers must succumb to the lure of the canonical and the mystification of the singular author. In *Sodometries* I limited my remarks on "O Happy dames" to a provocative paragraph, in part because I did not think I could convincingly argue the case for Mary Shelton's authorship, that it could only be raised as a possibility. In truth, I still think this is the case, but I think it is also the case for Wyatt. If it were obvious which poems were his, there would be no problem in establishing the canon.

This is a potentially embarrassing fact for any notion of sovereign authorship, and one upon which I would want to build. When one recognizes that it is not obvious what poems Wyatt wrote; that the canon is disputed; that attributions, even in Wyatt's lifetime, are contradictory; that manuscripts that seem to group poems by authors do not do so consistently; that even in the Egerton manuscript, which contains poems and corrections to them by Wyatt in his own hand, other hands were not inhibited from marking his poems, one arrives at a number of important conclusions: that there is no intrinsic evidence for authorship; that assignment of authorship is dependent upon extrinsic evidence, for example, on coincidences of attribution. Above all, it is dependent upon the notion that assigning authorship is what matters. And even the Egerton manuscript does not suggest that such a principle had been established in the 1530s, whereas *Tottel's Miscellany*, which, on its title page, advertises the name of the Earl of Surrey (although inside the book more poems are attributed to Wyatt than to Surrey) does so because Surrey's name is important to Tottel—not, however, simply as the name of an author, but as an authorizing name; it is an aristocratic title, a style that is announced and to which the poems are subsumed—a style, which, as everyone knows, is Tottel's imposition in terms of editorial changes, rewritings, the provision of titles for poems, and the like. Some of these features go back to manuscripts, and they reflect upon authorial habits in the period.[3] Wyatt's autograph manuscript testifies to numerous revisions; there is no guarantee that even he thought of producing authoritative and final texts of his poems or sought to regulate their form as they circulated from hand to hand.

These facts about manuscript production raise significant questions about the version of "O Happy dames" in the Devonshire manuscript. For even if Surrey were its original author, Shelton's version of it might make it, in some sense, her own. The manuscript provides a way of further thinking through this point, as well as some further evidence for why Shelton's authorship has not yet been given a proper hearing. The final dozen or so entries in the Devonshire manuscript, usually said to be in Shelton's hand, are texts transcribed from Thynne's 1532 edition of Chaucer.[4] In his "Unpublished Poems in the Devonshire MS.," Kenneth Muir referred to these as "a group of short poems in the same handwriting, some of them apparently composed by a woman" (p. 255), as he also opined was the case with another poem in the manuscript that opens, "For thylke grownde that bearyth the wedes wycke / Beareth eke these holsome herbes as ful ofte," a set of lines in fact from *Troilus and Criseyde*. Muir's conclusion about the value of the poems in the manuscript was that aside from the poems by Surrey and Wyatt and a poet who might be Wyatt's imitator, "the poetical level of the verse in the manuscript is not high" (p. 258). This judgment includes the Chaucer selections, and it is difficult not to believe that seeing a woman's hand kept Muir from recognizing Chaucer. It has also to be added, however, that Muir's failure reminds us that decontextualized Chaucer might not be recognizable. Moreover, some of the Chaucer in the manuscript is no longer thought to be Chaucer; and some that is, has been mistranscribed or, rather, has been rewritten in ways that seem intentional. All the verses anthologized from Thynne deal with women, and some have been reworded in order to make their representations far more positive than they are in the printed text. These revisions offer the strongest suggestion that in putting a text into her own hands, Mary Shelton also made it her own.[5] That Muir could not recognize Chaucer, out of context, scrawled in a woman's hand, is certainly fuel for the argument I want to make here. It leads one to doubt that if "O Happy dames" had not been claimed for Surrey by Tottel that its presence in the Devonshire manuscript would have led to that authorial ascription. There is, after all, no other poem among the 180 or 190 in the manuscript that is Surrey's (and only one other poem that ever has been claimed as his—by G. F. Nott in 1815, a claim that was refuted definitively in 1871, when it was shown that the signature after a poem that Nott read as "Surrey," in fact said "Somebody").[6]

Did Mary Shelton write "O Happy dames"? The arguments I have been making to problematize Surrey's authorship of the poem and to hold open a more capacious notion of authorship that would assign value to Shelton's hand, build on an assumption that, however, needs to be examined: that the version of the poem in the Devonshire manuscript is in fact in Mary Shelton's hand. Assignment of the poem to her hand was first made in a frustratingly brief account of the manuscript offered by Edward Bond in that 1871 article referred to above; not only is it difficult to know which leaves of the manuscript Bond thought Shelton wrote and why he thought so, but he assigns the final series of Chauceriana to the hand of Margaret Howard; indeed, he declares them to be her own compositions (as other poems in the manuscript certainly are).

Muir admits that he has "not been able to identify the numerous handwritings in which the MS. is written," although he claims that "Surrey's 'O happy dames' is scribbled by Mary Shelton" (p. 254). In his notes to the poems he prints from the manuscript, he refers to a number of them as being in the "same hand" without quite saying whose hand it might be; these poems in the "same hand" include the Chaucerian stanzas, but presumably not "O Happy dames." The "same hand," in other words, does not appear to be Mary Shelton's. In Raymond Southall's work on the manuscript—work distinguished by the fact that Southall did not think that establishing authorship was his prime task; indeed, he doubts that Wyatt's authorship is an ascertainable item—Southall finds three hands to predominate in the manuscript (he thinks there are at least twenty-three); he assigns "O Happy dames" to Mary Shelton, along with the Chauceriana and about twenty other leaves of the manuscript; hers is, for him, the main hand in the manuscript, followed by those of Mary Fitzroy (Surrey's sister and the wife of Henry Fitzroy, Henry VIII's illegitimate son) and Margaret Howard.[7] Southall offers no opinion on who provided much of the marginalia to the volume; it, moreover, is assigned to Shelton by Harrier, who, however, reassigns a number of the leaves of the manuscript that Southall thought were Mary Shelton's to other hands; he notes that Bond ascribed "O Happy dames" to Shelton, but he is willing to say only that it is "probably by Mary Shelton's hand" (p. 51). Moreover, he does not follow Southall in assigning her the Chaucerian verses, finding the "neat hand" of those leaves quite distinct from her "scrawl." However, as Paul Remley notes in a recent essay devoted to the question of Mary Shelton's hand in the manuscript, Harrier does elsewhere identify a neat hand as Shelton's, and, as Remley argues, the writer that could produce an italic signature and who at least twice, perhaps three times, inscribed her name in the volume in a cursive script that is not identical either to the italic signature or to the "scrawl," obviously could have done "neat" writing as well. For the point is, to reiterate: Mary Shelton did not have one hand. Moreover, differences in hands arise from numerous conditions (speed of writing, cut and quality of the quill being used) that often make it difficult to know whether different hands belong to different persons (hence Southall's "conservative estimate" of twenty-three hands in the manuscript does not in fact tell us how many writers contributed to it).

Remley assigns the final Chauceriana to Shelton and makes much of her rewritings as a kind of feminine (perhaps feminist) protest literature; so, too, he sees the marginalia as hers and serving the same function, as when she writes "forget this" beside a poem. (Others have assumed that such marginal remarks are meant to be directions for someone copying the manuscript, indicating which poems should or should not be copied, as in the frequent marginal notation, "and this"; Bond, on the other hand, took these comments to be Margaret Howard's responses to poems that particularly touched or angered her.) However, because Remley knows that it is exceedingly difficult to assign hands to bodies, he accepts only as Shelton's those pieces of text proximate to her signatures or which seem to him consistent with the version of Shelton that the marginalia (as he reads it) and the Chauceriana suggest—Shelton as a "subversive" voice of protest. Scrupulous about the material evidence of hands, Remley falls into a much too easy notion of a real person (with an agenda obviously shared by Remley) who dictates what in the manuscript is hers. Moreover, although Remley notes that Bond assigned "O Happy dames" to Mary Shelton and that "this view has persisted" (p. 48), he nowhere considers the possibility in his essay that the poem is in her hand, and thus implicitly calls the prevailing view into question, presumably because he does not find in "O Happy dames" evidence of the kind of "personal" "protest" he assigns to the name Mary Shelton. However, as Remley himself points out, we know scarcely anything about Mary Shelton, not even when she was born, and the few traces of her name that survive, including those instances in the Devonshire manuscript, have been read in numerous ways, most of which testify to the fantasies of modern scholars, usually (not surprisingly) about Shelton's supposed lovelife.[8] It is this paucity of evidence, however, which also renders suspect the notion that a real Mary Shelton can be extrapolated from the hands in the Devonshire manuscript.

I would not want to give the impression in reviewing these efforts to identify Mary Shelton's hand in the Devonshire manuscript that I feel capable of doing what these scholars, far more skilled as paleographers than I am or ever will be, can do. I think that it is clear that without some independent examples of Shelton's hand on documents that must have been written by her, we have little hope of being able to distinguish what exactly in the Devonshire manuscript is hers (and even such documents would not necessarily be conclusive since handwriting changes over time and differs, moreover, depending on the kind of text being written). In many respects, for the argument I have been making here, finding the real Mary Shelton is not the point. That the multiplicity of hands in the manuscript belong variously to three women is as useful for my purposes as the possibility of definitively ascribing texts to them; there are certainly poems in the manuscript by Margaret Howard, and just as certainly some by Mary Shelton. G. F. Nott remarked long ago that the hand of "O Happy dames" looks like that of Mary Fitzroy, and the example he provided in facsimile does bear a striking resemblance to the hand in the Devonshire manuscript (2: 591). There is a strong resemblance between the hands of these three women in this manuscript, and they are performing enormously important cultural work; a reduction of it to the question of who did what—and to the assumption that authorship is the most important category to be ascertained—limits one's understanding of the extent to which this manuscript participates in the creation of Tudor culture. This activity may not be, *pace* Remley, subversive, marginal protest; the rewriting instanced in the Chauceriana, for example, is not surprising in manuscript culture, which is not to suggest that how Chaucer is rewritten is inconsequential. More to the point may be the importance of recognizing these women's hands as participating in and shaping the materials of cultural transmission. The failure to recognize this fact—the persistence and importance of manuscript culture in the period—is a product of print culture, theirs and ours.

Tottel's version of "O Happy dames," as I mentioned above, is not the one offered in the Devonshire manuscript. There is, of course, no reason to suppose that he was avoiding reproducing in print a woman's hand and, indeed, the manuscript he worked from could have been another instance of the same phenomenon. However, it does have to be noted that every modern edition of Surrey reprints the poem from Tottel and not from the Devonshire manuscript; this *does* seem like an active suppression of the woman's hand.[9] There is no way to argue that the Devonshire manuscript offers a better text of the poem than Tottel does, if by better one means closer to Surrey's original, which is what better must mean to an editor of Surrey's work; but there is also no reason to assume in these terms that Tottel's text is any closer to the authorial holograph. We know that Tottel rarely prints its sources verbatim, and in most cases will be one step away from the manuscript(s) behind it. Ordinary editorial procedure would lead a modern editor in such instances to prefer a contemporary manuscript to the printed text, and in fact both of Padelford's 1920s editions of Surrey as well as Emrys Jones's 1964 Oxford edition do prefer manuscripts whenever possible. That is, in every instance but this one. That is, in the one case where a woman's scrawl has been identified as the manuscript hand.

What does the poem look like in the manuscript? Admittedly, it is a scrawl, or as Padelford writes in a note to the transcription he provided of the manuscript version in a 1906 essay on "The MS. Poems of Henry Howard, Earl of Surrey," "the hand is very slovenly" (p. 338).[10] However, once one admits the possibility that the hand that wrote this poem could also write neatly, the slovenly scrawl may simply indicate that it is not the neat hand of a copyist, not, that is, the neat copying hand. In the characteristic scrawl that most scholars agree is Mary Shelton's, that hand is found when she is composing, even when she is signing her name to one of her scrawled compositions. Mary Shelton's compositions in the manuscript commonly take the form of short verses, usually characterized by commentators as doggerel, a word that Shelton herself uses in one of these entries.[11] These entries often constitute *ex tempore* responses to some text in the manuscript.

The first thing therefore to remark about "o happy dames" in the Devonshire manuscript is that if it is in Mary Shelton's hand, it is in her composing hand. Moreover, as Padelford goes on to note, "words and even lines are scratched out to be replaced by slightly different spellings."[12] Were one dealing with a modern text, it would be easy enough to assume that these indicate a copyist recognizing and correcting a spelling mistake. However, there was no standardized spelling in the period; indeed what makes the texts certainly by Mary Shelton in the manuscript particularly elusive and difficult to transcribe is that their spellings allow quite alternative readings. If Shelton did not have any sense of correct or singular spelling (a fact, let me hasten to add, that is no sign of impoverished literacy, since, as has often been pointed out, modern editions of Renaissance texts often lose potential meanings by modernizing spellings and thereby deciding on one meaning when the old spelling preserves multiple possibilities), these crossings out and substitutions might then indicate her rethinking whether or not the word she just wrote is the word she wants, and then deciding that it is—or, perhaps, deciding that the respelling says better what she wants.[13] At any rate, I do not think such crossings out and substitutions of the same word constitute proof that the writer of these lines is attempting to be true to some text being copied.

Only once does a substitution suggest that the author may be a copyist, when "hartte" has been scratched out and "mynde" substituted—a substitution necessary to maintain the rhyme scheme. This is an "error" of the kind frequently noted in terms of texts reconstructed from memory, since "harte" does appear two lines down. Such accounts of mistaken transcription assume that the transcriber has memorized what is being copied and then errs by misremembering where the word properly belongs, often producing the kind of doubling that would have here had two "hart[t]"s, one clearly in the wrong place. The trouble with this explanation is that such errors also happen when one is writing, especially when writing quickly. The hand that wrote "hartte" and then crossed it out may be recognizing that it has gotten ahead of itself. There is a similar mistake noted by Padelford in the final line of the poem when, as the absent lover is imagined returning, the manuscript first read, "nowe he comes wylle allas no no," and then added above the line, between "wylle" and "allas," the words "he cume." "Now he comes wylle he cume allas no no" is a proper ten-syllable line, formally congruent with the final lines of each of the stanzas. But most of the lines in the poem have eight syllables, and the shorter version of the line is as intelligible as the longer one. Which is to say, it may not be an instance of Shelton leaving out what was in the version she was copying as of her rushing to a conclusion, still in the basic meter of the poem, and then reconsidering the end. I submit, therefore, as a real possibility, that the failure to use the Devonshire manuscript as the basis for modern texts of this poem is a refusal to grant what this account of the manuscript aims to suggest: the authority of the manuscript as (perhaps) a poem in the author's hand.[14]

But did a woman write "O Happy dames"? What is the gender of the speaker? As I indicated earlier, modern editors have followed Tottel in assuming that the speaker of the poem is a woman. Padelford provided an explanation of sorts for this (in his two editions of Surrey in the 1920s) by claiming that the poem was in all likelihood written by Surrey "for the Countess of Surrey, to voice her impatience at their separation during Surrey's absence on military duty in France" (an explanation that Jones repeats); alternatively, Padelford opines, perhaps, since it is in Shelton's hand in the Devonshire manuscript, Surrey wrote it for her, to express her desire for Thomas Clere, Surrey's companion in France, who died there in 1545. This explanation can be faulted on bibliographic grounds, since it assumes a somewhat later date for the Tudor entries in the Devonshire manuscript than is usual. Moreover, and much more to the point, this account assumes that women cannot write for themselves. Additionally, this explanation that a poem voicing intense desire for an absent male beloved must be written in a woman's voice aims to guarantee that there is nothing of Surrey's desire to be found in the text. Indeed, the only reason I have to want to go on thinking that this poem is by Surrey has precisely to do with the possibility for the representation of male–male eros that it represents, a possibility that I believe the current account of the poem as written for and as a woman seeks to erase, although I think even in its own terms some sense of gender transitivity can be reclaimed from the scenario that Padelford first suggested.[15]

Elizabeth Harvey has noted how often transvestite poems of the period involve placing a female speaker in the position authoritatively prescribed by the example of the poems that constitute Ovid's *Heroides*, one of which is a source for this poem as well, a woman lamenting the absence of her beloved, usually his betrayal and abandonment of her.[16] But as Ann Rosalind Jones has observed, there are instances of female-authored texts in the period that reclaim and reappropriate this Ovidian tradition.[17] In "o happy dames," the speaker initially addresses women "that may enbrayes / the ffrwte off your delyet"; the poem does not assume abandonment as the ordinary situation of women and accounts for happiness in erotically charged ways, as virtually every term in these lines suggests; some lines later, the speaker will once again invoke the situation of "owther lowers" who "en armes acrosse / rejoyes ther cheffe dellyet," imagining lovers embracing in the context of the speaker's description of sleepless nights and pained awakening to loss after dreaming of former delights. In that nocturnal, bedroom context, these embraces must also be sexual ones. The speaker sees women as sexual and is flooded with memories of union with the beloved, repeatedly aroused as the return of the beloved is anticipated, indeed is re-experienced. The final line of the poem, cited earlier, "nowe he comes wylle he cume allas no no," is the climactic instance in which he is almost present, and then is not. If this is a poem written by a woman, it represents female sexuality as unabashedly active and desiring, rather than contained by the familiar prescriptions or allowed to transgress (as in Padelford's scenario) only if one can assume that a man (preferably a husband) really wrote the poem.

It may be the forthrightness of this subject-position that has contributed to the supposition of male authorship, but, framed that way, it needs to be questioned for its reliance on a definition of gender difference plotted along the familiar axes of activity and passivity. Within the terms that the poem sets—in which the gender of the speaker is in fact never specified, and where it is only the presumption that if the desired object is male, the speaker must be female—what seems more to the point is the way in which the ordinary syntax of heteroerotic desire seems to have been reversed. If this places the speaker in the active male position, that need not mean that the poem is male authored. But it does mean that no matter who wrote it, the presumed hetero desire in the poem also vehiculates male–male desire. This, indeed, would be the case even in Padelford's scenario, since it assumes that in writing for his wife, Surrey was writing to himself; Padelford's plot thus inscribes an imaginary heteroerotics within a narcissistic cover for homoerotics.

More than the manipulation of subject/object positions in the poem allows for its gender transitivity, however. As the absent male is conjured up, he becomes an occupant of the speaker's mind, as, for instance, in the third stanza of the poem:

alas howe ofte in dremes I see
thoos yees that were my ffoode
wyche ssumetyme sso dellyted me
that yet they do me good
where with I wake with his retourne
whoosse abssente fflame dooth make me boren
but when I ffynde the lake lorde howe I mowren.

These lines display an intense incorporation and identification with the absent beloved; the seeing and the seen change positions, "thoos yees" become the speaker's I, still doing good, indeed ensuring the life of the speaker, as food and as the flame that still burns.

The fantasmatic identification and incorporation of the dream state also marks the writing of the poem in another way, guaranteeing that this is not the kind of straight autobiography that Padelford assumed. From the second stanza on, in which the absent beloved sails "en a shepe ffrawoghte wth remiemberances" to the fourth in which, projecting onto the beloved's absent state, the speaker exclaims, "loo whate amarryner lowe hays made me," the sea voyage of this poem is one that involves crossings of identity. The beloved contains the speaker and is thereby burdened by memory, and thus assumed to be in the same state of simultaneous connection and loss as is the speaker, whose transportations of the beloved, bringing him to mind, are also the exile of the speaker, at sea with the absent lover. These strong marks of identification in fact explain an otherwise puzzling feature of the poem, that it is impossible often to tell whether the speaker thinks the beloved is sailing away or sailing home. The traffic works in both directions, just as the "remiemberances" of the poem coupled with the failures and lack suggest a trading of presence and absence, of possession and dispossession, terms that could be marked as male and female, but, if so, only to note them as movable marks of gendered identity. If this is a poem by a woman, the positions usually gendered male and female are destabilized; indeed, insofar as it is easier to read this poem as (at the least) spoken by a woman, that position of writing seems to enable the other possibility that the poem voices—and not necessarily through a female speaker—the possibility of a male–male erotics.[18] This poem feels transgressive of the prescribed boundaries of female desire and expression; if it latches onto or produces this through the imagined occupation of a male desiring position, it also pushes beyond usual representational limits in the male–male desire avowed in the poem.

It is, of course, possible to read this poem as a male-authored one in which the presumed female speaker is simply a screen, in which there is no woman in the poem. However, other women are invoked in the poem, and the speaker seeks to occupy their positions of satisfied desire, which is one reason why it is difficult to read this poem and to erase the possibility that a woman is the speaker. Even if a male author has foisted his desiring position on to the women in this poem, it cannot be read, I think, as a male-authored text that simply appropriates women, since the text articulates a position for women as desiring subjects. And, of course, if this really is a poem written by Mary Shelton or one of the other women whose hands appear in the Devonshire manuscript, this enlargement of possibility, however much it is founded in a rewriting of an Ovidian tradition and in the gender transitive reversal of its syntax of male and female positioning, does not represent the marginal transgression and subversion that one might assume to be the only place possible for a woman writer; it is an occupation at the center.

Before concluding that a woman wrote this poem, however, we need to consider some further evidence for Surrey's authorship, for there are two other poems attributed to him that also have—and much more explicitly so than is the case with "O Happy dames"—speakers gendered female. One of these ("Good ladies, you that have your pleasure in exyle," Surrey, ed. Jones, no. 24) seems to be another version of that poem, involving the same situation; Padelford thought it certainly written for Surrey's wife, and the poem's inclusion of a reference to her Lord (as the beloved is insistently called) returning "And playng wheare I shall hym fynd with T. his lytle sonne" (l. 22), would seem to refer to their first child, Thomas, born in 1536. The poem appears in the Surrey section of Tottel, where it is titled "Complaint of the absence of her lover upon the sea" (no. 19), although the line that I have just cited appears only in the version of the poem in the Arundel Harington manuscript.[19] There, in fact, the poem is not attributed to Surrey; it is signed Preston. Ruth Hughey, the editor of the manuscript, opines that Preston may be the author of the poem; in all likelihood the full name to be attached to the ascription, she argues, is Thomas Preston, who offered himself to Cromwell's services in 1533 by sending him a "specimen" of his "fashion of writing." As Hughey observes, this may allude to his compositional skills—which would lend support to his authorship of the poem—but is much more likely to refer to his script. Why would a copyist (not the copyist, it should be added, whose hand appears in the Arundel Harington manuscript) sign that transcription of the poem? Hughey explains that letters often sent by others' hands, and in their hands, would have the copyist's name on it, as was the case when Preston served as one of Princess Mary's Gentleman Waiters and carried her letters. Following Padelford's scenario, Hughey concludes that when Surrey sent the poem to his wife, it was in Preston's hand. The problem with this explanation is that every example that she offers tracing Preston's activities locates him in England, not in France with Surrey. That is, if Thomas Preston did copy this poem for someone, the someone in question may have been Lady Frances de Vere, the Countess of Surrey. She did not accompany Surrey to France.

As for the other poem spoken by a woman assigned by modern editors to Surrey's authorship: this poem, which begins "Girt in my giltlesse gowne as I sit here and sow," does appear in Tottel, but was first included among the poems of uncertain authorship (no. 243). In its second printing, the poem was moved to the Surrey section, following one that begins "Wrapped in my careless cloke, as I walke to and fro" (Tottel, no. 26); there it is titled, "An answer in the behalfe of a woman of an uncertain aucthor." Although modern editors print "Girt in my giltlesse gowne" as Surrey's, Tottel lends no support for this ascription; clearly, he moved the poem to the Surrey section in recognition that it was an answer on behalf of the woman described in Surrey's poem. This poem also appears in the Arundel Harington manuscript, indeed in a version twice as long as that in Tottel. However, the presence of the poem in the Arundel Harington manuscript does not immediately support Surrey's authorship, since, as Hughey notes, the poem does not clearly belong in the Surrey section of the manuscript; the poem immediately following is not his, then there is a gap of eleven missing leaves in the manuscript (lost in the eighteenth century when they served as printer's copy for the *Nugae Antiquae*); the poems that follow this lacuna are Surrey's, but there is no way of knowing whether all the leaves missing were too, and hence no way of knowing where the Surrey group began and whether it included the poem in question. The very form of the poem furthermore makes Surrey's authorship doubtful; as Mary Shelton's practice in the Devonshire manuscript shows, other hands often penned responses. "Girt in my giltlesse gowne" is likely a woman's response to Surrey's poem.[20]

Finally, it is worth noting that "O Happy dames" probably once did appear in the Arundel Harington manuscript; the poem is printed in *Nugae Antiquae* (1769), presumably from one of the lost leaves of the manuscript. There it is headed, "By JOHN HARINGTON, 1543, *for a Ladie moche in Love.*" Hughey in fact prints the poem as Harington's,[21] although in her notes she indicates that she is "inclined to accredit the poem to Surrey" (p. 289). For my purposes here it is enough simply to notice this ascription to Harington; it registers the possibility that the manuscript was correct at least insofar as it ascribed "O Happy dames" to a hand other than Surrey's, just as it most certainly is in another's hand in the Devonshire manuscript. John Harington in fact often served as his own copyist in the Arundel Harington manuscript, and "by JOHN HARINGTON" at the head of the poem, like the name Preston appended elsewhere, may register his function as the poem's copyist, not as its author. In which case, if he wrote it "*for a Ladie moche in Love,*" "for" is not doing the work it did when Padelford said that Surrey wrote "O Happy dames" for his wife; "for" here would name Harington as the hand that made this copy of a female-authored text.

Mary Shelton's and Surrey's names appear together once in a line of a poem in the Surrey canon, an impassioned sonnet/epitaph on Sir Thomas Clere, Surrey's long-time companion after the death of Henry Fitzroy and the supposed "sweetheart" (as the editors are fond of saying) of Shelton. In that poem the fatal trajectory of Clere's life is traced along a path in which "Shelton for love, Surrey for Lord thou chase." It was, in fact, in the context of a reading of this epitaph that S. P. Zitner, to whom I alluded at the beginning of this chapter, referred to Shelton's scrawl; Zitner also noted what for him was only a muted homoeroticism in the "tactile immediacy" of another line in the poem, "Thine Earle halfe dead gave in thy hand his Will," assuring his readers that the line offered "no problem" since Surrey's relationship with his wife was quite "regular" and his devotion to Clere, and to Henry Fitzroy earlier, had been quite public (pp. 516, 524). Zitner's assumptions about "regularity" (or should we say straightness?) are based on the questionable belief that marriage and same-sex relations are necessarily incompatible, that open expressions of male–male love must necessarily not be erotic (they presumably must be secret and closeted). His account tallies with those we have observed explaining how Surrey wrote poems "for" the Countess.

It was left to Jonathan Crewe, following Zitner where he would not go, to read Surrey's homoerotics as explicit and to note that in this poem, in the line "Shelton for love, Surrey for Lord thou chase," Shelton is virtually "one of the boys," as Crewe puts it, her gender erased, or, if there, only as a sign of "cynical inclusion/exclusion," a kind of subliminal trace of a heteroerotic sanction for a "homosexual consummation" from which, Crewe opines, "Shelton has to be temporarily absent."[22] Crewe's reading, noting Surrey's virtual effacement of the woman in the poem—or claiming that as what is happening—restores Shelton as female to the line only for her, in Crewe's reading, to show up the fatality of homosexuality, which in this account not only kills men but also cynically abuses women. Yet, the line that names Shelton places Clere in the same position with her and with Surrey, behind each of them ("Shelton for love, Surrey for Lord thou chase"); places them, therefore, in a locus of substitution that is not the same thing as the erasure of difference. All three in the poem, as in life, are related to each other, cousins through the figure of Anne Boleyn, who appears as a kind of vanishing point in the poem—crowned in one line, and displaced as "battered Bullein" a few lines later—for a kind of gendered violence that Crewe fails to note, but that also structures relations in this poem. Clere is, in this poem, not merely the site of desire, he is also the site of identification for the poem's speaker, and the exchange of will is one place where this occurs. But what occurs there? "Thine Earle halfe dead gave in thy hand his Will." Clere writing; Surrey coming; Surrey half dead; Clere dead, and yet the place from which Surrey has his life. Clere, memorialized, the site of a remembrance: the site of writing that writes Surrey beyond his own life. The hand is that of the copyist who nonetheless is also the author. The one who comes behind also comes before. That hand might be Mary Shelton's.

I mean this almost literally; so, as a final note, let me add this. This poem on Sir Thomas Clere does not appear in Tottel, nor does it survive in any sixteenth-century manuscript. It is first recorded in 1605 in William Camden's *Remaines*, an inscription copied by Camden from the tomb of Thomas Clere. It is Camden who ascribed it to Surrey—to, as it happens, "the noble *Thomas* Earle of *Surrey*."[23] This renaming of Henry Howard as Thomas Howard is not an error caused by the fact that Clere's first name was Thomas, not a confusion of identity of the sort that the poem itself encourages. It is rather, as in the case of a Holbein drawing of Surrey, also mislabeled Thomas, the register of the fact that Henry Howard was only styled Earl of Surrey; his father Thomas and his son Thomas legitimately occupied the title. The Surrey style is not Surrey's proper name. Camden giving a name to an unsigned inscription on a tomb uncannily reminds us that it is out of traces that are, properly speaking, anonymous that Surrey is made. From other hands. Anonymous, Virginia Woolf noted some time ago, was often the name of a woman.[24]

GRAPHINA'S MARK

In her most extended treatment of Elizabeth Cary's *Tragedy of Mariam, The Fair Queen of Jewry*, Margaret Ferguson notices a unique fact about one of the characters in the play, that Graphina is "the only character whose name is not found in Josephus's text or in Lodge's translation of it" (Cary's sources).[1] In the "Introduction" and notes that she and Barry Weller supplied for their edition of the play, speculation about this name choice and the possibility that "her name may be intended to evoke writing (*graphesis* in Greek) as a 'silent' form of speech" are entertained.[2] This translation of the name in terms of its etymology—which I think entirely justified—has implications that I would like to address in the pages that follow. If Graphina's name does mean "writing," the addition of the diminutive, feminizing "ina" to the graphic root insistently genders writing as female; Graphina's name, translated literally, must mean something like "writing as a woman," or the character herself must, in some sense, be the equivalent of what her name means. Weller and Ferguson do not explicitly note the gendering of writing implicit in their gesture toward the etymology of Graphina's name. However, to define writing as a "silent" form of speech is congruent with this gendered realization/characterization; so defined, writing occupies the same idealized and prescriptive place that women do in the ideological terrain quickly mapped in the oft-cited phrase "silent, chaste, and obedient."[3] Writing is thus understood to occupy this female ancillary position; that Graphina herself refers to herself as a "handmaid" (2.1.59, 70) seems to assure this smooth translation of writing into woman. Writing as a woman would seem to translate into "writing is a woman."

There are arguments that one could fetch from Derrida's *Grammatology* (to look no further) that might cause one to pause at this gloss on *graphesis*/Graphina, for in equating writing with a silent and ancillary form of speech, the primacy of voice and the entirely secondary and derivative status of writing are affirmed.[4] Such a translation accedes all too quickly to the ideological production of the diacritical difference of speech and writing, whose overturning in deconstructive arguments meant to call into question what might otherwise seem the entirely natural relationship between voice and its representations. In this instance, moreover, the translation also naturalizes gender difference and the subordination of women to men. This is fully understandable, however: the note on Graphina's name means to remind us, I assume, about the massive burdens of exclusion experienced by women and in part justified by the time-honored formulas involving the suppression of women's speech and the control of their minds and bodies; it means, further, to raise the question how women come to have a voice in a period that seeks to keep them silent. These injunctions and disenablements cannot easily be dismissed, nor would a deconstructive argument (that remarks that such exclusions have no conceptual basis) deny them their real, material effects. Nonetheless there is always the danger that repeating such conditions reinforces them and makes virtually impossible either imagining resistance to them or even acts of their violation.

When writing is equated with an absence of speech, women's

writing is *eo ipso* declared already less than fully representative of women, a sign of absence, and somehow therefore in itself not entirely there. In such formulations, writing disappears into a representation of female silence, rather than testifying to the fact that some women did write and that these texts have undeniable material existence and therefore have a kind of priority over the law they violate. (Within a deconstructive argument, writing declares the ruination of the hierarchized difference between speech and writing by regarding both as secondary and derivative.) That is: rather than assume that the injunction against speech somehow overrides any textual production or that when textual production takes place it is always inside of and accommodating the law prohibiting it, one could argue that instances of writing by women reveal the limits of the law. Such an argument has its dangers, to be sure: the theoretical production of the equalization of writing and speech could lead to the false claims that the power differences between men and women are illusory. But it could also expose that such differences of power are connected not to gender difference per se but to its production as hierarchized difference.

In the pages that follow, I want to consider the implications that follow from the possibility, which I take as given, that in supplying the name Graphina for a character in her play—the only instance of such invention in *Mariam*—Cary is leaving a mark that is equivalent to her signature or, better, perhaps a mark that functions as a kind of generic signature making claims for women's writing. In her text, and for a character who appears quite briefly, speaking fewer than thirty lines, Cary offers the name that names her status as woman writer. As these circumstances might already suggest, such a mark of authorial propriety and textual ownership, reduced to so meager a gesture, suggests the limits of any argument that can be made about this representation of writing as a woman. Nonetheless, the lines are there, and they need to be read, unwelcoming as they may seem to be. Graphina is, after all, an extremely minor character in Cary's play, appearing only in one brief scene (2.1), and then, it appears, simply to echo her lover, Pheroras. It is on this basis that Dympna Callaghan remarks, in what could be said to be an expression of the critical consensus, "the unsullied femininity of the dramatically insipid Graphina" and goes on to conclude that "Graphina represents the play's ostensible ideal of femininity," the sole exception to her ideality being the fact that she is not *entirely* silent, since she does speak her twenty-seven lines, dutifully fulfilling the insistent request of Pheroras that she celebrate with him their incipient marriage, an event only made possible thanks to the supposed death of Herod (the structuring plot device of the first three acts of *Mariam*).[5]

Callaghan here follows the more extended, indeed, so far as I know, the only, reading of Graphina that takes her brief role in the play to require more than a glancing comment, the one offered by Margaret Ferguson in the essay alluded to above. Ferguson puzzles out what she refers to as "the strange little scene" that Graphina plays with Pheroras in a reading enormously attentive to possible destabilizations and ambivalences, to the sheer quirkiness registered in her description of the scene as strange. Finding that the scene "queries the logic of the 'chaste, silent, and obedient' topos," she notes, in particular, two dislocations: first, that Graphina's silence, against which Pheroras enjoins her to speak, "may function just as erotically as speech" (silent Graphina, in other words, whets the desire of her lover, and her silence therefore does not desexualize her or automatically guarantee her chastity); second, that her speech may function as the equivalent of proper silence, since when enjoined to speak, Graphina says what Pheroras tells her to say. Ferguson concludes that Graphina's name in the light of these "strange" opacities around the differential markers of speech and silence might signify " 'safe' speech, *private* speech," she italicizes, "both a nontransgressive mode of discourse (like private writing?) and a mutually satisfying love relation" (p. 48).

Implicitly, Ferguson's reading of the scene could seem to tally with my ambition here: to read Graphina as a kind of authorial signature. By reading the character as a sign of private writing, Ferguson connects Graphina to Cary's closet drama and the way in which it negotiates the injunctions against female speech by offering scripts for women that will never in fact be uttered in public.[6] However, such a reading virtually wills into oblivion the writing that is produced by making the only sign of its effectiveness its utterance or performance, a reading that perhaps too quickly discounts the work that Cary's genre performs and radically downplays the fact of publication and the possibilities of readership.[7] Moreover, in the analysis of the scene, the bias is toward a devaluation of Graphina's speech, a translation of it into silence, as the mere echo of the lover's demand. This evaluation jostles with the notion of mutual satisfaction that Ferguson appears to endorse, since it would seem as if the subordination of Graphina necessary to produce her silence as erotic and her speech as silence cannot easily be understood as testimony to Graphina's own desire, in which case it is difficult to know wherein mutuality would reside. Moreover, this production of Graphina seems to occupy the position and point of view of her lover.

There is, nonetheless, something, I think, to be said about the mutuality that Ferguson finds in this scene, but only if we attend a bit more closely to it and are willing to hold in suspension the law that would ensure that Graphina's lines must testify to the character's effacement by her lover's desire or, by extension, by the ideological demand that would seek to ensure that when a woman wrote or spoke she merely echoed commands and displayed her obedience.

"Why speaks thou not, fair creature? Move thy tongue, / For silence is a sign of discontent" (2.1.41–42): this is the injunction that Pheroras delivers, demanding Graphina's speech and interpreting her silence as disobedience, treating it as an indication that Graphina does not share his joy over their forthcoming marriage. While Herod, ruler of Palestine, brother of Pheroras, lived, he had intended to have Pheroras marry their niece. Disparagingly, Pheroras describes her to Graphina as a "baby" possessed of an "infant tongue" incapable even of sounding her own name (ll. 16–18). In forcing him into this infantile marriage, Herod would have plucked his hand "from fair Graphina's palm perforce" (l. 14), Pheroras remarks. However much the two prospective brides are distinguished (one forced on Pheroras, the other chosen), Pheroras's description also indicates a malleability on Graphina's part that might equally apply to the baby niece. In describing himself as the hand and her as the palm, he treats her hand as if in his grip (that the locution is possibly reversible, that it is his hand in hers will soon be considered). So, too, the command to speak, and therefore to distinguish herself from the silent niece, also voices the demand that her "fair" surface, which he describes for instance in noting the whiteness of her brow and the redness of her cheeks (l. 40), produce her as one who names herself, but only as his.

In these lines, Graphina is inscribed in a rivalry between Pheroras and Herod; for the niece had been promised to Pheroras so that the brothers might be allied through her, indeed to guarantee Pheroras's position as the "realm's copartner, kingdom's mate" (l. 26). But, in making the claims about his fair and chosen partner, Pheroras invokes a different form of partnership with Herod. Rather than partake in the kingdom and marry the woman chosen for him by his brother, Pheroras presents Graphina as a rival for Mariam, Herod's wife, and describes his desire for the lowborn Graphina as moving along the identical track that led Herod to an equally forbidden choice. (Herod had to divorce his wife Doris in order to marry Mariam, a royal scion; later in the play [4.8], Doris will claim that the divorce was ungrounded and that Mariam's marriage has been illegitimate and adulterous.)[8] In Pheroras's speech, two versions of how women might function between men and, consequently, two versions of male homosocial relations are set up. Incipiently, the form of male equalization that Graphina is enjoined to validate would seem to override modes of alliance tied to and ensuring aristocratic bloodlines. The reading of Graphina's brow and cheek—"I will boast / Graphina's brow's as white, her cheeks as red" (2.1.39–

40)—as comparable to Mariam's, makes her the sign of a class-transgressive beauty; and the equalization of Pheroras and Herod through Mariam and Graphina is founded in rivalry (between women and between men) rather than in a form of alliance between men dependent upon the subordination of women who are to be kept in their "baby" state of silence.

In spelling out these conditions for the production of Graphina's speech, I mean to open up possibilities (which a further reading of the play will need to confirm) that involve recognition of the ways in which the female characters in the play differentially occupy territories that are marked out through differential relations between men. Ferguson, certainly the most acute reader of female characters in the play, is by no means alone in contemplating *Mariam* almost exclusively in terms of the complicated diacritical differences that obtain among the women in the play. She, for instance, treats Salome's licentious speech and Graphina's ostensible silence as complexly intertwined, each moreover setting terms for the further differentiations that attend Mariam's speech and character in the play. Although such critical mappings are indeed crucial to any attempt to understand the ways in which gender is produced in the play and the complexities that are necessarily registered by the fact that the women in the play cannot be reduced to a singular instance of womanhood, they nonetheless assume a kind of gender separatism and an implicit gender essentialism despite gestures toward the multiplication of positions that women can occupy in the play. For the prevailing assumption that underlies such comparisons of women characters would seem to be that the gender opposition male/female is always and everywhere identically operative in the play. Or, more generally, that female speech/silence in the play always takes place under the aegis of the familiar patriarchal injunctions to silence, obedience, and chastity.[9]

That Graphina is, according to Pheroras, a token in male–male rivalry does not remove her from a position circumscribed by homosocial triangulation and subordination, to be sure. Nonetheless, this position is itself antagonistic to a more usual and legally legitimate working of that triangle: one in which the woman also guarantees class privilege; one in which male–male equalization is ensured by blood; one, moreover, in which Herod's delegation of half of his power to Pheroras only simulates equality, since the power is given by Herod as a reward for Pheroras's obedience. Pheroras's choice of Graphina, on the other hand, represents his assertion of an annihilative equality, since it overthrows the law of consanguinity: Pheroras would occupy his brother's position, not share it. This could mean that Graphina's role might function within a revised version of patriarchal social/sexual relations. Were something like this to be the case, then the mutuality of which Ferguson speaks might be discovered in the locus in which Graphina is urged to speak; possibly (and, admittedly, only momentarily, within the brief orbit of this scene), some of the impositions upon women in the more usual triangulation may have been alleviated.

These possibilities can be glimpsed in Graphina's lines insofar as she acknowledges that Pheroras's ability to produce her as desirable counters the opinions of others, who would find her class position tantamount to her undesirability. Such denigrating views are offered in the play, by Salome, who describes her as "one mean of birth, but yet of meaner mind" (3.2.12), and by Herod, who refers to her as a harlot (4.2.56). In those terms, she could be no legitimate conduit of power between men; rather, she could only exist as a prey to domination and ravishment, whereas, as she notes, Pheroras has respected her body. Indeed, Graphina names, ambivalently to be sure, as "last not best" (2.1.63), her elevation to a position of rivalry with a princess (the niece, but also Mariam). "Me your handmaid have you made your mate" (l. 59): this is central to her lines and crucial to the mutuality that the couple achieves. But it must be noted that in this transformation, Graphina no longer is the subservient and ancillary handmaid, nor can she be reduced to a site of passive inscription. Rather, as "mate," she gestures toward an assumption of place parallel to the one that Pheroras claims when he refuses the command of Herod. If this is the case, Graphina's supremely obliging and obedient speech might then also participate in a refusal of the law of the father and might have to be read as disobedient, if only because she, like Pheroras, depends upon a lapse or suspension of the paternal law. Certainly one can see that in enjoining Graphina to speak Pheroras desires to occupy the place of Herod, issuing implacable commands. But it is also possible to see that in claiming that position, Pheroras voids it precisely through his disobedience to Herod in choosing Graphina in the first place; so too, in marking what she has become through Pheroras's choice, a "mate," Graphina gestures toward the dissolution of the hierarchization that would ensure her gendered and classed subordination.

One could understand this situation by recalling, as Ferguson and other critics have done in remarking various aspects of *Mariam*, the conditions of internal resistance in the play, allied to Catholic practices of equivocation and demurral and to the limited rights of subjects to resist tyrants. Such reserves (in which outward conformity, or seeming conformity, is not matched by inner belief) might be attached to Ferguson's claims about private writing. Here, once again, such self-privation and refusal cannot leave a visible mark. Although I believe that such claims are certainly pertinent to the form of writing Graphina represents, we must take care not to erase female production or reduce it to a silence whose resistance can only be intuited.[10] Graphina speaks, or, more to the point, since this is what I take her speech to allegorize, she produces text, and at a site particularly marked as the woman's text.

In this respect it has to be seen that as Graphina details the ways in which Pheroras has elevated her to be his "mate" what she claims to be doing is simply to be reproducing his mind:

But since you will my imperfections bear,
In spite of doubt I will my silence break:
Yet might amazement tie my moving tongue,
But that I know before Pheroras' mind.

(2.1.51–54)

Claiming incomprehensibly to know beforehand what is in Pheroras's mind, Graphina produces herself as her reading of that otherwise amazed perception. Graphina stamps Pheroras with the mark of her imperfection and produces his mind as her preoccupied territory. The claim to be saying what he would hear is also the claim to know better than himself what she should say and incipiently to place his demand in the position of being handmaid to her speech. If this is mutuality—and it is entirely circular in its construction—it would seem to depend upon the destabilization of hierarchical and gendered difference. (Whose hand is in whose palm?) In this light more could be made of Graphina's claim to be his "mate," and not least when one notices that it echoes what Herod had designed for Pheroras, "to be his realm's copartner, kingdom's mate" (2.1.26). Reading the two uses of "mate" together, one finds that the term that names the normative male–male relationship to be secured through marriage to the princess also turns that relationship into a kind of marriage (the two types of marriage, patriarchal and mutual, which Lawrence Stone argued coexist in the period, are coimplicated in this conflation of the term "mate");[11] alternatively, the term "mate" that declares the mutuality of the marriage of Pheroras and Graphina also designates it as identical to a same-sex union. The relation of Pheroras and Graphina, their mutuality, occupies the terrain of male–male equalization precisely by evacuating the more usual determinate gender hierarchy that marks male/female relations (and which also serves everywhere else in the play to triangulate female–female relations and render them antagonistic).

The part of Graphina's speech to which we have attended—the lines in which she remarks what his choice means—is virtually parenthetical, framed as it is by this ventriloquization of Pheroras's mind. Graphina begins, moreover, by insisting that Pheroras not "mistake" her, and not read her silence as refusal or discontent; "You know my wishes ever yours did meet" (l. 48). So doing, Graphina, while seeming to acknowledge that she is always to be read correctly as the reflex of Pheroras, also marks as mistaken the very interpretive gesture he has made. The claim always to meet his wishes is thus tantamount to her declaring that no matter what he thinks he sees, he must see her as he desires her to be, the docile text. He is the one therefore who is being erased in order that her existence may be seen as his mirror. The vacuity of the glass that Graphina holds up to Pheroras leaves entirely intact the possibility that she is exactly as she has been "mistakenly" seen, resistant to Pheroras's joys or to her continuing subordination to him, and to his assumption that although he has made her his mate he nonetheless expects her to continue to produce herself as his handmaid, ancillary to his every wish, silent or speaking as he commands her to be. If Graphina is a blank text, a site to be inscribed by him, it is only through her offer of herself as such, indeed her demand that he see her as such, and therefore not see that the Graphina she is producing as his is her production of herself as his—as what she claims he wants to see and will see.

This is not the only way in which the lines are framed. First, Graphina claims that she has remained silent only fearing she might say "too little" (l. 50), that she might prove inadequate to a task that we must now, I think, describe as simulating herself along the lines of the desire that she ventriloquizes as his. However much, that is, the self-production here involves her production of his desire, it might nonetheless not be possible for Graphina, even in this position of control, quite to adequate the mind she is making up. And something like this must indeed be the case with the speech she offers, which hides throughout behind the mask of not saying anything on her behalf beyond the recognition of what he has done for her. As the speech closes, the sometime mate reiterates her subservient position: "But study cannot boot nor I requite, / Except your lowly handmaid's steadfast love / And fast obedience may your mind delight" (ll. 69–71). Throughout her speech, Graphina claims a need for further training, for more study, to equalize her remarks to his desire; now she claims that such adequation can never occur. Reiterating her subordination, she in fact is saying just what he would hear; that the mate knows her place.

But she also is saying that unless he takes what she fails to say to be the same as saying what he would hear, he will never hear her say what he wants to hear. The lines turn subservience and inadequation into refusal. They don't deliver. They mark the opacity of this writing, its sheer material resistance to subsumption into subordination and obedience. "I will not promise more than I can prove" (l. 72): this is Graphina's last line, the final frame to her speech. Afraid to give too little, she says, she gives even less. And he responds satisfied, remarking only his own inadequacy of "style" (l. 75) and "eloquence" (l. 76); so doing, Pheroras accedes to the mastery of her writing, and he turns from this to close by recalling his rivalry with Herod and to offer a strange conceit. Were Herod to live again, he says, nothing but death would bar him from marrying Graphina. The stakes have been raised; somehow what Graphina's speech/writing initiates in Pheroras is not merely a doubt that rivalry with Herod has been concluded with Herod's death, but a doubt about death itself and its finality. Reading this allegorically, one could say that Pheroras is now in the grips of a further indistinction wrought by problematizing the speech/writing distinction. For writing is not tied to the life and voice of the body; the upping of the ante into the counterfactuality of Herod's double life—"Should Herod's body leave the sepulchre, / And entertain the sever'd ghost again" (ll. 81–82)—translates the vexed and entirely unnatural relationship between writing and speech, body and spirit—and, I would add, between woman and man. It invites us further to contemplate whether the marking gendered as woman's writing stabilizes or throws into question what such a gendered marking means.

One place to take such questions, I think, is to the next scene of the play, between Constabarus and Babas's sons, which opens with a discussion of whether, because Constabarus has kept the boys, Herod's political enemies, hidden, they are obligated to him. Babas's first son proposes that their "lives, as sav'd by you, to you are due" (2.2.88), which would seem to be a version of the obligation that Graphina, as handmaid, owes to Pheroras. Constabarus, however, denies such subordination and obligation and reminds the boys that the ties of friendship do not take such hierarchical forms. "With friends there is not such word as 'debt' " (l. 100), he explains, going on to detail terms of commonality that would seem to be equivalent to the condition of "mate" voiced in the previous scene as describing what replaces the subordinate position of hand and handmaid:

> . . . amity is tied with bond of truth,
> All benefits are there in common set.
> Then is the golden age with them renew'd,
> All names of properties are banish'd quite:
> Division, and distinction, are eschew'd:
> Each hath to what belongs to others right.
>
> (ll. 101–6)

Friendship would seem to name the ideal form of a relationship of equality, one explicitly resistant, as Constabarus further notes, both to the law of the sovereign and of the father: "For neither sovereign's nor father's hate / A friendship fix'd on virtue sever can" (ll. 113–14). The alliance he has made with Babas's sons, although founded in a value that they derive from their father (as is explicitly declared [l. 121] and moreover implicit in the fact that they are named only in this lineal/genealogical fashion), is also an alliance opposed to Herod and made (like the marriage of Pheroras and Graphina) on no consanguineous basis. Indeed, within the structure of the play, Constabarus's secret resistance to Herod, which takes the form of sheltering these enemy boys, is paralleled by another secret, as he himself declares (1.6.483ff)—that Herod has ordered Mariam's death if he dies. Sohemus, supposedly a loyal servant to Herod, violates this secret, telling it to Mariam; this is a revelation that aims at abrogating the tyrant's right over the life and death of his subjects, the father's over his children, the husband's over his wife. That Herod's secret command expresses the excessive love he has for Mariam, and is meant to make her his sole property, contrasts with, even as it lends a sexual dimension to, the friendship that Constabarus declares at this moment. For, as Constabarus works out the parallel, he is in danger by harboring the political fugitives just as Mariam is by living beyond Herod's supposed death. Indeed, in imagining these *as* parallels, an equivalence is suggested with an event in the past, when Josephus was executed as Mariam's supposed lover, when he refused an earlier order to execute Mariam at the time of Herod's supposed death. Constabarus is in the position of Josephus, not for betraying Herod's secret command but for harboring his enemies. Thus, at the very least, a parallel obtains between secrets even as they are contrasted, much as the "matehood" that Pheroras diverts from Herod's designs is redesigned by Graphina to name their relationship.

This is, therefore, to imply that in the explicitness of an idealized and thoroughly conventionalized and acceptable male–male friendship, the play may be finding a vocabulary in which to rescript cross-gender relations. For however conventional Constabarus's description of friendship may be, it nonetheless also is posited against sovereign rule. Indeed, no sooner does he articulate this bond than he stops himself (which I take to be the sign of the political transgressiveness of his speech): "Too much of this," he says, " 'tis written in the heart, / And needs no amplifying with the tongue" (2.2.115–16). If Constabarus virtually retracts what he has said, he consigns his speech to that locus of resistance and reserve often associated with women's speech or recusant inwardness. That this site is nonetheless figured as a site of writing, however, is significant: for it suggests that we are here again in the region of Graphina's mark and that the economic relationship between speech and silence is remarked as a writing that is only retrospectively rendered invisible. Constabarus says that what he has just said is the same as the writing on his heart. Once again, we should note that such writing also testifies to an erotics ("Fool said my muse to me, look in thy heart and write"), and therefore to the possibility that relations between men, when reconceived outside the locus of patriarchal domination, may also figure as a potential form for reimagining cross-gender relationships.

The strongest objection to such a reading can easily be made by noting the virulently misogynist speech delivered by Constabarus in his final scene with Babas's sons, as they proceed to their deaths (4.6). Constabarus's relationship with the boys is what Salome, his wife, uses to have Herod kill him; implicitly, or at any rate, retrospectively, his secret ties to them register his antipathy to his wife—and to women in general, as his speech indicates, making Salome the model of all women. This is certainly how Babas's second son understands Constabarus's lines:

> Come, let us to our death: are we not bless'd?
> Our death will freedom from these creatures give:
> Those trouble-quiet sowers of unrest,
> And this I vow, that had I leave to live,
> I would forever lead a single life,
> And never venture on a devilish wife.
>
> (4.6.351–56)

Although it may seem simply perverse on my part to think that even in this highly objectionable context, it might be possible to defend the argument I am making about a nexus between certain male–male and male–female relations, there are several things to be noted here. First, the vow of renunciation of a wife, and of women in general, that ends this scene finds its parallel in Mariam's behavior. She too, after all, refuses to resume her position as Herod's wife and chooses death rather than continue the marriage. The "spiritual" union to which Babas's second son looks forward thus has as its complement her severing of the marriage tie and, with it, the principle of female subordination. Even as this speech and Constabarus's diatribe vilify women, they voice the desire for an absolute separation from women. (In this regard it is worth comparing too the scene between Constabarus and his rival Silleus [2.4], in which Constabarus refuses to fight over Salome; it ends in an incipient bond of friendship between the men; "I would from thee no foe, but friend depart," Silleus says, but his "heart to Salome is tied too fast / To leave her love for friendship" [ll. 392–4]; Constabarus, however, responds: "I ope my bosom to thee, and will take / Thee in as friend" [ll. 397–98]). Further, although Constabarus generalizes the condition of women from the example of Salome and Babas's second son ends by condemning "devilish" wives, "wife" and "woman" are not really identical locutions except under the patriarchal dispensation that rewrites women entirely through their relationship to the institution of marriage.[12] When Constabarus declares that " 'Twere better that the human race should fail, / Than be by such a mischief multiplied" (4.6.239–40), his anti-procreative remark also targets the deformations of marriage that assume that all women were made to do is to procreate.[13] In refusing the imperative to procreate, Constabarus's position is consistent with the anti-genealogical impulses of the writing on the heart, and with the forms of friendship that oppose the law of the father or the perpetuation of race/class hierarchies.

In this context, it seems necessary to take stock of the fact, often overlooked in criticism of the play that finds Salome's lines advocating divorce thrillingly proto-feminist, that her desire to be able to divorce is entirely directed to the possibility that she might marry again. Unlike Mariam, that is, who wishes no longer to have anything to do with Herod—or with any other men (so it would appear, when she announces that the death of Herod is not an inducement to a new alliance [1.2.201–2])—Salome's existence is entirely defined by the institution of marriage; even the rebelliousness of her promiscuous desire is situated within it.[14] She is the only woman in the play distressed by her brother's supposed death, and the only one who uses his return to further her ends.[15] All of which suggests how fully she is tied to him and therefore how the negativity that critics often read in her character has to do not simply with her as "evil" woman but as a woman whose will to power entirely operates within, even when it seems to violate, the patriarchal subordination of women.

Finally, to return to Constabarus's speech, I would note that his denunciation of all women offers one exception to the rule: Mariam.[16] Cursing all women, he curses them especially in their role vis-à-vis the "one" who gave them "Any grace," "And you yourselves will Mariam's life bereave" (4.6.313). Although Constabarus generalizes here, there is in fact only one woman who destroys Mariam, Salome. At the very beginning of the play, Constabarus had noted the parallel worked out in this conclusion: Salome is responsible for his death as she is for Mariam's. His crime, which is no crime, of hiding Babas's sons, is equivalent to Mariam's supposed guilt and real innocence (1.6.476–92). In other words, even as he vilifies women, Constabarus also identifies himself with Mariam. Furthermore, the scapegoating of women through the example of Salome serves to mystify the fact that Constabarus's accusations apply as well to Herod. The speech suppresses one cross-gender identification even as it broaches another, and in so doing, it may suggest possibilities in the conceptualizing of gender in the play not fully controlled by male–female opposition.

My argument here finds support in Laurie Shannon's recent essay on the political discourses of the play. Shannon recognizes the political value of male friendship in the play (she is even willing to associate Constabarus with constancy as a supreme moral value in *Mariam* [p. 149]); she concludes, in fact, by arguing for a strong identification between the play's protagonist and the male–male ideal: "Mariam refuses to say anything she does not mean, repudiating the modes of exchange to which women are consigned and instead fatally operating in the mode central to transcendent male friendship" (p. 152). This characterization of Mariam's public voice can I think be brought into the orbit I have been calling that of Graphina's mark, and the "fatality" that Shannon underscores reminds us that nowhere in the play is there a representation of female–female relationships equivalent to male–male ones.[17] This thesis seems to me far more plausible than the kind of femino-centric arguments of those who have seen, especially in the opening acts of the play that take place in Herod's absence, some domain of female empowerment, not least so given the fact that every scene in which two women appear—whether of Mariam with Alexandra, Mariam with Salome, or Mariam with Doris—is filled with antagonism, as these women's arguments are always shaped by their relationship with Herod.[18]

If the play does have utopic and egalitarian desires, as I believe it does, they occupy the terrain that I have marked as Graphina's, a transgression of the economies of gender subordination that moves toward a reoccupation of a terrain marked as male but re-marked so that female–male equality comes to occupy the position of male–male friendship. It is perhaps the operation of this paradigm that may explain some bizarre aspects of Herod's behavior late in the play, as, for instance, when his eagerness to see Mariam causes him to mistake his brother Pheroras for her (4.1.40–41), or when his self-accusations include the charge of fratricide (5.1.249).[19] The logic of these cross-genderings (in which Mariam *is* Pheroras, or Abel to Herod's Cain) could be said to have their origin in the strange scene with Graphina, and insofar (as in these last instances) as Mariam steps into a male position, there is even, through the route of cross-gendering, a glimpse at the possibility of female–female relationships modeled on the "matehood" of Pheroras and Graphina.

One further warrant for considering the possibility that male–male relations serve as a model for a reconceptualization of cross-gender relations might follow from the account about wooing felicity offered by Alexandra early in the play (1.2.155ff). This begins as allegory, Felicity a female deity sought by her female supplicant. Female–female empowerment is briefly entertained in this figuration, but, in order to woo Felicity, her male "minion," Anthony, must be supplicated (ll. 168–170). Alexandra's lines recognize power only in men, but they also designate Anthony's relation to the goddess through a term ("minion") commonly used to describe male–male relations (in fact, Anthony is marked in the play as Herod's "bosom friend" [2.2.170]).[20] Alexandra explains how she offered for Anthony's delectation a "table" (l. 164) containing two pictures, one of her son Aristobulus, the other of Mariam, and how he, caught between the excessive beauty of each, chose neither and pursued Cleopatra. Alexandra's speech is not, I think, to be taken as expressive of an ideal in the play; the debasement of her political maneuvering is marked when she denounces Mariam on the way to her beheading, a performance meant to ensure her survival under Herod (5.1.33–52). Still, what the speech glimpses is a moment of equivalence between hetero and homo desires. It imagines this, moreover, in terms of the equally titillating possibilities of representations of the two children; that is, rather than offering their bodies, Alexandra offers their pictures, a detachment of biological offspring from maternal source, a translation of them into the written sphere of the tablet.[21] That Anthony is baffled by this doubling ("Too much delight did bare him from delight" [1.2.185]), I take to indicate the mutual exclusiveness of what is nonetheless represented as equally possible choices of love objects. To choose both is impossible, yet that is the impossible and excessive desire whetted in him by the representation.[22] Perhaps, then, his baffled choice echoes the impossible yet desired substitution of cross-gender and same-gender relationships intimately connected to Graphina and to the terrain marked by Cary as women's writing.

That Anthony remains with Cleopatra, and that Alexandra ends her story by setting up Mariam as a competitor with the "brown Egyptian" (1.2.190), invites a consideration of the topic that Dympna Callaghan so importantly raises, the question of racial *marking* in the play. To her discussion, and its insistence that "women" in the play are continually re-marked though a lexicon of racialized difference, what I would add is the relationship between

Graphina's mark and these equally marked genealogical and racial imperatives. I highlight the term *mark* in part not only because it is insistently used by Callaghan in her discussion of "the mark of blackness" (p. 165), but also because the language of the play itself insists on a language of marking as well (Mariam, for example, refers to the "royal line" and how Herod "did style his heirs" [1.2.138–39]). To be considered, then, is the relationship between this racialized and textualized discourse.

"Virtue is white," Callaghan writes, "but white is really black" (p. 176). The summary paradox reveals that in celebrating the "fair" queen of Jewry, Mariam's race is remarked, that the play produces whiteness in a domain where, from an English point of view, no one is "white," neither Jew nor Edomite, the play's favored racialized sites for the production of difference (to be extended to the "brown" Cleopatra, the "Egyptian black" [5.1.239], "base Arabian" [1.6.380] Silleus, and, indeed, to the moral black/white distinction that can also be embodied, as when Herod tells Salome that, compared to Mariam, she is a "blackamoor" [4.7.462]). Certainly, to contemporary readers, one difficulty presented by readings of the play that celebrate its heroine lies in the fact that Mariam fully participates in this racialized discourse of difference, as when she reviles "base" Salome as "parti-Jew, and parti-Edomite, / Thou mongrel: issu'd from rejected race" (1.3.235–36; similarly, it is Constabarus who calls Silleus base). Salome's retort sounds a powerfully oppositional note:

> Still twit you me with nothing but my birth,
> What odds betwixt your ancestors and mine?
> Both born of Adam, both were made of earth,
> And both did come from holy Abraham's line.
>
> (1.3.239–42)

Part of the appeal of these lines lies in their egalitarian gesture ("When Adam delved and Eve span, Who was then the gentleman?") implicit in this recourse to an originary moment of non-differentiation. Moreover as Ferguson and Weller note, Salome's argument depends upon the etymological connection between Adam and Edom and upon the meaning of the name as "red earth"—the "crimson characters" (1.2.108) in which the play is written, the color associated with aristocratic blood distinction ("holy Abraham's line"), with the beauty and blush of the cheek, and with bloodthirstiness.[23] Mariam retorts by throwing Salome's "black acts" (l. 244) in her face, attempting to align morality with race, and Salome, in a move that in fact parallels Mariam's own blackening of others and self-whitewashing, notes in her *sola* scene that follows, that "tis long ago / Since shame was written on my tainted brow" (1.4.282–83) and that "shame is gone, and honour wip'd away" (l. 293).[24] As these citations might begin to suggest—and as a further tally of the language of "style," "line," "blot," and the like in the play would only further prove—racialized language in this play is repeatedly figured as textualized markings.

To read these in proximity to Graphina's mark is a complicated act. For if Graphina's mark is incipiently egalitarian, rooted in a writing on the heart, an affective bond not tied to race or genealogy, it also seems clear that Cary sides with Mariam in opposing Salome's egalitarianism (which seems to be offered as part of her self-serving self-promotion, which, as I have already argued, represents a position allied to patriarchal domination—even the equal descent from Abraham is marked as part of a determinate and patriarchal genealogical line; we might recall, too, Salome's denigration of Graphina's "base" status, which suggests the limits of her cross-class identifications). Thus, although there are reasons to transport the politico/sexual/gender domains linked through a textuality of "friendly" impulses to the anti-racial, anti-genealogical vocabulary of the play, one needs also to acknowledge the valorization of racialized difference in the play (itself undoubtedly to be linked to an incipient Catholic polemic that would just as strongly refuse the negotiability of terms of difference in favor of a sense of absolute spiritual Truth). It is within this heavily conflicted area of the "mark," the "blot," "line" and "style," most often explicitly associated with racial difference, that Cary invests her own self-textualization; that is, the play registers itself most fully *as text* through the deployment of racialized markers. If one could transport these textual markers to possibilities that Cary's vocabulary of racialized difference would not seem to countenance, one would still be making connections that the play's generalized (and conflicted) textuality offers.

The site of writing as a woman is not one that consistently puts pressure upon the sites of racialized writing (almost the opposite is the case). Yet, when Pheroras boasts that "Graphina's brow's as white, her cheeks as red" as Mariam's, or when he addresses her as "fair creature" (2.1.40–41), he produces her as the white surface rather than as the graphic mark. The resistance to whiteness, the refusal of blankness, the materiality of the text that Graphina embodies, could therefore be related to blackness in this text, and indeed to Callaghan's moral paradox that declares that there is in fact, and despite the play's desire to say otherwise, no whiteness in the play. All are marked black, the product of a "style" that, perhaps, resists the kind of absolute moral judgment against the play that Callaghan delivers when she concludes that it is "the metaphysics of race on which much of the play's production of femininity resides" (p. 177). If one relies upon the textual instability of the play itself, it can be read as potentially contributing to the progressive view that Callaghan argues.

In suggesting this, let me hasten to add the following: I do not make these arguments out of some desire to "save" the play. Rather, my aim is to make available critically ways of speaking about the play that move beyond moral condemnation or blame (this applies as much to the critics who address gender in the play as to Callaghan's discussion of race). In seeking to further some linkages between the scene of writing and the sex/gender system of the play—and in seeing these as potentially progressive elements in the play—I am not, I hope, desedimenting them from their participation in elements that are undeniably regressive. These are not limited to the racializations in the play. For by asserting racialized difference, the play also at such moments affirms genealogical difference and therefore sides with the class imperatives against which the ideal of friendship is offered. (In this context, it is useful to note that the term "friend" is used in the play not only to mark same-sex alliances; it also serves to designate consanguine and marital relationships.) Moreover, to reiterate: that ideal in this play is coincident with virulent misogyny, and it has to be owned that part of the way in which Cary seeks to rewrite woman in this play has to do with her support of values that are exclusively associated with male–male relationships.

This rewriting of "woman" by way of male friendship perhaps explains why the explicit links of textuality and race in the play function to align Mariam's declarations of her racial purity with Herod's denunciations of his own sister as black in comparison to Mariam's white. It may explain, too, why no positive female–female relations are represented in the play—and why, moreover, when female friendship is celebrated in the dedicatory poem to Elizabeth Cary (Cary's sister-in-law), it is represented as parallel to female–male relationships: "you are my next belov'd, my second friend" (l. 5). As this line suggests, the friendship between women is ranked below that between wife and husband, the "fainter beams" of the moon in comparison with the husband/Sun's. Yet, it also has to be remarked that the language of friendship (and of sister/brotherhood, which makes it difficult to know whether the Elizabeth Cary addressed was Henry Cary's sister or his sister-in-law) puts pressure on hierarchized and genealogically differentiated relationships. Moreover, the absence of Henry Cary is represented metaphorically in this poem as a "night" in which the "second light" of the dedicatee shines. In other words, this night also takes place during the day, and the female–female relationship replaces the marriage. Not surprisingly, this nocturnal scene is rewritten as a daylight one, and the female companion is equally whitened, marked as "unspotted" (l. 10). In this poem, too, the production of whiteness would seem to insist on a racialized purity that defends against the "blackness" of the poem's nocturnal female–female scenario and its strong marks of female–female identification (happily caught in the identical names of writer and recipient) and potentially erotic intimacy. All of which is to say that, in writing as a woman, Cary inevitably occupies differentially and conflictually a site that to be occupied at all cannot be entirely done from the position of suppressed, silent, and obedient woman. Uncomfortably, then, the empowerments of writing may also entail, as they do in *Mariam*, reinforcements of positions that one could quickly call "male"—so long as finally one will at least allow what this chapter has been arguing: that such a designation vastly simplifies the terrain of Graphina's mark.[25]

As a brief addendum to this essay into some of the problematics attending Cary's position as woman writer, it seems necessary to recall the two versions of histories of Edward II published in 1680, either or both of which may be hers.[26] As Dianne Purkiss argues in a review of the complex bibliographical dilemma represented by these publications, ascriptions of authorship to Cary have depended upon readings of the representation of Queen Isabel in the text.[27] This is, indeed, the case, and various arguments for Cary's authorship have been made on the basis of her presumed identification with this "strong" woman.[28] Purkiss is a bit more forthright than other critics in admitting that the "strong" Isabel does not emerge beyond a couple of brief mentions until halfway through the text (i.e., she is not clearly the protagonist of the text or the site of authorial investment). Purkiss also does her best with some uncomfortable evidence usually barely mentioned: that however much Isabel's rebellion against Edward is justified in the text, she also is finally condemned.[29] The text is equally ambivalent about Edward: passages of condemnation, frequently cited in the criticism, need to be juxtaposed with those in which his legitimacy as king—and the illegitimacy of overthrowing even a "bad" sovereign—are stressed.

This political opinion would seem at quite some distance from the position on tyranny that has been claimed to motivate *Mariam*. However, in the light of the argument I have been making—and without feeling that I can in any way argue conclusively for Cary's authorship of the Edward II materials—I would simply note that if the text has dual alliances, that by itself might not argue against its having been written by the author of *Mariam*. Moreover, Edward II and his minions Gaveston and Spencer provide strong test cases for the attractions of friendship as a model for male–female relations; that the texts condemn the abuses of Edward's minions (as they undoubtedly do) must be distinguished from the equally explicit defense of Edward's right to his affectional choice ("It is certainly no less honourable than just, that the Majesty of a King have the same full and free use of his Affections, without Envy or Hatred, which every man hath in his oeconomick Government" [p. 137]), a defense, it might be noted, in which male–male relations occupy the "oeconomick" domain of domestic life.[30] What is not condoned is the use of male–male relations as a tool of tyrannous abuse of subjects—or of the king's wife. But it has to be noted that Isabel's emergence as strong is also explicitly registered as her assuming the strength to outwit Spencer; a language of diabolism attached to male–male relations is transferred to her, as in the condemnation of her treatment of Spencer as that of "a Monster so monstrously used" (p. 129). Finally, it might be recalled that the final chorus of *Mariam* does not quite condemn Herod—rather it lectures him on the proper use of his power:

> Had he with wisdom now her death delay'd,
> He at his pleasure might command her death:
> But now he hath his power so much betray'd,
> As all his woes cannot restore her breath.

Now doth he strangely, lunaticly rave,
Because his Mariam's life he cannot save.

(5.283–88)

What this amounts to is power maintained through the suspension of the right to death—power possible only when it is not unleashed, a non-finalization that might be compared to the "life" of writing that suspends the distinction between life and death. (There is a rather pallid version of these sentiments condemning Edward's murder of those responsible for the death of Gaveston: "in point of extremity, it is more safe and Honorable to do less than we may, rather than all we may" [p. 74], a point reiterated in a self-styled "digression" on Edward's failures: "Lives cannot, being taken away, be redeemed" [p. 140]). It may therefore be the case that Cary's vision of a rehabilitation of the relations between men and women lies in this space. This is also, I have been arguing, the place of the woman writer for Cary: in the failure of the law and the necessary limits of its supposed absolute power Graphina can make her mark.

Elizabeth Cary was a prolific writer. That most of her texts are not at this time known (although one can hope that Donald Foster's claims to manuscript discovery are true and that others will follow)[31] does not mean they did not—or do not—exist. Solving the question of the authorship of the texts on Edward II will, I believe, have to await further discoveries that will make it increasingly possible for us to know what kind of writer Cary was. But this is not only an empirical question that depends upon the availability of texts. It also depends on how we conceive of women writers, what suppositions we bring to bear on their understanding of their own gendered position or their commitments to the representation of gender. In the light of the arguments I have been making here, and having more than a few reservations about the efforts of Weller and Ferguson (in the "Introduction" to their edition of *Mariam*) to claim some Shakespearian status for Cary's Senecan play; in the light of the possibility that the Edward II texts are hers, and given that they share with *Mariam* a dramatic sensibility more Marlovian than Shakespearian, it is my hope that some day we will have that early text that Cary's first biographer singles out as "of all she then writ, that which was said to be the best," "the life of Tamberlaine in verse."[32] This is, for obvious reasons, not a text that some critics who have championed Cary might particularly desire to have, since its protagonist is male and, at least in Marlowe's version of the story, a world conqueror who treats women as objects of pillage, but it would be intriguing, to say the least, to find whether Cary's treatment aligns Tamburlaine with her Herod, or whether even this outrageous figure was a site for identification and the investment of Graphina's mark.

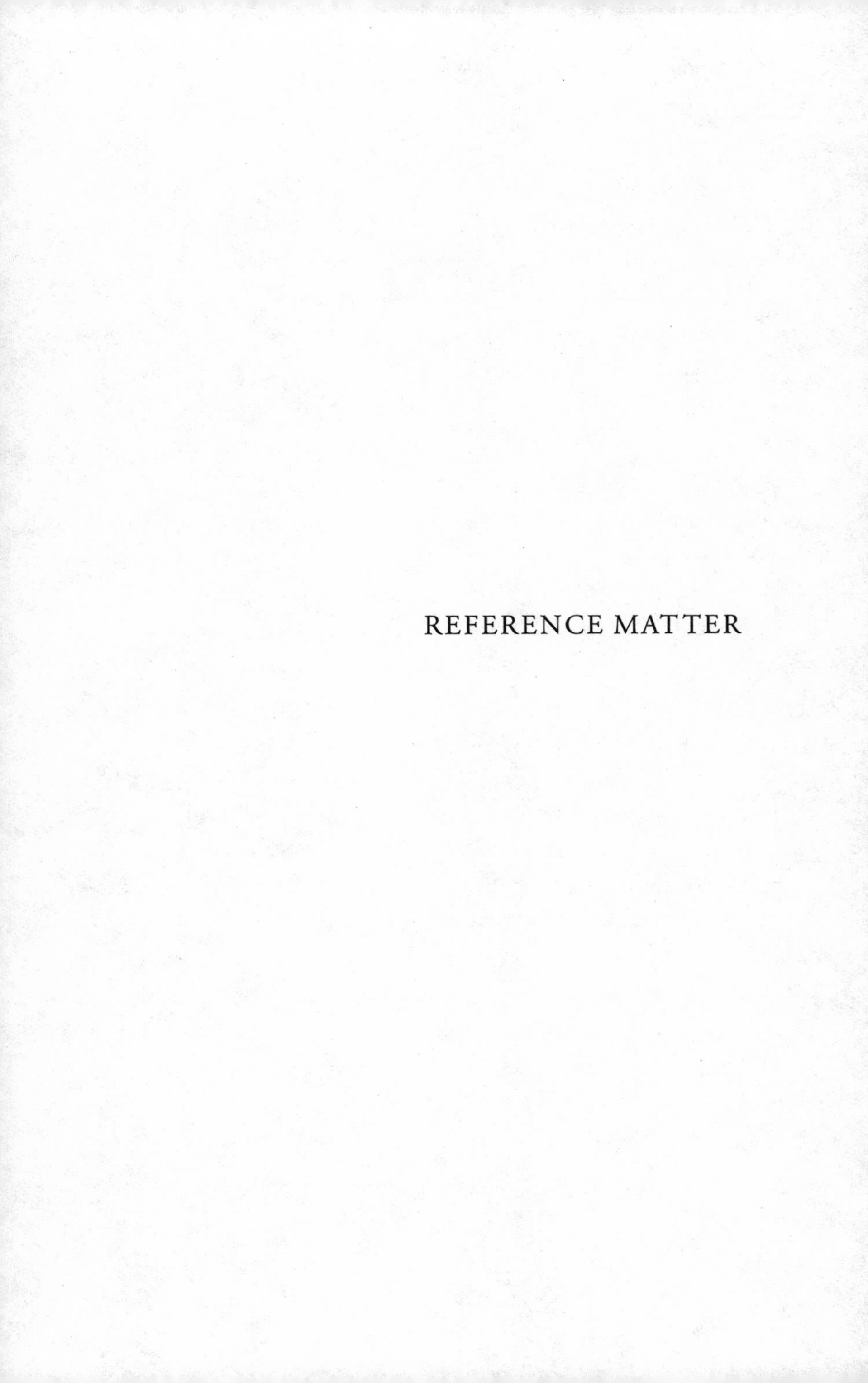

REFERENCE MATTER

NOTES

PART ONE: INTRODUCTION

1. Hobby, *Virtue of Necessity*, p. 204. Further page citations appear in the text.
2. In the United States, the landmark for this division is usually taken to be the 1982 Barnard conference, papers from which appear in Vance.
3. For a consideration of this collapse, as well as an urgent argument for an ongoing relationship between a feminist tradition in support of sexual freedom and queer theory, see Butler, "Against Proper Objects."
4. On this point, see the fundamental essay by Scott, "Gender: A Useful Category of Historical Analysis," in her *Gender and the Politics of History*, pp. 28–50.
5. The issue of race—addressed in some of the chapters of this book—has begun to be explored thanks to the essays in Hendricks and Parker, and is notably advanced in Hall.
6. See, e.g., Hackett, who tells the by now familiar story of the attack on Lady Mary Wroth launched by Edward Denny (p. 47), but fails to note that Wroth replied scathingly, rhyme for rhyme; who wor-

ries the question of Wroth's complicity with "a male or masculine gaze in ways which are oppressive to her own sex" (p. 58), ignoring thereby the evidence she also presents—of women as likely readers of romance—and thus the possibility that Wroth might be invested in such scenes. Rather than contemplating that relations between women could partake of the erotic charge of violence, Hackett opts for a reading of the text in terms of autoeroticism, thus collapsing relations between women into relations of the same, and before long violence and difference in the text is coded as male, whereas relations between women are described as scenes of "peaceful reciprocity" (p. 59) offering models of "female community or autonomy" (p. 60). One need not read far into Book One of the *Urania* to take stock either of the fierce antipathies of Antissia and Pamphilia, or to note that the resolution of their evasions, fighting, and lying is consummated in bed, but such dynamics—such erotics—are rendered impossible of notice if mutuality, support, and loving community must be discovered as the properly feminine.

7. See Davis, " 'Women's History.' " Davis opens her essay by pointing to this tradition that extends from Plutarch through Boccaccio and Christine de Pisan to the present (p. 83) and closes by urging a new direction: "from Women Worthies to a worthier craft" (p. 93). It is perhaps a mark of the direction that Hobby notes, that Davis's most recent book, *Women on the Margins*, while rich in context and contrastive materials, nonetheless is framed as a set of biographies of notable individual women.

8. I cite the subtitle of Haselkorn and Travitsky; questions of canon are addressed in Travitsky's "Introduction" to the volume.

9. Ferguson, "Moderation and Its Discontents," p. 360. Ferguson ends her review essay by commending Hobby for her self-critical postscript, a cue that I follow here.

10. See Guillory, esp. ch. 1. Guillory's arguments are not always as logical as they appear to be; he notes, for instance, of the inclusion of texts chosen in terms of categories of race or gender, that this points to the fact "of their being read now" not "that they have become canonical" (p. 17), but later admits that "changing the syl-

labus cannot mean in any historical context overth
canon, because every construction of a syllabus *ins*
again the process of canon formation" (p. 31). If th
is true, then it must follow that precisely when tex
in the syllabus they are involved in a process of car

11. See Ezell, *Writing Women's Literary History*, esp. chs. 3 and 4. Ezell mounts her evidence against such canonizing activities as the initial edition of *The Norton Anthology of Literature by Women*, which, as she demonstrates, is fully in line with Victorian anthologies of women writers that exclude earlier authors in favor of modern ones, and that choose which authors and which texts to represent on the basis of culturally normative notions of femininity.
12. Ballard, p. 54. Ballard's reference is noted in the headnote to Lanyer in Mahl and Koon, one of the earliest recent anthologies, p. 73.
13. I do not mean to imply here that the university is a site for the free exchange of ideas, or that it is some utopic space unrelated to the inequities of the culture; I mean only to affirm it is a site of possible contestation whose consequences in the world cannot be decided in advance.
14. For her work on this project, see Hobby, "Katherine Philips: Seventeenth-Century Lesbian Poet." The Philips described in this essay is not the celebrant of desexualized female friendships, as in conventional accounts, but one who reworks and reoccupies power relations toward the enunciation of same-sex desire.
15. As Maclean argues, marriage is the most restrictive domain governing women—definitionally as well as legally and socially. Nonetheless, it is not the only domain that defines women.
16. Donoghue, an important exception to this statement, overlaps only with the latest figure considered in this book, Aphra Behn.
17. See Wall, *Imprint of Gender*, ch. 5 *passim*, for extraordinarily rich discussions of women writers, which, nonetheless, also stop short of full consideration of questions of sexuality.
18. Wendy Brown's "Wounded Attachments" appears in her *States of Injury*, which furthers its arguments; it also is to be found in Rajchman, pp. 199–227, which contains a number of important

essays, including Scott, "Multiculturalism and the Politics of Identity," which argues strongly for the kind of expanded definition of gender that I seek to articulate and voices necessary suspicion about the evidence of experience for its inevitable policing and normativizing of identity categories and its reduction of social questions to individual ones (see esp. pp. 10–11).

19. On this point, see Moon.
20. I cite from the "Foreword" as it appears in Schleiner, pp. ix–x.
21. The second edition of *The Norton Anthology of Literature by Women* (1996) attempts to redress these and other shortcomings. It offers additional texts by some sixteenth- and seventeenth-century writers (e.g., Mary Sidney, Lanyer, Cavendish, Philips, Behn), and includes several authors not previously represented (e.g., Isabella Whitney, Elizabeth Cary, Mary Wroth); almost a hundred additional pages of this anthology feature pre-nineteenth-century writing.
22. See Traub, "The (In)significance of 'Lesbian' Desire."
23. Sedgwick, *Epistemology of the Closet*, p. 50; further page citations appear in the text.
24. "Renaissance" is a term that causes some misgivings for its honorific implications; however, "early modern" is also problematic in its implicit teleological valuation of modernity. It would also be inaccurate for the parameters of this project, which do not extend into the eighteenth century.

CANONIZING AEMELIA LANYER

1. Coiro, pp. 357–58. For a more recent intervention along similar, if less fully argued, lines, see Schnell, which also argues for social disparity and resentment as inevitably fracturing an idealized sisterhood of oppressed women.

   The process of canonization for Lanyer began with her inclusion in a number of anthologies of women's writing, among them: Gilbert and Gubar; Greer et al.; Mahl and Koon; Travitsky, *Paradise of Women*. Schleiner presents an excerpted version of *Salve Deus Rex Judaeorum* in an appendix.

2. Citations from Abrams, 1: 1045–46 (1986 ed.); 1: 1059 (1993 ed.).
3. It is the mention of this defense of Eve that constitutes the only substantive textual change in the headnote from the fifth (1986) to the sixth (1993) editions.
4. Coiro's argument is paralleled by Krontiris when she suggests that the limits to Lanyer's feminism may have been due to the fact that it was not "an efficacious strategy in soliciting female patronage" (p. 119); Krontiris thus sees that the intermittent feminism voiced in the poem is a classed and not simply a gendered articulation.
5. It would be impossible for a reader who knew nothing about the *querelle* to be aware that defenses of women, many of them authored by women, constitute a more plausible context for Lanyer.
6. See Mueller, esp. pp. 229–30, where she concludes that the speaker of the argument in defense of Eve, whom she takes to be Pilate's wife, embodies "femininity triumphant in masculine terms." However, on p. 233, she compares Lanyer to some feminist precursors, claiming that unlike them she does not presuppose Eve's inferiority.
7. Citations from Woods.
8. The fullest information about Lanyer's family history and service as court musicians is offered in headnote in Mahl and Koon.
9. Hutson, pp. 16, 14 cited.
10. See Rowse, *Poems of Shakespeare's Dark Lady*, pp. 11, 20, for the phrases cited. Rowse first presented his arguments about Lanyer in *Sex and Society*, pp. 96–117.
11. Nor does the fact that she was Italian on her father's side mean that she necessarily was "dark"—if "dark" even means brunette. Crewe has suggested the racial implications of "dark" as a euphemizing of "black" in *Trials of Authorship*, p. 183*n*4, an argument elaborated in forthcoming work. The fullest discussion of the racialization implicit in the sonnet tradition is to be found in Hall, ch. 2; she also glances at the figure of Cleopatra as used by women writers (including Lanyer and Cary) as an important site of difference among women, which could be further mobilized to disrupt the homogeneous notion of a community of women taken to be

exemplified in these texts. Although I do not address racialized difference in the discussion here, I turn to these questions in "Aphra Behn's Female Pen" and in "Graphina's Mark."

12. Cf. Schnell, who concludes, "she revered the upper classes and fantasized herself a member of them" (p. 34).
13. The feminist literature revaluing sex work is extensive; a necessary starting point is represented by Rubin, "Thinking Sex"; see also her interview with Butler, "Sexual Traffic," for contextualizations of that essay.
14. Daniel's poem cited from vol. 1 of Grosart.
15. Maurer takes to task the kind of biography of Lucy preserved in the *DNB* and supported by Wiffen, 2: 74–123; she instead echoes eighteenth-century condemnations of her character, as does Grimble, pp. 165–76. For a brief account that emphasizes the courtiership of Lucy and its basis in stunning indebtedness, see Byard.
16. On women as marriage brokers, see Erikson, p. 93, and Ezell, *Patriarch's Wife*; for an earlier period, see Harris, who has argued for and extensively documented the power at court of women. What is not to be endorsed in the arguments of Ezell and Harris, however, is the dissolving thereby of any effective notion of patriarchy; equally suspect is to assume that all female activity is necessarily subversive.
17. On this subject, see Peck; the role of women (including the Countess of Bedford) is briefly discussed on pp. 68–74.
18. In her letters to Lady Jane Cornwallis (in *The Private Correspondence of Lady Jane Cornwallis*), she complains that the Queen's illness (her final one, as it turned out) "makes me oftener a courtier than I intended" (p. 56), and, earlier, that she "cannot be sorry for her [the Queen's] frowns, which are now litle to me, all my court businesses being so dispatched as they will not requier my attendance ther" (pp. 44–45); she frequently excuses herself for failing to be able to visit Cornwallis by explaining that her movements and projects depend entirely upon the king (see, e.g., pp. 24, 47, 50, 52, 56, 58).
19. Epigram 76; cited from Parfitt.
20. Wall's citation (*Imprint of Gender*, p. 327) of Steinberg in this con-

text is apt; Christ's tumescence is a sign of his humanity, Steinberg argues; as Rambuss argues, such depictions of Christ must have sexual meaning.

21. For a similar argument, see McGrath, "Metaphoric Subversions," p. 103. McGrath (p. 104), in an unspecified way, does note the possibility of "erotically nurturing relationships with Christ and each other" (i.e., among women).

22. The feminization of Christ is also noted by McGrath, " 'Let Us Have Our Libertie Againe,' " pp. 342–44.

23. On her marriage, see Williamson, *George, Third Earl of Cumberland*, ch. 21, which includes a pathetic autobiographical letter in which the Countess describes her life up to 1589 as a "Pilgrimage of Grief" (p. 285). The letter adds to the sorrows of her marriage her failure to produce a living male heir.

24. For this stage of her life, see Williamson, *Lady Anne Clifford*. From this biography, it would be difficult to ascertain any information about Margaret Clifford's piety, which goes virtually unmentioned, although it is a quality frequently adduced by her daughter; Anne Clifford refers habitually to her as her "Blessed Mother." Although there are moments in *Salve Deus* in which the maternal bond is celebrated, it is certainly not the whole story. There is evidence to suggest that Anne was initially driven not entirely willingly by her mother. Thus, in her final letter to her mother, Anne refers to her husband as "the best, and most worthy man that ever breathed" and indicates that were it not for her mother's insistence, she might well have succumbed to Dorset's desire for her to accept a settlement rather than pursue her claims to inherit; the letter notes how "bitter against him" the Countess is and concludes: "Be assured that I will stand as constantly to my birthright as is possible for me, but I can do no more than I can, and therefore I can promise you no certainty of these matters" (Williamson, *Lady Anne Clifford*, p. 154).

25. See *The Private Correspondence of Lady Jane Cornwallis*, for her comparison between the death of her mother and the Lord Chamberlain's loss of his son (p. 65), or, for another instance in which piety and courtly self-interest coincided, her comments on the

death of the Marquis of Hamilton (pp. 118–19), and the discussion of these episodes in Lewalski, pp. 118–19.

26. Williamson, *Lady Anne Clifford*, p. 76.
27. See Clifford, p. 25. This is not the first time they slept together—an earlier incident is reported on p. 23—but it is apparently the first time they had sex.

APHRA BEHN'S FEMALE PEN

1. Munns, " 'I by a Double Right Thy Bounties Claim,' " p. 206, cited below.

 I take this first note as the opportunity to register my gratitude to Jonathan Brody Kramnick for his help with this chapter.
2. Behn, *Five Plays*, p. 7.
3. Woolf, p. 66. As Woolf writes a bit earlier, "She made, by working very hard, enough to live on. The importance of that fact outweighs anything she actually wrote, even the splendid 'A Thousand Martyrs I have made,' or 'Love in Fantastic Triumph sat' " (p. 64).
4. Cf. Munns, " 'Good, Sweet, Honey, Sugar-Candied Reader,' " in which Munns describes Behn's double-bind as involving a female gender whose display opens her to charges of sexual promiscuity, but whose flaunting of a male part falters since it is something "she does not literally possess" (p. 53). However, if the part is her pen, then she does possess it. The terms of this dilemma could be recast theoretically following the argument of Butler in "The Lesbian Phallus and the Morphological Imaginary" (in her *Bodies That Matter*, pp. 57–91), which throws into question the kinds of literalistic possession underlying Munns's argument, but which also argues for possession which registers and ramifies within the symbolic/linguistic domain.
5. See the initial chapter in Ballaster, *Seductive Forms*.
6. On this subject, see L. Brown, pp. 25 ff. Brown's essay is a complex reworking of this position, taking the mediating figure of the woman (by which Brown seems to mean the white woman) and the slave (by which Oroonoko only seems to be meant) as being in an unrecognized position of "mutuality" and reflection (see

pp. 62–63); the link between them seems to reside in their commodification.

7. On the first page of the "Introduction" to *Nobody's Story*, Gallagher warns against a misconstrual of her title that I might seem to be making, that she is not "lamenting the unjust absence of women from the eighteenth-century literary canon," that "the 'nobodies' of my title are not ignored, silenced, erased, or anonymous women. Instead, they are literal nobodies: authorial personae, printed books, scandalous allegories, intellectual property rights, literary reputations, incomes, debts, and fictional characters. They are the exchangeable tokens of modern authorship" (p. xiii). Although I share Gallagher's impulse not to think of women writers as marginalized, I must demur from the portrait of nobody as a universal authorial condition. Not only does gender get collapsed in this formulation, but I find it difficult to assimilate the items in Gallagher's list to any coherent notion of a "nobody" except insofar as all are involved in kinds of abstraction. The difference between a literal nobody and the silent, erased, and anonymous woman lacks terms, I find, to make the desired distinction. Some of my argument below with Gallagher is motivated by an earlier version of one of the chapters on Behn in *Nobody's Story* (ch. 1), which appeared as "Who Was That Masked Woman." Gallagher has modified some of her earlier positions in the direction of a consideration of the enablements of Behn's strategies, and with a far greater recognition of her success than was apparent in the first version of her argument.

8. All citations of Behn's shorter fiction are from volume 3 of Todd, the most recent volume to have appeared in this ongoing editorial project. The final sentence of *Oroonoko* recoups this devaluation of the pen.

9. As Jones and Stallybrass argue contra Laqueur, "gender was *not* primarily defined within medical discourse in the Renaissance" (pp. 106–7). For a critique of Laqueur's complicity with the one-gender system, see Traub, "The Psychomorphology of the Clitoris," pp. 84–85. For further hesitations about the uniformity of the one-gender model, see Daston and Park, pp. 420 ff, and the

review of Laqueur by Park and Nye, which forcefully argues for a less homogeneous understanding of early modern medicine, one that has a version of both the single- and the two-gender model, as well as for a sense of the continuities within medical thought from Aristotle to Freud rather than the break Laqueur argues. This review also takes Laqueur to task for a model of feminist historiography that fails to see the relevance of gender to questions of sexuality, and which, in "rescuing" women from the depradations of medicine, also exacerbates the vicitimization of women by not recognizing that the medical model was not as uniform or as pervasive in its effects as is claimed.

10. See Foucault, pp. 106–7.
11. On this point see *inter alia*, Hobby, *Virtue of Necessity*, pp. 114–27, for one of the earliest critical articulations of this thematic in Behn's plays. Although Hobby stresses this point, she also points briefly and usefully to the fact that Behn enjoyed a fair amount of success as a playwright and had close ties to the court and to royalist culture.
12. For considerations that lie behind these statements, see McKeon, "Historicizing Patriarchy," a masterful redaction of the historical literature toward a powerfully synthetic schematicization of the relations of gender, sexuality, and class in the period.
13. The most historically refined account of the molly house is to be found in Bray, ch. 4; see also essays by Trumbach, and Norton.
14. As Hunt points out, there is reason to doubt the notion of an exclusively male homosexual subculture and good reason to explore the existence of a heterogeneous community that included male transvestites, female heterosexual prostitutes, and "sexually noncomformist groups," among them actresses; it is also a social grouping that includes the "unrespectable poor" as well as a range of laborers (p. 370).
15. Traub, "The Perversion of 'Lesbian' Desire."
16. Donoghue's book is avowedly about representations, and she assembles a large range of texts that demonstrate awareness of female–female sexual relations.

17. N. Armstrong's rather counterintuitive arguments treat domestication and female literacy as entwined sites of empowerment.
18. A parallel could be drawn with Margaret Cavendish's *Blazing World*, in which the Empress, disabused of her desire to form a cabal, nonetheless enters into a "platonic" seraglio relationship with the Duchess of Newcastle.
19. I am prompted in these remarks by Kramnick's review of Donoghue, which notes how problematic it is to move from the massive discursive evidence that Donoghue marshals to the social realization of lesbianism.
20. The argument here could be compared to that of Pollak. Although to a certain extent, Pollak posits a homosexual basis to male homosocial relations that she regards as oppositional to (or the secret truth of) heterosexual relations, she also details how Sylvia's empowerment in *Love Letters* occurs through her ability to occupy hetero- and homosexual desiring positions, the latter especially when, disguised as a boy, she works her charms on males who, while preferring women, certainly don't exclude boys as sexual objects.
21. Gallagher characteristically sees such identification as involving an erasure of gender: "fantasies of absolutism, carried to their logical conclusion, tended to enlarge rather than fill the void of female identity," she summarizes the argument of "Embracing the Absolute" in *Nobody's Story*, p. 51*n*6. Gallagher comes to this conclusion precisely because of the assumption that gender difference is unbreachable and *eo ipse* oppositional.
22. For Behn's identification with Hellena, see the conclusion to Lussier, pp. 236–39, as well as the argument offered by Kavenik (p. 184) that Hellena's sexuality can be connected to Behn's male and libertine stance. On identification with Angellica Bianca, see Diamond.
23. Behn, *Five Plays*, p. 204.
24. A twist on this might be read in *The Lucky Chance*, in the final coupling of Gayman and Julia. Julia is sold to Gayman by her husband; thus despite her own attempts to preserve her honor and

her marriage, the very institution of marriage is responsible for her debauchery; Gayman, although devoted to Julia, is a kind of inadvertent rake. Lured by money (as is Julia's husband), he engages in a bargain with the devil (engineered by Julia) in which it is unclear to him whether he has sex with a man in drag, a repellent woman, or Julia herself.

25. Frank's essay is part of a forthcoming book that examines critical writing—by Dryden and by women critics—for the ways in which these instabilities of sex and gender operate.
26. For a parallel argument with Gallagher on the issue of patronage that Behn eventually found, and "her adoption of the male playwright's voice," see Payne, p. 117.
27. The argument I make here is congruent with that of Hutner, "Re-visioning the Female Body."
28. On this point, see Holland, p. 41.
29. Behn, *Five Plays*, p. 154, emended to include lines dropped in that edition.
30. See Staves, ch. 5, "The Authority of Nature's Laws."
31. For somewhat similar arguments to those advanced here, see Markley, who argues for the relationship between Behn's royalism and the figure of the seductive rake, whose "power to relinquish the power of 'Custom' " (p. 131) is bestowed upon the women seduced, often by causing " 'a kind of Rape' [the phrase comes from *The City Heiress*] in order to enable the possibility of 'mutual Love' " (p. 132), a possibility Markley argues is available to women who have abandoned the ideological construction of sexual repression. In Markley and Rothenberg, a similar argument is offered, although there Behn is critiqued for the inequalities that she therefore advocates.
32. Poems are numbered and cited following Todd, vol. 1.
33. This is also true in the incomplete no. 92, where the figure of Cupid intervenes between Behn and her "lovely Charmer" (l. 2).
34. In no. 92, the fair Lady is also imagined as an armed Diana.
35. Donoghue, p. 58. I would demur from Donoghue's monolithic "society" in this formulation; "society" here means those who sub-

scribe to the imperatives of propriety governed by marriage. In Behn's "society," these are hardly guiding presumptions.

36. Hoyle's sexuality is the subject of a good deal of critical discussion; see, e.g., Goreau, pp. 203–6; Duffy, pp. 138–47; often labeled "bisexual," he is as often taken to expose the ills of heterosexuality because of his homosexuality. That is, since a number of Behn's texts seem to testify to a less-than-happy relationship with Hoyle, his rejection of her is taken to demonstrate both the fact of male domination and of male disinclination. For one example of this argument, see Salvaggio, pp. 256–58, which continually conflates homosexual and homosocial, and therefore allows Salvaggio to make Hoyle an exemplary instance of heterosexual masculinity.

The possibility of a facilitation of female–female erotics by way of male homosexuality makes sense of what is otherwise a non sequitur in Barash's discussion of "To the fair Clarinda," where, to the question, was Behn "*really* a lesbian," Barash replies "that one of her male lovers was bisexual" (p. 173).

37. For a forceful critique of this assumption, see Warner.

38. See Moira Ferguson, ch. 2, "*Oroonoko*: Birth of a Paradigm," pp. 27–49.

39. The major theorization of the possibilities of romance for women readers and writers, albeit in a contemporary context, is offered by Radway.

40. See Sussman, p. 230, for the sentence cited above; Margaret Ferguson, "Juggling the Categories," a sentence from which is cited in the text below.

41. In framing the discussion this way, I depend upon McKeon, *Origins of the English Novel.*

42. Or so Sussman argues, implicitly following the discussion of L. Brown. While Behn's harem romance hardly qualifies as a genuine slave narrative, it is worth recalling the arguments of Judy, which counters the construction of an African-American canon of slave narratives with an African-Arabic text unintelligible in the usual terms of analysis. Inadvertently, Behn's romance points to this other tradition.

43. For an essay that lambasts *Oroonoko* for its complicities with white feminism, see Ballaster, "New Hystericism." For a review of criticism that regards the relationship between the narrator and Imoinda as a textual aporia, see Fogarty.
44. On these questions, see Fuss, *Identification Papers*.
45. Cf. McKeon, "Historicizing Patriarchy," pp. 312–15, for an incisive discussion of the role of femininity in the making of masculinity in the period; in keeping male and female gender separate in his discussion, however, McKeon does not broach the co-implication I suggest here.
46. Traub, "The Psychomorphology of the Clitoris," pp. 93–97. On this point, see also Hobby, "Katherine Phillips," p. 189. One text influential in promulgating the association of lesbianism with non-European women is Paré, pp. 188–89.
47. See Goreau, p. 232. Worth comparing is the conclusion to Behn's "The Black Lady," which is about a black-haired woman, who having been impregnated, is about to be sent to the poor house when she agrees, instead, to marry the man who got her pregnant; as the story closes, the police who have arrived to find the black lady are directed instead to a black cat that has just kittened. The substitution seems pointedly erotic, and perhaps depends on something like the "black ace" locution for its wit.
48. See Ballaster, *Seductive Forms*, ch. 3, " 'A Devil on't, the Woman Damns the Poet': Aphra Behn's Fictions of Feminine Identity," pp. 69–113. A portion of this chapter appears as " 'Pretenses of State': Aphra Behn and the Female Plot," in Hutner, *Rereading Aphra Behn*, pp. 187–211.
49. Margaret Ferguson, "News from the New World," p. 188*n*67. Another moment of almost explicit lesbian desire may be when the narrator tells Imoinda stories about nuns, considering that in Behn's fiction (e.g., *The Fair Jilt*), nunneries are regularly the breeding grounds for promiscuous sex (Behn also puns on the nunnery/whorehouse possibility, as in *The Unfortunate Happy Lady*, which features a madam ogling its heroine's body); this is also the case in *The Rover*, and there Hellena's initiation into sexual desire is at the hands of the abbess.

50. Behn, *Love Letters*, p. 226.

51. The point I am arguing could find support in the work of Bersani or its mobilization toward what de Lauretis (p. 26) characterizes as a deromanticized (that is to say, unredemptive) endorsement of perversity.

PART TWO: INTRODUCTION

1. All citations from Montaigne facsimile edition, A2r. Commentators on Florio discussed below include Hannay, "Introduction," *Silent but for the Word*; Lamb, "The Cooke Sisters"; Parker, *Shakespeare from the Margins*.

2. Parker, *Shakespeare from the Margins*, p. 140. It is particularly odd finding Parker taking this position, when, in the note that appears on the final page of her "Gender Ideology, Gender Change," Parker takes this passage in Florio, as well as one in which he equates words with women, to reflect "humanism and its anxieties of virility" (p. 364*n*62). Thus, in the essay, Parker takes these and other remarks about women to reflect on men (and, indeed, shows how often in Montaigne, the supposed impossibility of men turning into women is evidenced—in male impotency and in a vernacular incapable of standing up to Latin) and never entertains their implications for women.

3. While Lamb has the support of the *OED* in reading "hatchet" as a verbal form meaning "to cut with a hatchet," it seems equally possible that Florio's "hatchet" represents the past participle of "hatch," to bring forth young. Indeed, "hatchet" might even suggest the making of a graphic mark, a hatch.

4. For some information on Gwinne and Diodati in relation to Florio, see Matthiessen, pp. 113, 118.

5. For one feminist attempt to capitalize on these definitions, see de Lotbinière-Harwood.

6. Basnett-McGuire summarizes the import of translation in the period, and notes these various episodes (pp. 55–58); she concludes: "Translation was by no means a secondary activity, but a primary one, exerting a shaping force on the intellectual life of the age, and at times the figure of the translator appears almost as a revolution-

ary activist rather than the servant of an original author or text" (p. 58).

7. For some loose formulations along these lines, see the comments of Eugene Vance offered in the roundtable on translation recorded in Derrida, *Ear of the Other*, p. 137.
8. Among the many recent studies to consider translation in a colonial context, one important theoretical account is Niranjana; an excellent book on a Renaissance example is Raphael.
9. Wayne, p. 27.
10. Wall, *Imprint of Gender*, p. 337. On this point, see also Orgel.
11. For a full argument along these lines, see my *Writing Matter*, which details the impossibility of maintaining the limits prescribed by humanist educational programs. In asking questions of the "literal" here, I also follow questions raised in that book, in which the "letter," in manifold senses of the term (as alphabetic character, epistle, literature) cannot be stabilized to a singular determination. For further consideration of the worries caused by the cultivation of a style incapable of control, see Halpern, ch. 1, esp. pp. 45–60.
12. This is the question that Krontiris (pp. 76–77) worries, and it follows from her assumption that women writers who translate hide behind the original or efface themselves in their literal translations. What they deliver, "consciously or not" (p. 77), is the original text.
13. On this point, see Lamb, "The Cooke Sisters," p. 124.
14. Bornstein, p. 134.
15. Erasmus as cited in Sowards, p. 83.
16. Hyrde, preface to M. Roper, as reproduced in DeMolen, p. 100.
17. Ibid.
18. Vives, pp. 49–50.
19. See Correll, esp. pp. 243–46, for the theoretical formulation.
20. At the level of generality of the critique of origin, Derrida need not especially be privileged, since his work is part of a modern problematic that echoes through post-Freudian psychoanalysis and post-Marxist social thought, among others. If there is a reason to privilege Derrida, it is, as many have noted, because the question of translation is one to which he often returns. Indeed, a text like "Plato's Pharmacy" in *Dissemination* makes its intervention

into western philosophy precisely through the problem of translation, there through *pharmakon*, that impossible word for poison/cure. For a revaluation of Florio's work as translator indebted to Derridean protocols of reading, see Conley.

21. The title, "Living On / Border Lines," names one or two texts—"Border Lines" runs along the bottom of the page and includes frequent addresses to the translator and to the problematic of translation.

22. See Derrida, *Ear of the Other*, p. 121, for the connection between "Living On / Border Lines" and Benjamin. Benjamin figures often in Derrida's extemporized remarks in the roundtable on translation in *Ear of the Other* and is the subject of his "Des Tours de Babel."

23. Benjamin refers to this as "pure language," which he glosses at one point as "the foreignness of languages" (p. 75), that is, of all languages, including one's own. It is this dividedness that means that the "pure" is not simply a transcendental originary concept but a *différance*, never revealed *as such*, only revealed in the movements of the mark, from language to language, in translation. All languages, including one's own, are, therefore, not one, are therefore translations.

24. I think here particularly of her poem, "To the Angell Spirit," addressed to the dead Sidney on the completion of their joint project of translating the psalms (the text of the poem is included in Waller, *"The Triumph of Death"*). I take her writing to represent this joint project even in works in which Sir Philip's hand is not so literally to be found. Wall writes with acuity about this relationship in *Imprint of Gender*, pp. 310–19, offering arguments that resonate with my own. This is not surprising in the least; the chapter that follows on Mary Sidney was heavily influenced by Wall's "Isabella Whitney," now included in *Imprint of Gender* and extended in Wall's treatment of Sidney there. I wrote "The Countess of Pembroke's Literal Translation" before Wall's book appeared.

25. This figuration of marriage is read in Benjamin in "Des tours de Babel," pp. 191–200; everywhere Derrida reads the original/translation relation as this form of coupling, pulling the relationship of textual production into the orbit of heterosexual reproduc-

tion. This is most egregiously the case in his reading of Benjamin's figure of translation as a royal robe, which Derrida takes to be a wedding gown ("Des tours," pp. 193 ff). Although there may well be something to be said for the gown, with its pleats and folds, as a textual dress, why a potentially transvestite figure must be translated into a wife remains to be asked, not least because this heterosexualizing reading also recurs to the familiar reading of translation as a woman.

MARGARET ROPER'S DAUGHTERLY DEVOTIONS

1. I cite Erasmus and Roper from *Moreana*. The 1524 date for the work is established by Hyrde's prefatory letter; the earliest edition extant dates from 1525/26.
2. Gee judges Roper's work "a mature achievement of its kind" (p. 265); he notes prior publications of translations by women that he does not regard as truly anticipating Roper's accomplishment as a humanist translator; he concludes by placing her in a second stage of a tripartite developmental scheme in the history of translation on the grounds that she never proceeded to original work.
3. All citations from McCutcheon's introduction to the selections from Roper are to Wilson.
4. I will go on to argue against this reduction, but it is worth noting that among those excluded from this family portrait are Margaret Roper's husband, William, as well as their children.
5. Correll's sophisticated understanding of the imbrications of class ambition and gender in humanist writing can be compared with the "discovery" that motivates Jardine, *Erasmus, Man of Letters*, that the saintly father of humanism was also a self-promoter; similar arguments also can be found in Jardine and Grafton.
6. These are letters no. 128 and 108 in Rogers, *Correspondence of Sir Thomas More*. English translations of them can be found in Rogers, *St. Thomas More*. For a reading of these injunctions similar to McCutcheon's, see Jardine, "Cultural Confusion," esp. p. 5: "I hardly need point out that whether or not Margaret Roper would have liked to 'seek for the praise of the public,' that option was, in

the interests of propriety, simply not open to her, and her father was bound to insist on the fact." Jardine thus ignores the facts, argued below, for Roper's public persona, including her publication and epistolary circulation.

7. The letter is no. 2211 in Allen and Allen. It is translated into French and English in "Correspondance entre Erasme et Margaret Roper." All English citations of the Roper-Erasmus correspondence are drawn from this article. Future references to Latin texts will be to Allen and Allen. The drawing also is alluded to in a letter to More (Allen and Allen, no. 2210). It is, of course, no great sign of the empowerment of women to note that Margaret Roper's letters facilitated More's relations with other men; but, again, one needs to ask whether this circulation of her texts could be limited solely to that purpose.
8. Cave, pp. 24 ff.
9. English citations from this letter also are drawn from "Correspondance entre Erasme et Margaret Roper," p. 33. Béné notes that in his dedication of Ovid's *Nux* to John More (1523), a scene of emulation with his sister is imagined; however, Béné fails to read the dedication to Prudentius in this light, stressing rather its significance as a sign of Erasmus's friendship with More and his favorite daughter and as a pedagogical tract suited to Margaret Roper and revelatory of Erasmus's Christian humanism.
10. Reynolds, *Margaret Roper*, pp. 28–29.
11. This section I cite from the translation provided by Sowards, p. 83.
12. Ibid., p. 79.
13. Stapleton, p. 103.
14. These strategies are carried over to the dialogue between the abbot and the learned lady, the latter almost certainly modeled on Roper. There, the learning of the woman represents her as a challenge to the clergy, although she is also represented as a wife and mother, in order to forestall the possibility nonetheless intimated in the colloquy, that a woman could arrive at the position of the male humanist; see Erasmus, *Colloquies*, p. 223.
15. Roper's name does not appear in print; nonetheless she is not all that difficult to discern as the author through the remarks about

her made in Hyrde's preface. Moreover, she was named as the author in legal proceedings occasioned by the unlicensed publication of the book, thus providing a further avenue for public knowledge of the identity of the "vertuous and well lerned gentylwoman of .xix. yere of age" named on the title page of the first licensed edition. For an account of the legal proceedings, see Reed, esp. pp. 166–70. As Warnicke comments, Roper's publication "exceeded even her father's view of the proper bounds of women's activity" (p. 25).

16. Besides McCutcheon and Gee on this topic, see also Verbrugge. Gee emphasizes the fluency of the translation and attributes it to humanist training in double translation; McCutcheon stresses the heightening of the father-child relationship; Verbrugge emphasizes the distancing between God and the abject petitioner.

17. On this topic, see Stevens. Marius places Erasmus's relationship with More in the context of a phase in his life in which Erasmus's "ache" for love took the form of "saccharine letters to other young men" (p. 79; see p. 81 on this as a determinate for Erasmus's response to More); Stevens's essay handily provides terms for moving the discussion beyond the embarrassment that Marius confesses.

18. On Pierre Le Moyne's 1647 commendation and its subsequent anglicization, see Maber; I cite Paulet from p. 49 of this article.

19. W. Roper, p. 239.

20. See Crewe, *Trials of Authorship* ch. 3, "Remembering Thomas More: The *Encomium moriae* of William Roper," pp. 79–100.

21. Without attempting to resolve the question of attribution, Wright has commented on the reasons why sixteenth-century (and modern) editors have tended to treat the letter as More's, the weight of male authority attached to authorship; she argues that the writing function assumed by Roper in the letter is to mediate between More and royal authority, thus serving as an intermediary between men. Although Wright does note instances in the letter in which Roper is producing More, she emphasizes Roper's subsumption within male-controlled discourse.

22. See W. Roper, pp. 243–44.

23. Although Erasmus comments on the suitability of the task of

writing the *Precatio Dominica* to his temperament, he makes quite clear in the prefatory letter to Jostus Ludovicus Decius (Allen and Allen, no. 1393), who asked him to do it, that bonds of friendship, gift exchanges, and connections to the Polish court were also determining factors.

24. Halkin, p. 175. Indeed, shortly after the *Precatio Dominica* appeared, a committee was formed to censor any passages that fell "short of the truth" before it was published in Paris (Farge, p. 177, who adds in a note that the *Precatio* was the subject of discussion six times in the course of 1524).

25. At the simplest level, of course, the desire to persuade More to accept the oath is related to the possibility that Margaret Roper would have a future; once More was executed for treason, there would be no chance for any of the family. But, of course, the relations between More and his family cannot simply be reduced to such practical considerations, and there is much in the dynamic I have been describing that would lead to the more insidious desires of the daughter sketched here.

26. Stapleton, on the other hand, robs the kiss of its impact by including farewell kisses between More and Margaret Giggs and with his son as well (pp. 181–82). Erasmus also describes the scene between More and his daughter, filling it in with tears, unspeakable grief on Margaret's part, and words from More counseling patience. (See *Expositio Fidelis*, Allen and Allen, 11: 372.)

27. It is uncritically endorsed by Marius: "There can be no question that Margaret was the woman he most adored . . . and she as clearly adored him in return. She was an intelligent and loving woman who gave him all a perfect wife might give except the temptation to engage in sexual intercourse—the act that he believed threatened the salvation of his soul" (p. 228). The kind of opacity around father-daughter incest evident here is under constant pressure in the essays in Boose and Flowers.

28. For a reading of connections between pedagogy, anal erotics, and writing in Bacon that could be compared to the argument here, see Hammill.

29. The story is told in W. Roper, pp. 212–13, in which he reports the

physicians "much marvelling of themselves that they had not before remembered it." So far as I have been able to determine the administration of enemas was not a normal procedure in the sweating sickness, not even when the patient had reached the state of unconsciousness that usually portended death. An early manuscript (ca. 1485) account of the disease does recommend purgation before the administration of any medication (see Creighton, 1: 242); Caius alludes to "avoidance" (26v) without specifying whether emetics or enemas are involved. Emetics are recommended in one German pamphlet of ca. 1528 (see Hecker, p. 272). On the whole, as Hecker emphasizes, English treatment of the disease involved bed rest, warm covering, and herbals; he remarks that Caius's recommendation that the patient not be removed from the bed even if defecation occurs is not exceptional; that diarrhea was a frequent symptom of the disease would seem to be further proof that enemas would rarely have been administered (p. 282).

Stapleton's account of Margaret Roper's sweating sickness attributes her cure simply to More's prayers (p. 66), a sanitizing hagiographic gesture repeated in Chambers, who refers to the remedy without naming it (p. 183).

30. The first version appears in Harpsfield, p. 164; the latter is reported in Reynolds, *Margaret Roper*, p. 105.

31. The nourishing value of enemas is affirmed by Montague. In Lieberman, the etymological meaning of enema, "to send in" (p. 217), provides one link between enemas and letters. The fullest historical treatment of the procedure and apparati is offered by Friedenwald and Morrison. The particular attention to feeding and overindulgence of bodily appetite in Roper's *Devout treatise* may be connected to the prevailing conception about the sweating sickness (voiced in Caius, who sees the disease "in bodies corrupt by repletion" [13v] and affirmed by Hecker) that the disease was especially one visited upon the affluent and caused by overconsumption. It is usually assumed that Roper suffered the disease in its 1528 outbreak, which is of course several years after the writing of the *Devout treatise*, but it is also possible that she was struck in its 1517

outbreak—there is a letter from More to Erasmus at this time that reports his family safe so far from it, though it had killed Henry VIII's Latin secretary (Rogers, no. 41).

32. Freud comments on the primordiality of anal birth in his analysis of the Wolfman's version of the primal scene as *a tergo* intercourse, a point emphasized in Edelman's reading of the case, pp. 173–91. It is for this reason suspect simply to follow the strand in Freud's thought that equates the anus with and as a version of the vagina, as Ronell does, or as Dixon does in her treatment of enema scenes in Renaissance Dutch paintings, pp. 147–53. The specificity of the anus is thereby lost, and with it a heterosexualizing collapse is performed. Although Paster's treatment of scatology often tends in this direction as well, she does document an Elizabethan and early Jacobean formation in which vaginal "intercourse" and anal "purging . . . may well have been, or been felt or somehow counted as, the same" (p. 142). In *Trials of Authorship*, Crewe limits his remarks on the clyster to a footnote in which he reads the scene as involving the fantasy of penetration of Roper's body and as akin to the sadomasochism of More's temperament (p. 179). Although Crewe's reading of incestuousness aims at derailing certain conventional oedipal assumptions, he does not use the specificity of this fantasy of anal penetration to further his argument.

33. Roper perhaps acknowledges his wife's agency in his will, when he portions out blame and blessing, hoping to be buried with his wife, "whose soul our Lord pardon," and father-in-law, "whose soul Jesus bless" (Reynolds, *Margaret Roper*, p. 140). His request was not fulfilled.

THE COUNTESS OF PEMBROKE'S LITERAL TRANSLATION

1. Coogan, p. 324.
2. Rees, p. 83.
3. Waller, *English Poetry*, p. 159. Cf. his discussion of the poem in his "Introduction" to *"The Triumph of Death,"* pp. 12–14, and in his *Mary Sidney*, pp. 144–50.
4. On the logic of citationality and iterability, I depend upon Der-

rida's classic 1971 essay "Signature Event Context," and his subsequent exchange with John Searle, conveniently gathered in *Limited Inc.*

5. Hannay, *Philip's Phoenix*, p. 109.
6. Lamb, *Gender and Authorship*; the poem is discussed on pp. 138–41, where the judgment that it is "disturbing" is reached.
7. Waller, "The Countess of Pembroke and Gendered Reading," p. 343. For a similar account in which the countess is reduced to a position of silence that the critic teases into speech, see Waller's "Struggling into Discourse," e.g., pp. 245–46, for an account of the countess's writing couched entirely in the negative ("she wrote no prose romance. . . . She wrote no original drama"); "it is the critic's responsibility to make those silences speak," Waller concludes, not noting that the critic also has produced the silences.
8. Jones, *Currency of Eros*, pp. 2–3.
9. A revised version of her essay appears in Wall, *Imprint of Gender*, pp. 279–310, where it is followed by a section on the Countess of Pembroke (pp. 310–19), which extends the argument about the entitlements of the position of mourning in much the same way as I do here. Wall's focus is on the dedicatory poem to Sir Philip Sidney, "To the angell spirit," and on how the Countess of Pembroke's "coupling" with her dead brother enables her to assume a writing position that, however apparently secondary it is, also produces a stance in which she can write—and produce a version of her brother. Wall is attentive to the sexualization of this coupling, which she finally declares a textualized event; in treating this joining of the living and the dead, and the amalgammation of these muses into a maimed and repieced textual body, Wall all but moves into the territory of gender crossing that I map in this essay.
10. "It [the translation of Petrarch] reflects, one might speculate, her own deeply idealized love for her brother, the impossibility of its consummation and the realisation that his poetic inspiration for her is the only real and lasting fruit of her love," Waller writes in his biography, *Mary Sidney*, p. 144, concluding that Laura's final farewell to the poet may be "expressive of Mary's own farewell to her brother" (p. 150).

11. Hannay, *Philip's Phoenix*, p. 259*n*41. Waller reviews his original account of the incestuous relationship between brother and sister in his biography *Mary Sidney* (p. 100) in "The Countess of Pembroke and Gendered Reading," pp. 335–36. Lamb also balks at Waller's account; see *Gender and Authorship*, pp. 69–71.
12. For further thoughts on the logic of the preposterous, see Edelman, "Seeing Things: Representation, the Scene of Surveillance, and the Spectacle of Gay Male Sex," in *Homographesis*, pp. 173–91, and Goldberg, *Sodometries*, pp. 4f, 180f, 184, 188, 192.
13. I summarize the arguments of the second chapter of Butler, *Gender Trouble*.
14. Commenting in his *Mary Sidney* on lines of a dedicatory poem to her dead brother accompanying the psalm translation, Waller finds them "personal and disturbing" (p. 99), indeed "peculiarly personal" marks of "intense intimacy": "It is as if a veil is being lifted very briefly, unwillingly, even unconsciously. Her love for her brother passes even her own understanding. With caution, we may recall Aubrey's speculation" (p. 100).
15. Crewe, *Hidden Designs*, pp. 76–88, who notes Waller's "dirty" version of the open secret of the relationship of brother and sister. For Crewe's further thoughts on the powerful social logic of incest, see his account of the relationship of Margaret More Roper and Sir Thomas More in *Trials of Authorship*, pp. 79–100.
16. Lamb, *Gender and Authorship*, p. 18.
17. Sidney, *Arcadia*, p. 57. I am grateful to Charles Barker for discussion of this text.
18. See, e.g., Duncan-Jones's description of Sidney as "the darling of so many older men" (p. 42), or her conclusion that "friendships with older men were what Sidney was best at" (p. 254). For further thoughts on Duncan-Jones's account of Sidney's relations with men, see my review of her biography.
19. For another instance of this, see the letter of the Countess of Pembroke to Sir Tobie Matthew reproduced in Hannay, *Philip's Phoenix*, p. 199; the letter is about manuscript circulation, and in it, the countess recalls that she has forgotten Sir Tobie's "Otherself," his friend George Gage, and then comments on her pleasure

that "two so worthie, and so well-paired Friends" include her in their circle. The countess's attitude here gives the lie to Hannay's remark that she would have "resented Nashe's accusation that Harvey courted Sidney as a '*Cyparissus* or *Ganimede*' (sig. O3v). Accusing Harvey of homosexual impulses toward Sir Philip was not the way to endear himself to Sidney's family" (p. 140). On the relations between the homosocial and the homosexual in the Elizabethan period, the best guide remains Bray, although the term "homosocial" and its relevance to the Renaissance are best explored in the chapter on Shakespeare's sonnets in Sedgwick, *Between Men*. See also my *Sodometries*, including the discussion of the Countess of Pembroke's writing there (pp. 81–101) and the "Introduction" to *Queering the Renaissance* for more general considerations of the relations between gender, sexuality, and writing in the period.

20. John Donne, "Upon the translation of the Psalmes by Sir Philip Sydney, and the Countesse of Pembroke his Sister," in *Divine Poems*, pp. 33–35; line numbers are provided in my text.

21. See Crewe, *Trials of Authorship*, p. 179*n*10.

22. Cf. Fisken, particularly her comments on blood and ink on p. 269, and her conclusion that "through her writing Mary Sidney forged a bond with her brother that his death could not sever" (p. 272).

23. Citations of "Triumphis Mortis," from Neri, pp. 555–69; book and line numbers are provided in the text. The Countess of Pembroke's *The Triumph of Death* is similarly cited from Waller, *"The Triumph of Death,"* pp. 67–79.

24. "Here [Mary Sidney] has treated 'altri' as masculine plural, failing to realize that it is of course singular and is an allusion to Petrarch himself" (Rees, p. 85).

25. "To thee pure spirite, to thee alones addres't," in Waller, *"The Triumph of Death,"* pp. 92–95, l. 45. It is these lines that led Waller to his speculations of incest.

26. Mistaking a second person singular as first person, as Rees (p. 85) notes.

27. See, e.g., Wilkins. Much the same is the case in the modernized text of the Countess's *Triumph* offered in Brooks-Davies,

pp. 291–99, where a number of decisions about the beginnings and ends of speeches are questionable; this is nonetheless the best edition of the poem, offering ample and useful notes.

PART THREE: INTRODUCTION

1. Riley, p. 113.
2. On this point, see Goldberg, *Writing Matter*; for the identification of the gender of the writer on the basis of the hand, see also Marotti, pp. 25–26. For the importance of manuscripts for female authorship in the period, see Ezell, *Patriarch's Wife*, esp. ch. 3; and idem, *Writing Women's Literary History*, ch. 2, esp. pp. 50–65.
3. For some similar worries, see Kamuf, esp. p. 298, where Kamuf opposes to the seemingly tautological "writing as a woman" the inevitable non-identity posited by similitude. For Kamuf, self-identity as a woman represents a closure within inevitably male-marked or biologically determinate definitions of woman, whereas the *mise-en-abyme* structure of the "as" allows for a non-identification in such terms, which may open a space for gendered difference that is not caught in such predeterminations.
4. Harvey argues that such transvestite performances only seem to offer women's voices, that, in fact, they are produced by and appropriated for the purposes of the male writers.
5. Fuss, *Essentially Speaking*.
6. Riley cites Maclean, pp. 87–88, on p. 25; pp. 44–46 in Maclean may also be consulted for further examples of the ways in which different differences necessarily open possibilities in the very incoherence of definitions of gender difference, and their production in different domains of thought and with relation to different institutional sites. These conflicted terrains can be related to the arguments about the one-sex model offered by Laqueur, as they are pertinent even to the critique of Laqueur offered in Daston and Park, who argue that Laqueur's model, which allows for degrees of difference, coexists with medical models based in absolute gender oppositions (see esp. pp. 420–24).
7. Kelly's essay, "Did Women Have a Renaissance?" first published in 1977, is now available in *Women, History and Theory*, pp. 19–50.

For an argument that women achieved "spiritual prominence" in the period, and that this must call Kelly's claims into question, see King, pp. 238–39. King's assertions point to a worrisome feature of Riley's argument, the possibility of seizing upon mind or spirit as if accomplishments in that realm could simply transcend the material limitations of most women's lives.

8. Early printing, for instance, exhibits many of the vagaries of production of manuscripts. Most notable, in this context, and as is suggested by the extant copies of Aemilia Lanyer's *Salve Deus Rex Judaeroum*, print runs could be quite small—not very much in excess of and possibly even more limited than the circulation of some texts in manuscript—and different printings would be different books, tailored, as in the case of Lanyer, to different recipients. Moreover, as Thomas demonstrates, printed texts find their way into manuscripts, where they are treated in exactly the same way as manuscripts are—that is, without a sense that the printed text is any more permanent than a manuscript or that it displays more authorial ownership than a text copied—and often revised in so doing—in a manuscript context.
9. See *Sodometries*, p. 60, for the particular question of female authorship to which I return in this essay.
10. All citations in the text are from Rollins.

MARY SHELTON'S HAND

1. All citations in my text are from Rollins.
2. Zitner, p. 513; Harrier, pp. 24, 27.
3. On this point, see the basic and influential essay by Saunders. For a recent essay stressing the ways in which modern authorship does not govern Renaissance manuscripts, see Thomas.
4. This was first established by Seaton.
5. This thesis is developed by Remley, pp. 55–58. Marotti includes in his brief treatment, "Women and the Manuscript System," in *Manuscript, Print, and the English Renaissance Lyric*, pp. 48–61, a consideration of the Devonshire manuscript that rehearses some of the standard information about its female contributors, ending with citations of some of the Chauceriana as exemplary of poems

in praise of women (pp. 55–57); Marotti gives no indication of the presumed authorship of these pieces, nor is he quite certain that they are to be taken straight; for one he holds open an "ironic reading," another is said to engage in hyperbole (p. 57).

6. See Nott, 1: 162–63, and Bond, pp. 654–55.
7. Southall, "The Devonshire Manuscript"; and idem, *Courtly Maker*, pp. 15–25, 171–73.
8. Remley, pp. 42–43, sorts out many of the confusions to be found in previous scholarship about Shelton's ancestry, including being mistaken for a sister who was possibly Henry VIII's mistress; Ives (pp. 86, 242–32), for example, names the Shelton of the Devonshire manuscript "Madge," and conflates her with Margaret Shelton, Mary's sister. Mary Shelton's relationship with Thomas Clere is, however, the most common shorthand way scholars have to identify her; "Mary Shelton is best known as the sweetheart of Surrey's friend Thomas Clere," Harrier writes (p. 26), opening a paragraph in which he assigns her the wrong parents; "Mary Shelton, who was beloved of Sir John Clere," Foxwell identifies her in an appendix on the history of the Devonshire manuscript in her edition of *The Poems of Sir Thomas Wiat*, 2: 244–45, basically repeating her point in *Study of Sir Thomas Wyatt's Poems* that "Mary Shelton's name appears in connection with the Howards" (p. 127); Padelford, in *Poems of Henry Howard Earl of Surrey*, is Harrier's immediate source, when he describes her as "Mary Shelton, the sweetheart of Sir Thomas Clere" (p. 186 [1920 ed.], p. 215 [1928 ed.]).
9. The editions I have in mind are those of Padelford, and Surrey, ed. Jones, which is the text used for citations.
10. Citations of the poem from the manuscript depend on and reproduce Padelford's transcription of it on pp. 337–38.
11. The comment, "ryme dogrel how many myle to meghlemes," occurs after a poem (no. 40 in Muir, p. 277) that may be Mary Shelton's.
12. Padelford, "MS. Poems of Henry Howard," p. 338.
13. See McLeod's essays on this subject.
14. There are, as well, the usual reasons for preferring the manuscript version to Tottel: it is less regular in meter; some of the variants,

though not in any way obviously superior to the version in Tottel, are also obviously just as good as what Tottel prints. The untitled manuscript, as might be expected, gives evidence of the poem in a less smoothed out version than that offered by Tottel.

15. The best study of gender transitivity in Surrey, and in this poem in particular, remains Anthony Scott's unpublished essay, "The Fatality of Surrey's Desire." Nott, in his 1815 edition, provides in his titles and notes to the poems some oddly interesting comments along these lines. His apparatus is entirely dominated by the notion that all of Surrey's poems are part of his romance with Geraldine; thus, although Nott believes that "O Happy dames" was written for someone else, he thinks it gave Surrey the opportunity in this poem nonetheless to voice his longing for Geraldine (see 1: 12, 262). Nott thus reads the genders in the poem as completely reversible. Of another poem to which I turn below, "Girt in my giltlesse gowne," which Nott titles "The Fair Geraldine retorts on Surrey the charge of artifice" (1: 31), Nott expresses the hope that someone else wrote this poem for Geraldine, going on to say however that "she who can wound the feelings of a deserted Lover by copying what another dictates, makes the insult her own, and has little to plead in her defence" (1: 314). Nott, that is, takes the question of surrogacy a great deal more seriously than Padelford does, and recognizes the investment of the hand in writing, in this case, I assume, because of the high cultural value that Nott ascribes to Renaissance poetry.

16. The other poems in Tottel explicitly labeled as spoken by a woman (all by "uncertain authors") follow this paradigm; one (no. 190, "The Ladye Praieth the Returne of her Lover Abidying on the Seas") though close in subject matter to "O Happy dames," posits an unfaithful lover and an abandoned woman; such also is the case with no. 222, "The Lady Forsaken of her Lover, Prayeth his Returne, or the End of her own Life." Number 275, "The beginning of the Epistle of Penelope to Ulisses," translates Ovid.

17. See A. R. Jones, *Currency of Eros*, p. 43, on Isabella Whitney.

18. The contemporary situation to which this might be likened is the

production of male homoerotic pornography—K/S zines—by and for women; on this, see Russ.

19. See Hughey, *The Arundel Harington Manuscript*, 1: 132 for the text of the poem; and 1: 30–31 and 2: 112 for Hughey's comments on Preston summarized below.
20. It is also worth noting that none of the poems supposedly spoken by a woman and supposedly authored by Surrey are to be found in BL Add 36529, the fullest sixteenth-century manuscript collection of Surrey's writing.
21. In Hughey, *Sir John Harington*, pp. 131–32. Hughey's comment below is from this book.
22. Crewe, *Trials of Authorship*, p. 66.
23. Camden, p. 50.
24. Woolf, p. 49.

GRAPHINA'S MARK

1. Margaret Ferguson, "Running On with Almost Public Voice," p. 47. An abbreviated version of this essay appears as "The Spectre of Resistance," and some of the arguments about Cary are anticipated in "A Room Not Their Own," pp. 105–11.
2. All citations of Cary are from Weller and Ferguson; I quote here from an endnote, p. 160.
3. The prescriptive literature is reviewed in Hull.
4. On these points, see pt. I, "Writing Before the Letter," in Derrida, *Of Grammatology*.
5. Callaghan, p. 177. For a similar evaluation, see N. Miller, p. 208.
6. However, it is worth noting that although it is unlikely that *Mariam* was written for the public stage, it could have been performed privately, at home. Moreover, thinking of the play as closet drama overprivatizes the genre; Cary's play is a Senecan drama and part of a neoclassical revival that proved enormously stageworthy in France (it leads, after all, to classic French theater as well as to English Restoration tragedy). The form of the play might of itself testify to rather large and public ambitions. For a congruent attempt to rethink closet drama, see Straznicky.

7. For an acute brief summary of Senecan drama as a site of political critique, see Shannon, esp. pp. 144–47. See also Lewalski, pp. 191–94; and Gutierrez, pp. 237–38.
8. At least one commentator on the play, Krontiris (p. 90), argues that Doris here is expressing Cary's point of view. Herod's marriage to Mariam also is class transgressive, though in the opposite direction to Pheroras's, since Mariam, as the scion of the royal line of Palestine, elevates him and legitimates his occupancy of the position of king of Palestine given to him by the Romans.
9. As Wiegman forcefully observes: "In reading multiplicity and heterogeneity at the reportedly deessentialized (but always female) body and finding unicity and homogeneity at the un(der)theorized (but always male) body, feminist theory has both guaranteed the primacy of gender and discussed its complexities in very narrow terms" (p. 12). As she further observes, the point in desedimenting a monolithic masculinity is not "to claim for the masculine some kind of equal fracturing that would discount the hierarchical power of patriarchy, but to locate the myth of masculine *sameness* that functions as feminism's most intense reinscription of patriarchy's own illusory logic," assuming "that the demystification of woman's common oppression was inextricable from a critique of man's totalized hegemony" (p. 180). It is my hope that such principles underlie the analysis conducted here.
10. This form of resistance is one, for example, that even James I countenances in *The Trew Law of Free Monarchies* when he considers what subjects of tyrants are to do: "following and obeying his lawfull commands, eschewing and flying his fury in his unlawfull, without resistance, but by sobbes and teares to God" (McIlwain, p. 61); flight—or petitions to God—are allowable because such forms of resistance are tantamount to invisibility and thus assumed to have no political efficacy. (For further considerations of questions of conscience, see Goldberg, *James I and the Politics of Literature*, ch. 3, esp. pp. 113–20.) Yet the examples of Catholics in the period, brought to public notoriety (as in the Gunpowder Plot, for example, or their repeated refusals to sub-

scribe to the Oath of Allegiance, or to do so equivocally), can hardly be confined to such sites of private resistance, and, as Rowlands details, women were often publicly resistant. In this context, one could compare the scene of Cary's own resistance to the judges when she was examined about her two young sons, whom she had abducted and sent to France to join a monastery. Cary, as reported by her biographer, resisted her inquirers, not by remaining silent, but by capitalizing on the equivocations possible in the language of their demands. Thus, when they showed her the order prohibiting unlicensed departures, she replied that since she was not a border officer, she had not violated the law (see *The Lady Falkland, Her Life*, in Weller and Ferguson, p. 259). Not exactly lying, Cary told them a truth that satisfied their questions and yet which refused to give them the answer they sought. Their exasperated question, "if she meant to teach them law" received a telling answer, that she was a lawyer's daughter—hence, that the law itself is not univocal, and that a woman can claim to be doing nothing more than what her father did and yet disobey the instruments of royal authority.

11. Stone argues for the gradual replacement of the "restricted patriarchal nuclear family" by "the closed domesticated nuclear family," the latter of which is marked by the mutuality of "companionate" marriage.

12. As in the succinct formula in *The Law's Resolution of Women's Rights* (1632), that "all of them [i.e., women] are understood either married or to be married and their desires are subject to their husband" (cited from anthologized selection in Klein, p. 320).

13. The anti-generative position is, of course, perilously close to an annihilative wish for a world without women; the potentially progressive impulse to relieve women of the burden of biological reproduction is possible in these lines insofar as the heroine of the play also wishes to have done with marriage. How unimaginable such a prospect is can be seen, of course, in the fact that Mariam's divorce from Herod is also suicidal.

14. For a typical counterview, see Travitsky, "The *Feme Covert*," who

describes Salome as a female villain produced by Cary's "internalization of negative imagery and of patriarchal constructs of women" (p. 192).

15. That Pheroras denounces Constabarus, at Salome's behest, and in order to keep Graphina, suggests how limited the utopic prospect of 2. 1. is; whatever is to be read in Graphina's mark can also be misread—as her lines demonstrate—as a sign of her utter compliance with his demands (for an interpretation of the play that depends on this [mis]reading of Graphina's silence, see Kennedy, pp. 116–17, 125, 126); and however much male–male relations hold out a model for male–female relations, Pheroras and Graphina do not come to embody this, nor does any other married couple in the play.

16. This exception is also noted by Beilen, p. 171.

17. In the closing pages of her essay (pp. 152–53), Shannon usefully points to the ideal of female friendship voiced in the prefatory poem to *Mariam*; acutely noting the absence of such relations from the play (although the problem is not, I believe, that women cannot speak to each other as men can, but rather that their subordinate position in the gender hierarchy continually determines their positions even when they do speak to each other), she contrasts what the play depicts with the relations in this poem and the possibilities they represent: "the existence of a new audience of women and . . . a feminist or reforming wisdom" (p. 153).

18. It is possible, too, as Angela Burns and Helen Tartar have reminded me, to read an erotic charge in these rivalries between women (a point also relevant to the invidious making of comparisons in Lanyer's *Salve Deus*). No utopic consequences follow from this, of course; yet this would also seem to enable Cary to write as a woman. This would apply to the representation of the woman writing in *Mariam* insofar as it involves making distinctions among women, even, through Constabarus, misogynistically attacking conventional women. Possibly, too, these were life strategies, as may be suggested by the biography of Cary by one of her daughters, with its continual recording of Cary's self-alienation and self-division, a depressiveness attached to conventional roles—as submissive wife, as mother, and as a noblewoman subject to

regimes of dress and social behavior—that also seems to have been one of Cary's resources finally to live outside her marriage and to announce her conversion to Catholicism.

19. Cf. also the Butler's self-accusation for betraying Mariam, in which he likens himself to Achitophel (4.5.275), thereby putting Mariam in the position of Absalom.

20. It also is apparently some version of "friendship" that ties Herod to Caesar; this is implicit in the description that Babas's Second Son offers of his childhood visit to Rome, and his witnessing of the mild, sweet, and clement behavior of Octavius "then a page" (2.2.183) and Julius Caesar. This description serves to eroticize a scene of friendship and also to suggest the ways in which Palestinian/Roman relationships of power work. Herod stands at the nexus of these, and his marriage to Mariam attempts to give a double basis to his power, both the "friendship" relations of Rome as well as the ancestral relationships in which Mariam is an heir to David's throne.

21. Since Alexandra went to Anthony to denounce Herod for killing her father and her son, the picture she offers of Aristobulus is the image of a corpse.

22. Weller and Ferguson hear here an Ovidian echo, the lament of Narcissus, that plenty makes him poor; this is plausible, but I would resist recasting this scene of blockage as narcissistic.

23. Cf. the discussion between Herod and Salome about Mariam's cheek in 4.7, in which Herod asks Salome to describe the "mark" (l. 399) and when she figures the cheek as an enticing and entrapping "crimson bush" (l. 401), he refuses the figuration: "you mark'd it not" (l. 404), which Salome refigures as Mariam's refusal to blush although "foul dishonours do her forehead blot" (l. 406).

24. A particularly complex instance of a double writing of marking/unmarking is possible through the term "blot," which can mean either, as when Antipater claims that "foul adultery blotteth Mariam's brow" (2.3.278). This (un)marking is narrativized when Doris tells Mariam that her "soul is black and spotted" (4.8.575), and then goes on to claim that "no stain" (l. 593) but rather her virtues caused Herod to abandon her. The double

mark (black and white) is continually refigured in Herod's accusation of Mariam as a "white enchantress" (4.4.176) who hides "black revenge" (l. 184), who rather than being "plain as water" (l. 197), transparent, hides a "stain" (l. 199), which is her name (l. 230), and yet, whom to kill, would be "to muffle Jewry in the foulest black / That ever was an opposite to white" (ll. 237–38).

25. I hope, too, that my essay is not misperceived as repeating comments of the sort that Beilen quotes, p. 157, about Cary as a "masculine" writer. I don't mean to suggest the kind of either/or in which, if Cary works inside any patriarchal constructions, she then must be seen to have abandoned her gender, or that in order to be true to it she must inhabit a femininity somehow outside or entirely opposed to masculinity. Thus, I would endorse Belsey's remark on *Mariam* that "there is no space outside discourse from which women may silently intuit an alternative definition" to patriarchy (p. 164) and that it therefore "is always possible to interrogate the dominant definitions" (p. 165); where I would demur from Belsey is her supposition that Mariam is a "unified, autonomous subject" (p. 173) and that it is from that position that interrogation occurs. I would argue instead that "patriarchy" is sufficiently fissured to allow the subject position of the woman/writer.

26. The texts in question are: *The History of the Life, Reign, and Death of Edward II*, ascribed to E. F., and *The History of the most unfortunate Prince King Edward II*, said to have been found among the papers of and supposed to have been written by Henry Viscount Falkland. Citations below are from the first (the longer) of the these texts.

27. Purkiss, "Introduction," *Renaissance Women*, p. xxvii. This book contains a modern edition of E. F.'s *Edward II*. Lewalski also reviews the textual question in *Writing Women*, Appendix A; as do Weller and Ferguson in their "Introduction" to *Mariam*, pp. 12–16.

28. See, e.g., Krontiris, pp. 92–101; Lewalski summarizes her reading this way: Isabel "is portrayed with much sympathy as a strong, noble, intelligent woman who is a match for and finally victorious over her principal antagonist, Spencer; whose marital infidelity is entirely understandable and scarcely culpable; and who can and

does act effectively in the public arena as rhetorician, military commander, and reforming ruler; and whose guilt is recognized but largely deflected" (pp. 210–11).

29. Weller and Ferguson, on the other hand, find Isabel to be a "monster of cruelty" ("Introduction," p. 38), which may be part of the reason they remain agnostic on the question of whether Cary wrote these Edward II materials.

30. In this light, moreover, one would perhaps not have to take the position that Purkiss does, of regretting how "obnoxiously blind" Cary is "to the possibility of a homosexual subjectivity" ("Introduction," p. xxix). Although Purkiss is surely to be applauded for her recognition that Cary's gender concerns may not carry over to questions of sexuality, "homosexual subjectivity" is hardly something one can find represented in texts by Cary's contemporaries; on the other hand, as this passage indicates, *Edward II* does not condemn male–male relations out of hand.

31. Foster believes he has found Cary's translations of Blosius and Seneca, as well as a much longer version of her poem on the death of Buckingham.

32. *The Lady Falkland Her Life*, in Weller and Ferguson, p. 190.

BIBLIOGRAPHY

Abrams, M. H., ed. *The Norton Anthology of English Literature*. New York: W. W. Norton, 1986, 1993.

Allen, P. S., and H. M. Allen, eds. *Opus Epistolarum Des. Erasmi Roterodami*. 12 vols. Oxford: Clarendon Press, 1906–58.

Armstrong, Isobel, ed. *New Feminist Discourses*. London: Routledge, 1992.

Armstrong, Nancy. *Desire and Domestic Fiction*. Oxford: Oxford University Press, 1987.

Athey, Stephanie, and Daniel Cooper Alarcon. "*Oroonoko*'s Gendered Economies of Honor/Horror: Reframing Colonial Discourse Studies in the Americas." *American Literature* 65 (1993): 415–43.

Ballard, George. *Memoirs of Several Ladies of Great Britain*. Detroit: Wayne State University Press, 1985.

Ballaster, Ros. "New Hystericism: Aphra Behn's *Oroonoko*: The Body, the Text, and the Feminist Critic." In Isobel Armstrong, pp. 283–95.

———. *Seductive Forms: Women's Amatory Fiction from 1684 to 1740*. Oxford: Clarendon Press, 1992.

Barash, Carol. "The Political Possibilities of Desire: Teaching the Erotic Poems of Behn." In Fox, pp. 160–76.

Basnett-McGuire, Susan. *Translation Studies*. London: Methuen, 1980.
Behn, Aphra. *Five Plays*. Ed. Maureen Duffy. London: Methuen, 1990.
———. *Love Letters Between a Nobleman and His Sister*. Ed. Maureen Duffy. New York: Penguin Books / Virago Press, 1987.
Beilen, Elaine V. *Redeeming Eve*. Princeton: Princeton University Press, 1987.
Belsey, Catherine. *The Subject of Tragedy*. London: Methuen, 1985.
Béné, Charles. "Cadeau d'Erasme à Margaret Roper: Deux hymnes de Prudence." In Murphy, Gibaud, and DiCesare, pp. 469–80.
Benjamin, Walter. "The Task of the Translator." In idem, *Illuminations*, ed. Hannah Arendt; trans. Harry Zohn. New York: Schocken Books, 1969, pp. 69–82.
Bersani, Leo. *The Freudian Body*. New York: Columbia University Press, 1986.
Bond, Edward A. "Wyatt's Poems." *Athenaeum* 2274 (May 27, 1871): 654–55.
Boone, Joseph, and Michael Cadden, eds. *Engendering Men*. New York: Routledge, 1992.
Boose, Lynda E., and Betty S. Flowers, eds. *Daughters and Fathers*. Baltimore: Johns Hopkins University Press, 1989.
Bornstein, Diane. "The Style of the Countess of Pembroke's Translation of Philipe de Mornay's *Discours de la vie et de la mort*." In Hannay, *Silent but for the Word*, pp. 126–34.
Brant, Clare, and Diane Purkiss, eds. *Women, Texts and Histories, 1575–1760*. London: Routledge, 1992.
Bray, Alan. *Homosexuality in Renaissance England*. London: Gay Men's Press, 1982.
Brink, Jean R., ed. *Privileging Gender in Early Modern England. Sixteenth Century Essays and Studies* 23 (1993).
Brooks-Davies, Douglas, ed. *Silver Poets of the Sixteenth Century*. London: J. M. Dent, 1994.
Brown, Laura. *Ends of Empire*. Ithaca: Cornell University Press, 1993.
Brown, Wendy. *States of Injury*. Princeton: Princeton University Press, 1995.
Butler, Judith. "Against Proper Objects." *differences* 6 (1994): 1–26.
———. *Bodies That Matter*. New York: Routledge, 1993.

———. *Gender Trouble: Feminism and the Subversion of Identity*. New York: Routledge, 1990.

Byard, Margaret. "The Trade of Courtiership. The Countess of Bedford and the Bedford Memorials: A Family History from 1585 to 1607." *History Today* 29 (Jan. 1979): 20–28.

Caius, John. *A Boke or Counseill against the Disease called the Sweate* (1552). Ed. Archibald Malloch. New York: Scholars' Facsimiles & Reprints, 1937.

Callaghan, Dympna. "Re-reading Elizabeth Cary's *The Tragedie of Mariam, Faire Queene of Jewry*." In Hendricks and Parker, pp. 163–77.

Camden, William. *Remaines of a Greater Worke*. London, 1605.

Canfield, J. Douglas, and Deborah C. Payne, eds. *Cultural Readings of Restoration and Eighteenth-Century Theater*. Athens: University of Georgia Press, 1995.

Cary, Elizabeth. *The Tragedy of Mariam*. Ed. Barry Weller and Margaret W. Ferguson. Berkeley: University of California Press, 1994.

Cave, Terence. *The Cornucopian Text*. Oxford: Clarendon Press, 1979.

Chamberlain, Lori. "Gender and the Metaphorics of Translation." *Signs* 13 (1988): 454–72. Reprinted in Venuti.

Chambers, R. W. *Thomas More*. Ann Arbor: University of Michigan Press, 1958 (1935).

Clifford, D. J. H., ed. *The Diaries of Lady Anne Clifford*. Phoenix Mill, Eng.: Alan Sutton, 1990.

Coiro, Ann Baynes. "Writing in Service: Sexual Politics and Class Position in the Poetry of Aemilia Lanyer and Ben Jonson." *Criticism* 35 (1993): 357–76.

Conley, Tom. "Institutionalizing Translation: On Florio's Montaigne." *Glyph Textual Studies* 1 ("Demarcating the Disciplines"): 45–60.

Coogan, Robert. "Petrarch's *Trionfi* and the English Renaissance." *Studies in Philology* 67 (1970): 306–27.

Correll, Barbara. "Malleable Material, Models of Power: Woman in Erasmus's 'Marriage Group' and *Civility in Boys*." *ELH* 57 (1990): 241–62.

"Correspondance entre Erasme et Margaret Roper." *Moreana* 12 (1966): 29–46, 121.

Creighton, Charles. *A History of Epidemics in Britain*. 2 vols. London: Frank Cass, 1965 [1894].

Crewe, Jonathan. *Hidden Designs*. New York: Methuen, 1986.

———. *Trials of Authorship*. Berkeley: University of California Press, 1990.

Culler, Jonathan, ed. *On Puns*. Oxford: Basil Blackwell, 1988.

Daston, Lorraine, and Katharine Park. "The Hermaphrodite and the Orders of Nature: Sexual Ambiguity in Early Modern France." *GLQ* 1, no. 4 (1995): 419–38.

Davis, Natalie Zemon. " 'Women's History' in Transition: The European Case." *Feminist Studies* 3 (1976): 83–103.

———. *Women on the Margins: Three Seventeenth-Century Lives*. Cambridge, Mass.: Harvard University Press, 1995.

Deconstruction and Criticism. New York: Continuum, 1984.

de Lauretis, Teresa. *The Practice of Love*. Bloomington: Indiana University Press, 1994.

de Lotbinière-Harwood, Susanne. *Re-belle et Infidèle / The Bilingual Body*. Montreal: Les éditions de remue-ménage; Toronto: Women's Press, 1992.

DeMolen, Richard L., ed. *Erasmus of Rotterdam*. New York: Twayne Publishers, 1971.

Derrida, Jacques. "Des Tours de Babel." In Graham, pp. 165–205.

———. *Dissemination*. Trans. Barbara Johnson. Chicago: University of Chicago Press, 1981.

———. *The Ear of the Other*. Ed. Christie V. McDonald; trans. Peggy Kamuf. New York: Schocken Books, 1985.

———. *Of Grammatology*. Trans. Gayatri Chakravorty Spivak. Baltimore: Johns Hopkins University Press, 1974, 1976.

———. "Living On / Border Lines." In *Deconstruction and Criticism*, pp. 75–176.

———. "Signature Event Context." In *Limited Inc*. Evanston, Ill.: Northwestern University Press, 1988.

Diamond, Elin. "*Gestus* and Signature in Aphra Behn's *The Rover*." *ELH* 56 (1989): 519–41.

Dixon, Laurinda S. *Perilous Chastity*. Ithaca: Cornell University Press, 1995.

Donne, John. *Divine Poems*. Ed. Helen Gardner. Oxford: Clarendon Press, 1978.

Donoghue, Emma. *Passions Between Women: British Lesbian Culture, 1668–1801*. London: Scarlet, 1993.

Duberman, Martin, Martha Vicinus, and George Chauncey, Jr., eds. *Hidden from History: Reclaiming the Gay and Lesbian Past*. New York: Meridian, 1989.

Duffy, Maureen. *The Passionate Shepherdess*. London: Methuen, 1977.

Duncan-Jones, Katherine. *Sir Philip Sidney: Courtier-Poet*. New Haven: Yale University Press, 1991.

Duyfhuizen, Bernard. " 'That Which I dare Not Name': Aphra Behn's 'The Willing Mistress.' " *ELH* 58 (1991): 63–82.

Edelman, Lee. *Homographesis*. New York: Routledge, 1994.

Epstein, Julia, and Kristina Straub, eds. *Body Guards*. New York: Routledge, 1991.

Erasmus, Desiderius. *The Colloquies of Erasmus*. Trans. Craig R. Thompson. Chicago: University of Chicago Press, 1965.

———. *Precatio Dominica in Septem Portiones Distributa. Moreana* 7 (1965): 9–64.

Erikson, Amy Louise. *Women and Property in Early Modern England*. London: Routledge, 1993.

Ezell, Margaret J. M. *The Patriarch's Wife*. Chapel Hill: University of North Carolina Press, 1987.

———. *Writing Women's Literary History*. Baltimore: Johns Hopkins University Press, 1993 .

F., E. *The History of the Life, Reign, and Death of Edward II*. London: Charles Harper & Thomas Fox, 1680.

Farge, James K. *Orthodoxy and Reform in Early Reformation France*. Leiden: E. J. Brill, 1985.

Ferguson, Margaret. "Juggling the Categories of Race, Class, and Gender: Aphra Behn's *Oroonoko*." In Hendricks and Parker, pp. 209–24.

———. "Moderation and Its Discontents: Recent Work on Renaissance Women." *Feminist Studies* 20 (1994): 349–66.

———. "News from the New World: Miscegenous Romance in Aphra Behn's *Oroonoko* and *The Widow Ranter*." In Miller, O'Dair, and Weber, pp. 151–89.

———. "A Room Not Their Own: Renaissance Women as Readers and Writers." In Koelb and Noakes, pp. 93–116.

———. "Running On with Almost Public Voice: The Case of 'E.C.' " In Howe, pp. 37–67.

———. "The Spectre of Resistance." In Kastan and Stallybrass, pp. 235–50.

Ferguson, Moira. *Subject to Others*. New York: Routledge, 1992.

Fisken, Beth Wynne. " 'To the Angell spirit . . .': Mary Sidney's Entry into the 'World of Words.' " In Haselkorn and Travitsky, pp. 263–75.

Fogarty, Anne. "Looks That Kill: Violence and Representation in Aphra Behn's *Oroonoko*." In Plasa and Ring, pp. 1–17.

Foster, Donald W. "Resurrecting the Author: Elizabeth Tanfield Cary." In Brink, pp. 141–75.

Foucault, Michel. *The History of Sexuality: An Introduction*. Trans. Robert Hurley. New York: Pantheon, 1978.

Fox, Christopher, ed. *Teaching Eighteenth-Century Poetry*. New York: AMS Press, 1990.

Foxwell, A. K., ed. *The Poems of Sir Thomas Wiat*. 2 vols. London: University of London Press, 1913.

———. *A Study of Sir Thomas Wyatt's Poems*. New York: Russell & Russell, 1964 (1911).

Frank, Marcie. "Fighting Women and Loving Men: Dryden's Representation of Shakespeare in *All for Love*." In Goldberg, *Queering the Renaissance*, pp. 310–29.

Friedenwald, Julius, and Samuel Morrison. "The History of the Enema with Some Notes on Related Procedures." *Bulletin of the History of Medicine* 8 (1940): 68–114, 239–76.

Fuss, Diana. *Essentially Speaking*. New York: Routledge, 1989.

———. *Identification Papers*. New York: Routledge, 1995.

Gallagher, Catherine. "Embracing the Absolute." *Genders* 1 (1988): 24–39.

———. *Nobody's Story: The Vanishing Acts of Women Writers in the Marketplace, 1670–1820*. Berkeley: University of California Press, 1994.

———. "Who Was That Masked Woman: The Prostitute and the Playwright in the Comedies of Aphra Behn." In Hutner, *Rereading*, pp. 65–85.

Gee, John Archer. "Margaret Roper's English Version of Erasmus's *Precatio Dominica* and the Apprenticeship Behind Early Tudor Translation." *RES* 13 (1937): 257–71.

Gerard, Kent, and Gert Hekma, eds. *The Pursuit of Sodomy*. New York: Harrington, 1989.

Gilbert, Sandra, and Susan Gubar, eds. *The Norton Anthology of Literature by Women*. New York: W. W. Norton, 1985.

Goldberg, Jonathan. *James I and the Politics of Literature*. Baltimore: Johns Hopkins University Press, 1983.

———. Review of Duncan-Jones. *LGSN* 19, no. 2 (July 1992): 22–24.

———. *Sodometries: Renaissance Texts, Modern Sexualities*. Stanford: Stanford University Press, 1992.

———. *Writing Matter: From the Hands of the English Renaissance*. Stanford: Stanford University Press, 1990.

Goldberg, Jonathan, ed. *Queering the Renaissance*. Durham: Duke University Press, 1994.

Goreau, Angeline. *Reconstructing Aphra*. New York: Dial Press, 1980.

Graham, Joseph F., ed. *Difference in Translation*. Ithaca: Cornell University Press, 1985.

Greer, Germain, et al., eds. *Kissing the Rod*. New York: Noonday, 1988.

Grimble, Ian. *The Harington Family*. New York: St. Martin's Press, n.d.

Grosart, Alexander B., ed. *The Complete Works in Verse and Prose of Samuel Daniel*. 5 vols. New York: Russell & Russell, 1963 (1885).

Guillory, John. *Cultural Capital: The Problem of Literary Canon Formation*. Chicago: University of Chicago Press, 1993.

Gutierrez, Nancy A. "Valuing *Mariam*: Genre Study and Feminist Analysis." *Tulsa Studies in Women's Literature* 10 (1991): 233–51.

Hackett, Helen. " 'Yet Tell Me Some Such Fiction': Lady Mary Wroth's *Urania* and the 'Femininity' of Romance." In Brant and Purkiss, pp. 39–68.

Hall, Kim. *Things of Darkness: Economies of Race and Gender in Early Modern England*. Ithaca: Cornell University Press, 1995.

Halkin, Léon-E. *Erasmus: A Critical Biography*. Trans. John Tonkin. Oxford: Basil Blackwell, 1993.

Halpern, Richard. *The Poetics of Primitive Accumulation*. Ithaca: Cornell University Press, 1991.

Hammill, Graham. "The Epistemology of Expurgation: Bacon and *The*

Masculine Birth of Time." In Goldberg, *Queering the Renaissance*, pp. 236–52.

Hannay, Margaret. *Philip's Phoenix*. New York: Oxford University Press, 1990.

Hannay, Margaret, ed. *Silent but for the Word*. Kent, Ohio: Kent State University Press, 1985.

Harpsfield, Nicholas. *The Life and Death of Sir Thomas More*. In Reynolds, *Lives*, pp. 51–175.

Harrier, Richard. *The Canon of Sir Thomas Wyatt's Poetry*. Cambridge, Mass.: Harvard University Press, 1975.

Harris, Barbara J. "Women and Politics in Early Tudor England." *Historical Journal* 33 (1990): 259–81.

Harvey, Elizabeth. *Ventriloquized Voices: Feminist Theory and English Renaissance Texts*. London: Routledge, 1992.

Haselkorn, Anne M., and Betty S. Travitsky, eds. *The Renaissance Englishwoman in Print*. Amherst: University of Massachusetts Press, 1990.

Hecker, J. F. C. *The Epidemics of the Middle Ages*. Trans. B. G. Babington. London: George Woodfall & Son, 1846.

Hendricks, Margo, and Patricia Parker, eds. *Women, "Race," and Writing in the Early Modern Period*. London: Routledge, 1994.

Herman, Peter, ed. *Rethinking the Henrician Era*. Urbana: University of Illinois Press, 1994.

The History of the most unfortunate Prince King Edward II. London: A. G. & J. P., 1680.

Hobby, Elaine. "Katherine Philips: Seventeenth-Century Lesbian Poet." In Hobby and White, pp. 183–204.

———. *Virtue of Necessity: English Women's Writing, 1649–88*. Ann Arbor: University of Michigan Press, 1989 (1988).

Hobby, Elaine, and Chris White, eds. *What Lesbians Do in Books*. London: Women's Press, 1991.

Holland, Peter. *The Ornament of Action*. Cambridge, Eng.: Cambridge University Press, 1979.

Howe, Florence, ed. *Tradition and the Talents of Women*. Urbana: University of Illinois Press, 1991.

Hughey, Ruth. *Sir John Harington of Stepney*. Columbus: Ohio University Press, 1971.

Hughey, Ruth, ed. *The Arundel Harington Manuscript of Tudor Poetry*. 2 vols. Columbus: Ohio University Press, 1960.

Hull, Suzanne W. *Chaste, Silent and Obedient*. San Marino, Calif.: Huntington Library, 1982.

Hunt, Margaret. "Afterword." In Goldberg, *Queering the Renaissance*, pp. 359–77.

Hutner, Heidi. "Revisioning the Female Body: Aphra Behn's *The Rover*, Parts I and II." In Hutner, *Rereading*, pp. 102–20.

Hutner, Heidi, ed. *Rereading Aphra Behn*. Charlottesville: University of Virginia Press, 1993.

Hutson, Lorna. "Why the Lady's Eyes Are Nothing like the Sun." In Brant and Purkiss, pp. 13–38.

Irigaray, Luce. *Speculum of the Other Woman*. Trans. Gillian C. Gill. Ithaca: Cornell University Press, 1985.

Ives, Eric. *Anne Boleyn*. Oxford: Basil Blackwell, 1986.

Jardine, Lisa. "Cultural Confusion and Shakespeare's Learned Heroines: 'These are old paradoxes.'" *Shakespeare Quarterly* 38 (1987): 1–18.

———. *Erasmus, Man of Letters*. Princeton: Princeton University Press, 1993.

Jardine, Lisa, and Anthony Grafton. *From Humanism to the Humanities*. Cambridge, Mass.: Harvard University Press, 1986.

Jed, Stephanie H. *Chaste Thinking*. Bloomington: Indiana University Press, 1989.

Jones, Ann Rosalind. *The Currency of Eros: Women's Love Lyric in Europe, 1540–1620*. Bloomington: Indiana University Press, 1990.

Jones, Ann Rosalind, and Peter Stallybrass. "Fetishizing Gender: Constructing the Hermaphrodite in Renaissance Europe." In Epstein and Straub, pp. 80–111.

Jones, R. F. *The Triumph of the English Language*. Stanford: Stanford University Press, 1953.

Judy, Ronald. *(Dis)forming the American Canon*. Minneapolis: University of Minnesota Press, 1993.

Kamuf, Peggy. "Writing Like a Woman." In McConnell-Ginet, Borker, and Furman, pp. 284–99.

Kastan, David, and Peter Stallybrass, eds. *Staging the Renaissance*. New York: Routledge, 1991.

Kavenik, Frances M. "Aphra Behn: The Playwright as 'Breeches Part.' " In Schofield and Macheski, pp. 177–92.

Keller, Lynn, and Cristanne Miller, eds. *Feminist Measures*. Ann Arbor: University of Michigan Press, 1994.

Kelly, Joan. *Women, History and Theory*. Chicago: University of Chicago Press, 1984.

Kennedy, Gwynne. "Lessons of the 'Schoole of wisedom.' " In Levin and Robertson, pp. 113–36.

Kimmel, Michael S., ed. *Love Letters Between a Certain Late Nobleman and the Famous Mr. Wilson*. New York: Haworth, 1990.

King, Margaret. *Women of the Renaissance*. Chicago: University of Chicago Press, 1991.

Klein, Joan Larsen, ed. *Daughters, Wives, & Widows*. Urbana: University of Illinois Press, 1992.

Koelb, Clayton, and Susan Noakes, eds. *The Comparative Perspective on Literature*. Ithaca: Cornell University Press, 1988.

Kramnick, Jonathan Brody. Review of Donoghue. *LGSN* 22, no. 2 (Summer 1995): 29–30.

Krontiris, Tina. *Oppositional Voices*. London: Routledge, 1992.

Lamb, Mary Ellen. "The Cooke Sisters: Attitudes Toward Learned Women in the Renaissance." In Hannay, *Silent but for the Word*, pp. 107–25.

———. *Gender and Authorship in the Sidney Circle*. Madison: University of Wisconsin Press, 1990.

Levin, Carole, and Karen Robertson, eds. *Sexuality and Power in Renaissance Drama*. Studies in Renaissance Literature 10. Lewiston, N.Y.: Edwin Mellen Press, 1991.

Levin, Carole, and Jeanie Watson, eds. *Ambiguous Realities*. Detroit: Wayne State University Press, 1997.

Lewalski, Barbara Kiefer. *Writing Women in Jacobean England*. Cambridge, Mass.: Harvard University Press, 1993.

Lieberman, William. "The Enema: Some Historical Notes." *Review of Gastroenterology* 13 (1946): 215–29.

Lussier, Mark. " 'Marrying the Hated Object': The Carnival of Desire in Behn's *The Rover*." In Brink, pp. 225–40.

Maber, R. G. "Pierre Le Moyne's Encomium of Margaret Roper, Translated by John Paulet, Marquis of Winchester (1652)." *Moreana* 23 (1986): 47–52.

Maclean, Ian. *The Renaissance Notion of Woman*. Cambridge, Eng.: Cambridge University Press, 1980.

Mahl, Mary R., and Helen Koon, eds. *The Female Spectator: English Women Writers Before 1800*. Bloomington: Indiana University Press, 1977.

Marius, Richard. *Thomas More*. New York: Vintage Books, 1984.

Markley, Robert. " 'Be Impudent, Be Saucy, Forward, Bold, Touzing, and Leud': The Politics of Masculine Sexuality and Feminine Desire in Behn's Tory Comedies." In Canfield and Payne, pp. 114–40.

Markley, Robert, and Molly Rothenberg. "Contestations of Nature: Aphra Behn's 'The Golden Age' and the Sexualizing of Politics." In Hutner, *Rereading*, pp. 301–21.

Marotti, Arthur. *Manuscript, Print, and the English Renaissance Lyric*. Ithaca: Cornell University Press, 1995.

Matthiessen, F. O. *Translation: An Elizabethan Art*. Cambridge, Mass.: Harvard University Press, 1931.

Maurer, Margaret. "The Real Presence of Lucy Russell, Countess of Bedford, and the Terms of John Donne's 'Honour is so sublime perfection.' " *ELH* 47 (1980): 205–34.

McConnell-Ginet, Sally, Ruth Borker, and Nelly Furman, eds. *Women and Language in Literature and Society*. New York: Praeger, 1980.

McCubbin, R. P., ed. *'Tis Nature's Fault*. Cambridge, Eng.: Cambridge University Press, 1985.

McGrath, Lynette. " 'Let Us Have Our Libertie Againe': Amelia Lanier's 17th-Century Feminist Voice." *Women's Studies* 20 (1992): 331–48.

———. "Metaphoric Subversions: Feast and Mirrors in Amelia Lanier's *Salve Deus Rex Judaeorum*." *LIT* 2 (1991): 101–13.

McIlwain, Charles Howard, ed. *The Political Works of James I*. Cambridge, Mass.: Harvard University Press, 1918.

McKeon, Michael. "Historicizing Patriarchy." *Eighteenth-Century Studies* 28 (1995): 295–322.

———. *The Origins of the English Novel*. Baltimore: Johns Hopkins University Press, 1987.

McLeod, Randall. "Spellbound: Typography and the Concept of Old-

Spelling Editions." *Renaissance and Reformation*, n.s. 3 (1979): 50–65.

———. "UnEditing Shak-speare." *Sub-Stance* 33/34 (1982): 26–55.

———. "Unemending Shakespeare's Sonnet III." *SEL* 21 (1981): 75–96.

Miller, David Lee, Sharon O'Dair, and Harold Weber, eds. *The Production of English Renaissance Culture*. Ithaca: Cornell University Press, 1994.

Miller, Naomi J. *Changing the Subject: Mary Wroth and Figurations of Gender in Early Modern England*. Lexington: University Press of Kentucky, 1996.

Montague, J. F. "History and Appraisal of the Enema." *Medical Record* 139 (1934): 91–93, 243–47, 297–99, 458–60.

Montaigne, Michel de. *The Essayes* (1603). Trans. John Florio. Menston: Scolar Press, 1969.

Moon, Michael. " 'The Gentle Boy from the Dangerous Classes': Pederasty, Domesticity, and Capitalism in Horatio Alger." *Representations* 19 (1987): 87–110 .

Mueller, Janel. "The Feminist Poetics of Aemilia Lanyer's 'Salve Deus Rex Judaeorum.' " In Keller and Miller, pp. 208–36.

Muir, Kenneth. "Unpublished Poems in the Devonshire MS." *Proceedings of the Leeds Philosophical and Literary Society* 6 (1947): 253–82.

Munns, Jessica. " 'Good, Sweet, Honey, Sugar-Candied Reader': Aphra Behn's Foreplay in Forewords." In Hutner, *Rereading*, pp.42–62.

———. " 'I By a Double Right Thy Bounties Claim': Aphra Behn and Sexual Space." In Schofield and Macheski, pp. 193–210.

Murphy, C. M., H. Gibaud, and M. DiCesare. *Miscellanea Moreana*. Binghamton, N.Y.: Medieval & Renaissance Texts and Studies, 1989.

Neri, Ferdinando, ed. *Rime e Trionfi di Francesco Petrarco*. Turin: Unione Tipografico, 1966.

Niranjana, Tejaswini. *Siting Translation*. Berkeley: University of California Press, 1992.

Norton, Rictor. *Mother Clap's Molly House*. London: Gay Men's Press, 1992.

Nott, G. F., ed. *The Works of Henry Howard and of Sir Thomas Wyatt*. 2 vols. London: T. Bensley, 1815.

Orgel, Stephen. "The Renaissance Artist as Plagiarist." *ELH* 48 (1981): 476–95.

Padelford, Frederick Morgan. "The MS. Poems of Henry Howard, Earl of Surrey." *Anglia* 29 (1906): 273–338.

Padelford, Frederick Morgan, ed. *The Poems of Henry Howard Earl of Surrey*. Seattle: University of Seattle Press, 1920; rev. ed., 1928.

Paré, Ambroise. *On Monsters and Marvels*. Trans. Janis L. Pallister. Chicago: University of Chicago Press, 1982.

Parfitt, George, ed. *Ben Jonson: The Complete Poems*. New Haven: Yale University Press, 1975.

Park, Katherine, and Robert Nye. "Destiny Is Anatomy." *New Republic*, Feb. 18, 1991, pp. 53–57.

Parker, Patricia. "Gender Ideology, Gender Change: The Case of Marie Germain." *Critical Inquiry* 19 (1993): 337–64.

———. *Shakespeare from the Margins*. Chicago: University of Chicago Press, 1996.

Paster, Gail Kern. *The Body Embarrassed*. Ithaca: Cornell University Press, 1993.

Payne, Deborah C. " 'And Poets Shall by Patron-Princes Live': Aphra Behn and Patronage." In Schofield and Macheski, pp. 105–19.

Peck, Linda Levy. *Court Patronage and Corruption in Early Stuart England*. London: Routledge, 1990.

Petrarch, F. *Triumphis Mortis*. In Neri, pp. 555–69.

Plasa, Carl, and Betty J. Ring, eds. *The Discourse of Slavery*. London: Routledge, 1994.

Pollak, Ellen. "Beyond Incest: Gender and the Politics of Transgression in Aphra Behn's *Love-Letters Between a Nobleman and His Sister*." In Hutner, *Rereading*, pp. 151–86.

Prior, Mary, ed. *Women in English Society*. London: Methuen, 1985.

The Private Correspondence of Lady Jane Cornwallis. London: S&J Bentley, Wilson, & Fley, 1842.

Purkiss, Dianne, ed. *Renaissance Women: The Plays of Elizabeth Cary; The Poems of Aemilia Lanyer*. London: William Pickering, 1994.

Quint, D., M. W. Ferguson, G. W. Pigman III, and W. A. Rebhorn, eds. *Creative Imitation*. Binghamton, N.Y.: Medieval & Renaissance Texts & Studies, 1992.

Radway, Janice. *Reading the Romance.* Chapel Hill: University of North Carolina Press, 1984; reissued, 1991, with a new preface.

Rajchman, John, ed. *The Identity in Question.* New York: Routledge, 1995.

Rambuss, Richard. "Pleasure and Devotion: The Body of Jesus and Seventeenth-Century Religious Lyric." In Goldberg, *Queering the Renaissance*, pp. 253–79.

Raphael, Vicente L. *Contracting Colonialism.* Durham: Duke University Press, 1993.

Reed, Arthur W. "The Regulation of the Book Trade Before the Proclamation of 1538." *Transactions of the Bibliographical Society* 15 (1917–19): 157–84.

Rees, D. G. "Petrarch's 'Trionfo della Morte' in English." *Italian Studies* 7 (1952): 82–96.

Remley, Paul. "Mary Shelton and Her Tudor Literary Milieu." In Herman, pp. 40–77.

Reynolds, E. E., ed. *Lives of St. Thomas More.* London: Dent, 1963.

———. *Margaret Roper, Eldest Daughter of St. Thomas More.* New York: P. J. Kenedy & Sons, 1960.

Riley, Denise. *"Am I That Name?": Feminism and the Category of "Women" in History.* Minneapolis: University of Minnesota Press, 1988.

Rogers, Elizabeth Frances, ed. *The Correspondence of Sir Thomas More.* Princeton: Princeton University Press, 1947.

———. *St. Thomas More: Selected Letters.* New Haven: Yale University Press, 1961.

Rollins, Hyder Edward, ed. *Tottel's Miscellany.* 2 vols. Cambridge, Mass.: Harvard University Press, 1965.

Ronell, Avital. "*Le Sujet Suppositaire*: Freud and Rat Man." In Culler, pp. 115–39.

Roper, Margaret More. *A devout treatise upon the Pater noster. Moreana* 7 (1965): 9–64; Reprinted in DeMolen, pp. 96–124.

Roper, William. *The Life of Sir Thomas More.* In Sylvester and Harding, pp. 197–254.

Rowe, Kenneth Thorpe. "The Love of Sir Philip Sidney for the Countess of Pembroke." *Papers of the Michigan Academy of Science Arts and Letters* 25 (1939): 579–95.

Rowlands, Marie B. "Recusant Women, 1560–1640." In Prior, pp. 149–80.

Rowse, A. L., ed. *The Poems of Shakespeare's Dark Lady*. New York: Clarkson N. Potter, 1979 (1978).

———. *Sex and Society in Shakespeare's Age*. New York: Charles Scribner's Sons, 1974.

Rubin, Gayle. "Thinking Sex." In Vance, pp. 267–319.

———. Interview with Judith Butler, "Sexual Traffic." *differences* 6 (1994): 62–99.

Russ, Joanna. "Pornography by Women for Women, with Love." In idem, *Magic Mommas, Trembling Sisters, Puritans and Perverts*. Trumansberg, N.Y.: Crossing Press, 1985, pp. 79–99.

Salvaggio, Ruth. "Aphra Behn's Love: Fiction, Letters, and Desire." In Hutner, *Rereading*, pp. 253–70.

Saunders, J. W. "From Manuscript to Print." *Proceedings of the Leeds Philosophical and Literary Society* 6 (1951): 507–28.

Schleiner, Louise. *Tudor and Stuart Women Writers*. Bloomington: Indiana University Press, 1994.

Schnell, Lisa. " 'So Great a Difference Is There in Degree': Aemilia Lanyer and the Aims of Feminist Criticism." *MLQ* 57 (1996): 23–35.

Schofield, Mary Anne, and Cecilia Macheski, eds. *Curtain Calls: British and American Women and the Theater, 1660–1820*. Athens: Ohio University Press, 1991.

Scott, Joan Wallach. *Gender and the Politics of History*. New York: Columbia University Press, 1988.

———. "Multiculturalism and the Politics of Identity." In Rajchman, pp. 3–12.

Seaton, Ethel. "The Devonshire Manuscript and Its Medieval Fragments." *RES* 7 (1956): 55–56.

Sedgwick, Eve Kosofsky. *Between Men*. New York: Columbia University Press, 1985.

———. *Epistemology of the Closet*. Berkeley: University of California Press, 1990.

Shannon, Laurie J. "*The Tragedie of Mariam*: Cary's Critique of the Terms of Founding Social Discourses." *ELR* 24 (1994): 135–53.

Sidney, Sir Philip. *Arcadia*. Ed. Maurice Evans. Harmondsworth, Eng.: Penguin, 1977.

Southall, Raymond. *The Courtly Maker: An Essay on the Poetry of Wyatt and His Contemporaries*. New York: Barnes and Noble, 1964.

———. "The Devonshire Manuscript Collection of Early Tudor Poetry, 1532–41." *RES* 15 (1964): 142–50.

Sowards, J. K. "Erasmus and the Education of Women." *Sixteenth-Century Journal* 13 (1982): 77–89.

Stapleton, Thomas. *The Life and Illustrious Martyrdom of Sir Thomas More*. Trans. Philip E. Hallatt; ed. E. E. Reynolds. Bronx, N.Y.: Fordham University Press, 1966.

Staves, Susan. *Players' Sceptres*. Lincoln: University of Nebraska Press, 1979.

Steinberg, Leo. *The Sexuality of Christ in Renaissance Art and in Modern Oblivion*. New York: Pantheon, 1983.

Stevens, Forrest Tyler. "Erasmus's 'Tigress': The Language of Friendship, Pleasure, and the Renaissance Letter." In Goldberg, *Queering the Renaissance*, pp. 124–40.

Stone, L. *The Family, Sex and Marriage in England, 1500–1800*. New York: Harper, 1979.

Straznicky, Marta. "Reading the Stage: Margaret Cavendish and Commonwealth Closet Drama." *Criticism* 37 (1995): 355–90.

Surrey, Henry Howard, Earl of. *Poems*. Ed. Emrys Jones. Oxford: Clarendon Press, 1964.

Sussman, Charlotte. "The Other Problem with Women: Reproduction and Slave Culture in Aphra Behn's *Oroonoko*." In Hutner, *Rereading*, pp. 212–33.

Sylvester, Richard S., and Davis P. Harding, eds. *Two Early Tudor Lives*. New Haven: Yale University Press, 1962.

Thomas, Max. "Reading and Writing the Renaissance Commonplace Book: A Question of Authorship?" In Woodmansee and Jaszi, pp. 401–15.

Todd, Janet, ed. *The Works of Aphra Behn*. 3 vols. London: William Pickering, 1995.

Traub, Valerie. "The (In)significance of 'Lesbian' Desire in Early Modern England." In Goldberg, *Queering the Renaissance*, pp. 62–83.

———. "The Perversion of 'Lesbian' Desire." *History Workshop Journal* 41 (1996): 23–49.

———. "The Psychomorphology of the Clitoris." *GLQ* 2 (1995): 81–113.

Travitsky, Betty S. "The *Feme Covert* in Elizabeth Cary's *Mariam*." In Levin and Watson, pp. 184–96.

Travitsky, Betty S., ed. *The Paradise of Women*. New York: Columbia University Press, 1989 (1981).

Trumbach, Randolph. "The Birth of the Queen: Sodomy and the Emergence of Gender Equality in Modern Culture." In Duberman, Vicinus, and Chauncey, pp. 129–40.

———. "London's Sodomites: Homosexual Behavior and Western Culture in the Eighteenth Century." *Journal of Social History* 11 (1977): 1–33.

———. "Sex, Gender, and Sexual Identity in Modern Culture: Male Sodomy and Female Prostitution in Enlightenment London." *Journal of the History of Sexuality* 2 (1991): 186–203.

———. "Sodomitical Assaults, Gender Role, and Sexual Development in Eighteenth-Century London." In Gerard and Hekma, pp. 407–29.

———. "Sodomitical Subcultures, Sodomitical Roles, and the Gender Revolution of the Eighteenth Century." In McCubbin, pp. 109–21.

———. "Sodomy Transformed: Aristocratic Libertinage, Public Reputation and the Gender Revolution of the Eighteenth Century." *Journal of Homosexuality* 19 (1990): 105–24.

Vance, Carole S., ed. *Pleasure and Danger*. Boston: Routledge and Kegan Paul, 1984.

Venuti, Lawrence, ed. *Rethinking Translation*. London: Routledge, 1992.

Verbrugge, Rita. "Margaret More Roper's Personal Expression in the *Devout Treatise Upon the Pater Noster*." In Hannay, *Silent but for the Word*, pp. 30–42.

Vives, J. L. *Instruction of a Christian Woman*. In Watson, pp. 29–136.

Wall, Wendy. *The Imprint of Gender*. Ithaca: Cornell University Press, 1993.

———. "Isabella Whitney and the Female Legacy." *ELH* 58 (1991): 35–62.

Waller, Gary. "The Countess of Pembroke and Gendered Reading." In Haselkorn and Travitsky, pp. 327–45.

———. *English Poetry of the Sixteenth Century*. London: Longman, 1986.

———. *Mary Sidney, Countess of Pembroke: A Critical Study of Her Writings and Literary Milieu*. Salzburg: Institut für Anglistik und Amerikanistik, 1979.

———. "Struggling into Discourse: The Emergence of Renaissance Women's Writing." In Hannay, *Silent but for the Word*, pp. 238–56.

Waller, Gary, ed. *"The Triumph of Death" and Other Unpublished and Uncollected Poems by Mary Sidney*. Salzburg: Institut für Sprache und Literatur, 1977.

Warner, Michael. "Homo-Narcissism; or, Heterosexuality." In Boone and Cadden, pp. 190–206.

Warnicke, Retha M. *Women of the English Renaissance and Reformation*. Westport, Conn.: Greenwood Press, 1983.

Watson, Foster, ed. *Vives and the Renascence Education of Women*. New York: Longmans, Green, 1912.

Wayne, Valerie. "Some Sad Sentences: Vives' *Instruction of a Christian Woman*." In Hannay, *Silent but for the Word*, pp. 15–29.

Weller, Barry, and Margaret W. Ferguson, eds. *Tragedy of Mariam*. Berkeley: University of California Press, 1994.

Wiegman, Robyn. *American Anatomies: Theorizing Race and Gender*. Durham: Duke University Press, 1995.

Wiffen, J. H. *Memoirs of the House of Russell*. 2 vols. London: Longman, Rees, Orme, Brown, Green, and Longman, 1883.

Williamson, George C. *George, Third Earl of Cumberland*. Cambridge, Eng.: Cambridge University Press, 1920.

———. *Lady Anne Clifford: Her Life, Letters and Work*. Kendal, Eng.: Titus Wilson & Son, 1922.

Wilkins, Ernest Hatch, ed. and trans. *The Triumphs of Petrarch*. Chicago: University of Chicago Press, 1962.

Wilson, Katharina M., ed. *Women Writers of the Renaissance and Reformation*. Athens: University of Georgia Press, 1987.

Woodmansee, Martha, and Peter Jaszi, eds. *The Construction of Authorship*. Durham: Duke University Press, 1994.

Woods, Susanne, ed. *The Poems of Aemilia Lanyer*. Oxford: Oxford University Press, 1993.

Woolf, Virginia. *A Room of One's Own*. New York: Harcourt Brace Jovanovich, 1929.

Wright, Nancy. "The Name and Signature of the Author of Margaret Roper's Letter to Alice Alington." In Quint et al., pp. 239–57.

Zitner, S. P. "Truth and Mourning in a Sonnet by Surrey." *ELH* 50 (1983): 509–29.

INDEX

In this index an "f" after a number indicates a separate reference on the next page, and an "ff" indicates separate references on the next two pages. A continuous discussion over two or more pages is indicated by a span of page numbers, e.g., "57–59." *Passim* is used for a cluster of references in close but not consecutive sequence.

Library of Congress Cataloging-in-Publication Data

Goldberg, Jonathan.
Desiring women writing : English Renaissance examples / Jonathan Goldberg.
p. cm.
Includes bibliographical references (p.) and index.
ISBN 0–8047–2982–4 (cloth : alk. paper). —
ISBN 0–8047–2983–2 (pbk. : alk. paper)
1. English literature—Early modern, 1500–1700—History and criticism.
2. English literature—Women authors—History and criticism. 3. Women and literature—England—History—16th century. 4. Women and literature—England—History—17th century. 5. Women—England—History—Renaissance, 1450–1600. 6. Femininity (Psychology) in literature. 7. Desire in literature. 8. Renaissance—England. I. Title.
PR113.G65 1997
820.9'9287'09031—dc21 97–4112
CIP

This book is printed on acid-free paper
Original printing 1997
Last figure below indicates year of this printing
06 05 04 03 02 01 00 99 98 97